How We Fight

MIND ASSOCIATION OCCASIONAL SERIES

This series consists of carefully selected volumes of significant original papers on predefined themes, normally growing out of a conference supported by a Mind Association Major Conference Grant. The Association nominates an editor or editors for each collection, and may cooperate with other bodies in promoting conferences or other scholarly activities in connection with the preparation of particular volumes.

Director, Mind Association: M. Fricker

Publications Officer: Julian Dodd

Recently Published in the Series:

Thick Concepts
Edited by Simon Kirchin

Metaphysics and Science
Edited by Stephen Mumford and Matthew Tugby

Wittgenstein's *Tractatus*
History and Interpretation
Edited by Peter Sullivan and Michael Potter

Philosophical Perspectives on Depiction
Edited by Catharine Abell and Katerina Bantinaki

Emergence in Mind
Edited by Cynthia Macdonald and Graham Macdonald

Empiricism, Perceptual Knowledge, Normativity, and Realism
Essays on Wilfrid Sellars
Edited by Willem A. deVries

Spheres of Reason
New Essays in the Philosophy of Normativity
Edited by Simon Robertson

Dispositions and Causes
Edited by Toby Handfield

Images of Empiricism
Essays on Science and Stances, with a Reply from Bas C. van Fraassen
Edited by Bradley Monton

Philosophers on Music
Experience, Meaning, and Work
Edited by Kathleen Stock

How We Fight

Ethics in War

EDITED BY
Helen Frowe
and Gerald Lang

OXFORD
UNIVERSITY PRESS

OXFORD
UNIVERSITY PRESS

Great Clarendon Street, Oxford, OX2 6DP,
United Kingdom

Oxford University Press is a department of the University of Oxford.
It furthers the University's objective of excellence in research, scholarship,
and education by publishing worldwide. Oxford is a registered trade mark of
Oxford University Press in the UK and in certain other countries

First Edition published in 2014

Published in the United States of America by Oxford University Press
198 Madison Avenue, New York, NY 10016, United States of America

British Library Cataloguing in Publication Data
Data available

Library of Congress Control Number: 2013952011

ISBN 978–0–19–967343–8

Gerald Lang dedicates this volume to his mother, and to the memory of his father, William Arthur Lang (1919–2006).

Helen Frowe dedicates this volume to her mum, Julia, who never underestimates the importance of a Bellini at sunset.

Acknowledgements

These papers arose from a conference on just war theory held at the University of Sheffield in August 2010. We are very grateful to all the attendees, and to the sponsors of the event: the Leverhulme Trust, the Mind Association, and the Aristotelian Society. We are also grateful for support from the Wallenberg Foundation during the book's final stages. We would like to thank Peter Momtchiloff at Oxford University Press for his advice and encouragement, along with two anonymous referees who provided us with helpful comments on the draft papers. Special thanks are also due to David R. Mapel, who helped us to referee papers for the volume. Finally, we'd like to thank the authors for letting us publish their splendid papers.

Contents

Notes on Contributors

SABA BAZARGAN is Assistant Professor of Philosophy at UC San Diego.

HELEN FROWE is Wallenberg Academy Research Fellow in Philosophy at the University of Stockholm.

ADAM HOSEIN is Assistant Professor of Philosophy at the University of Colorado, Boulder.

F. M. KAMM is Professor of Philosophy at Harvard University.

GERALD LANG is Lecturer in Philosophy at the University of Leeds.

KASPER LIPPERT-RASMUSSEN is Professor of Politics at Aarhus University.

JEFF MCMAHAN is Professor of Philosophy at Rutgers University.

VICTOR TADROS is Professor of Law at the University of Warwick.

SUZANNE UNIACKE is Professor of Philosophy at the Centre for Applied Philosophy and Public Ethics, Charles Sturt University.

NOAM ZOHAR is Associate Professor of Philosophy at Bar Ilan University.

Introduction

Helen Frowe and Gerald Lang

I.1 Why Just War *Theory*?

Warfare has never suffered from a lack of commentary or interest, and the moral costs of war have never been overlooked. At the same time, there is so much that is eye-catching, horrifying, remarkable, obviously deplorable, and simply strange about war, and there are so many different historical and political angles from which one can approach it, that systematic and theoretically sophisticated moral thinking about it must simply take its place in the cultural queue. In our own time, and in our own culture, the ethics of war has attracted significant public interest in the aftermath of the attacks of 9/11, the wars in Iraq and Afghanistan, humanitarian interventions in Kosovo and Libya, and the earlier failures to intervene in Rwanda and Bosnia. These events have furthered the need for careful and orderly thinking about the moral foundations of war and armed conflict, and the essays in this volume are offered as a contribution to that endeavour.

Both academics and ordinary citizens have looked to traditional 'just war' principles in order to assess the morality and legality of these events. Just war theory is traditionally divided into three stages: justice prior to war (*jus ad bellum*), justice during war (*jus in bello*), and justice after war (*jus post bellum*). While the last of these stages is still a comparatively novel addition to the philosophical literature, *jus ad bellum* and *jus in bello* have been extensively studied.

Jus ad bellum and *jus in bello* are further divided into various sub-principles. *Jus ad bellum*, which appraises the morality of going to war, is normally taken to consist of at least seven conditions. First, there must be a just cause for war: war must be a response to some specific act of wrongdoing, such as a territorial invasion of some other sovereign nation. Second, there is the legitimate authority condition, which says that war can only be declared by political authorities who represent a political community. Third, there must be a formal declaration of war. Fourth, the war must be declared with the right intention, and not for some unstated and illegitimate reason, such as a concern with electoral popularity or an illicit grab for resources. Fifth, there is the proportionality condition: the value of the rectification of wrongdoing represented by the just cause has to be proportional to the disvalue of the harms which are expected to be inflicted in the course of the war. Sixth, there must be a reasonable prospect of success: political leaders must not take their soldiers to what can be reasonably expected to be their doom. Seventh, and finally, the declaration of war must be a last resort. War must not, in other words, be the continuation of policy by other means, and all other feasible non-violent ways of seeking remedy for the wrongdoing must already have been attempted (and failed).

Jus in bello is normally taken to consist of two principal requirements. First, there is the requirement of discrimination, according to which only 'non-innocent' individuals, or individuals who participate in combat, may be killed, while 'innocent' individuals, or individuals who don't participate in combat, may not be (deliberately) attacked. The discrimination requirement yields, in turn, the doctrine of the *moral equality of combatants*, which awards non-innocent combatants on both sides of the conflict permission to kill opposing combatants, and the doctrine of *non-combatant immunity*, which insists that civilians or non-combatants be shielded from physical danger. Second, there is the requirement of proportionality, which in this region of just war theory concerns means, not ends: the expected disvalue generated by the means employed in warfare must be proportionate to the expected value of the goods achieved by fighting.

Just war theory has a long and complex pedigree, reaching far into medieval and ancient thought. As a result of this ancestry, however, it arrives in our own time as a fairly mongrel patchwork of ideas, principles, and pragmatic fixes. Though it is surely better to have some sort of non-crazy and widely adhered to framework for minimizing the dangers of unrestrained war than to have no framework at all, the serviceability of just war theory remains moot. For many contemporary theorists, the principles of just war theory have been found lacking, and to be in need of extensive revision. Even those who are inclined to uphold some version of just war theory usually recognize that the just war framework requires more perspicuous and reliable foundations. (The publication, in 1977, of Michael Walzer's *Just and Unjust Wars* was a significant landmark in that project of critical reconstruction.)

Many traditional accounts of just war theory regard war as a unique activity that cannot be captured by the moral rules of ordinary life. After all, the actors, the aims, and the stakes involved in war have no recognizable counterparts in everyday life. These versions of just war theory are strongly collectivist, holding that there is a distinctive way in which moral responsibility can be ascribed to states, rather than to the individual members of states. They assign collective, state-based goals, such as the defence of sovereignty, the status of a just cause. And they identify legitimate authority—generally taken to require being a head of state—as a pre-requisite of waging a just war. Furthermore, moral and legal responsibility for waging war is typically attributed to a nation's political leaders, rather than, say, the combatants who carry out the killing and maiming that war entails, or the citizens who supply money and materials that facilitate their country's war effort.

This understanding of just war theory has been challenged by the spread of democracy, education and methods of mass communication, which have fundamentally altered the way in which people regard the relationship between the citizen and the state, as well as the responsibility of citizens for the actions of their political leaders. Moreover, it is difficult to fit terrorist campaigns—increasingly the focus of military policy and a prominent feature of the war in Afghanistan—into the traditional just war framework, given that framework's state-based view of political violence. Faced with these developments, many philosophers (and scholars in other disciplines) have sought to revise, improve or radically alter our understanding of the morality of waging and fighting war, seeking an account of the ethics of war appropriate to our time.

Foremost amongst this growing body of work are the writings of Jeff McMahan, whose individualist approach to the ethics of war has had a profound influence on both those who share and those who reject his view that war is an extension of ordinary life, to be judged by our ordinary moral rules.[1] The label 'individualism' should not be taken to imply that McMahan thinks individuals lack duties towards other individuals, or that collectives don't matter. Individualism primarily denotes a methodological approach to war, whereby the rules that apply to war have to be grounded or justified, if they are going to be grounded or justified at all, in principles that have primary application to individuals in everyday life. The most obvious sub-department of applied everyday ethics which is relevant to war is the morality of self-defence and self-preservation. If war is hell, as General Sherman is reputed to have said, then the ethics of self-defence might show us how, nonetheless, war can sometimes be justified.

Through an application of this approach, McMahan's has claimed that *jus ad bellum* and *jus in bello* cannot be morally evaluated independently of one another. In particular, McMahan holds that the permissibility of *in bello* actions rests largely on whether one's war has already satisfied the *ad bellum* conditions. If just combatants, or combatants whose cause for fighting has been certified by *jus ad bellum*,

[1] See, in particular, McMahan's *Killing in War* (Oxford: Clarendon Press, 2009).

are confronting unjust combatants, or combatants whose cause for fighting has not been ratified by *jus ad bellum*, then a strong moral asymmetry between these combatants seems to be immediately in place. Just combatants have done nothing to make themselves liable to be killed, since they fight for a just cause, and have been given moral clearance to fight. Unjust combatants, by contrast, are liable to be killed, since they threaten combatants who are not liable to be killed.

McMahan's views have an immediately destabilizing effect on the doctrine of the moral equality of combatants, which insists upon a symmetrical, two-way permission to kill by just combatants and unjust combatants alike. If McMahan's critique is on the right lines, then just war theory is plainly in trouble. Some writers disagree with McMahan, of course. And regardless of the success of McMahan's line of argument, we are left with many other issues to consider.

In ten essays, this volume presents a substantial body of new work by some of the leading philosophers of war. The essays are concerned with a mixture of topics concerned with both *jus ad bellum* and *jus in bello*. Alongside explorations of classic *in bello* topics, such as the principle of non-combatant immunity and the distribution of risk between combatants and non-combatants, the volume also addresses how the fighting of a war might affect our judgements concerning whether that war meets the *ad bellum* conditions. All of these essays reflect a broadly 'analytical' approach to the morality of war, where the rules of war are examined through the micro-foundations of liability and non-liability of the individuals encompassed by those rules. The discussions are unashamedly philosophical, and tend to approach these applied issues from a theoretical perspective that researchers not working in this field sometimes find peculiar.

It strikes some people as especially odd to employ abstract examples when dealing with a topic such as war, because history provides us with a wealth of 'real life' examples that seem to capture the sorts of situation that philosophers discuss, such as the inflicting of collateral damage or the waging of an unjust war. Others might even find the philosophical literature's appetite for abstract cases distasteful; as evidence of a lofty refusal among philosophers to acknowledge the hard politics and the visceral tragedies of war.

We believe these charges are unmerited. There are two relevant points. First, philosophers, no less than scientists, are entitled to test moral principles in ways which diverge from their particular application to real world situations. This is in order to exclude distorting factors and other sorts of extraneous information, so that we can get to know how resilient these principles are, and discover their proper scope of application. There need be no denial that, when the time has come to apply these principles to real conflicts, complex questions of uncertainty and empirical fact have to be factored in. The vital point is that, even before such worldly accommodation is attempted, we need to have a lucid understanding of the principles and rules which we propose to apply to that world.

Second, while real life often does provide us with examples of the sorts of situation discussed by philosophers, the theoretical discussions are not always best illuminated by the use of those examples. Once one invokes a particular conflict to illustrate an idea, it is hard not to import one's thoughts about the general justness of that conflict, and the overall behaviour of the relevant parties, into one's attitude towards any particular event within that conflict. If, for example, one thinks that the United Kingdom's claim to the Falkland Islands is unsound, this is likely to colour one's judgements about the morality of any action undertaken in the course of the Falklands war in 1982, such as the sinking of the Argentinean Belgrano warship. The same is true of wars that are typically thought to be just, such as the Allied war against Nazi Germany. Rather than considering, say, the general ethical issues surrounding the use of nuclear bombs, readers might be tempted to consider whether using a nuclear bomb was permissible in the only circumstances in which nuclear bombs have actually been used. Of course, it is an important question what we should think of these real life cases, but one aim of (much of) moral and political philosophy is to provide general principles that inform our reasoning about particular cases, and it is hard to do this when mired in the details of particular cases. By abstracting away from real life examples, we are able to focus on what strike us as the salient or interesting features of a moral problem for the purposes of answering a specific question, and this will allow us to produce more informed and lucid responses to new occurrences of war, or to new calls to go to war.

I.2 Pacifism, Punishment, and War

In his essay, Saba Bazargan engages with some recent debates on pacifism. When it comes to serious deliberation about warfare, pacifism may seem to be the obvious default position: how exactly can warfare qualify for moral permissibility, given its indulgent accommodation of the sort of violence and destruction which is so roundly condemned elsewhere in our moral thought? If war is special—if it makes available terms and conditions for military violence that are not on offer to other types of violence—then the question arises as to why this is so.

Pacifism comes in different degrees of strength. The strongest form of pacifism denies that any kind of violence, even an individual's self-defensive violence against a culpable and dangerous aggressor, is permissible. Most pacifists do not hold this extreme position, however. Pacifists are more likely to permit individual self-defensive violence, but to deny that the conditions for large-scale conflict are ever in place. The relevant prohibitions will also tend to be *contingent*. There *could* perhaps be a world in which a war was justly fought, but our world, for one reason or another, is not like that.

Bazargan considers two forms of contingent pacifism: 'proportionality-based' pacifism and 'epistemic-based' pacifism. Proportionality-based pacifism makes the proportionality condition in *jus in bello* much more stringent than it has usually been taken to be in just war theory. There are different routes to this greater stringency. First, this form of pacifism may hold that the killing of civilians (or non-combatants) in war is excessive, even if the deaths of non-combatants qualify as 'collateral damage'; as merely foreseen, rather than deliberately aimed at. On this line of thought, non-combatants are protected by much more robust constraints than just war theory grants to them. Second, proportionality-based pacifism may insist on a less cavalier attitude to combatant liability. Combatants are typically young, ignorant, and economically oppressed. Their presence in the army reflects various forms of duress, if not outright conscription. Given these facts, they do not lose their non-liability to be killed just as soon as they are given a rifle and some ammunition. Third, proportionality-based pacifism may hold that a more extensive set of harms should be included in the proportionality calculation: namely, the harms caused by both armies, not just the army whose mobilization may ensue from these deliberations. (This form of proportionality involves revision to the *jus ad bellum* form of proportionality condition.)

Bazargan is not convinced that these lines of argument present insurmountable difficulties for non-pacifism. He does not see any convincing argument for the extremely weighty restriction against civilians' deaths which proportionality-based pacifism insists upon. He doubts that the non-ideal circumstances in which combatants are recruited into armed conflict can straightforwardly endow them with moral immunity: war is a morally risky activity, and the moral stakes for those who participate in it are extremely high. And, while he supports proportionality calculations which take the harms caused by the opposing side into consideration, he argues that these particular harms can be offset by the values upheld by war: the lives saved, or the freedoms upheld.

That does not extinguish the prospects for contingent pacifism, however. Bazargan is more encouraging towards epistemic-based pacifism, which denies permission to go to war to nations with flawed war-mongering records. Epistemic-based pacifism does not forbid wars where we have good reasons for thinking them just. It denies, rather, that we have good reasons for thinking the war just if the government sponsoring it has a history of unreliable judgements in this area.

In contemporary thinking about just war, wars which are considered just are overwhelmingly wars that are defensive in nature. (Even wars of humanitarian intervention, whose status is controversial, can be described as having other-defensive aims, if not self-defensive aims.) But, as Victor Tadros notes in his contribution, punitive wars have often been fought. Can they, in theory, be justified?

Tadros focuses on the permissibility of deterrence-based wars. To explain the ideas, imagine there are three opposing nations: X, Y, and Z. There are two forms of deterrence-based wars: special deterrence and general deterrence. In special deterrence, Y's aim in attacking X is to deter X from launching a future attack on Y. In general deterrence, by contrast, Y's aim in attacking X is to protect Y by deterring Z from launching a future attack on Y. As Tadros notes, general deterrence raises deeper issues than special deterrence. Wars of special deterrence may be assimilated, with a tweak or two, to preventive wars, which can themselves be assimilated, with a tweak or two, to ordinary defensive wars. These wars may be permissible just as long as there is evidence that an attack is planned. (This evidence may certainly be difficult to collect if the attack is not imminent, but the difficulty of justifying such wars will be primarily epistemic or informational, rather than moral.) But what about wars based on general deterrence? If Y attacks X to prevent itself from being attacked by Z, then it would seem that X is not just *harmed* by Y, but *used* by Y. In everyday morality, being used by others violates the so-called 'means principle', and is normally forbidden outside catastrophe-threatening scenarios.

If it can be established that general deterrence is sometimes justified in the individual case, then the prospects for wars of general deterrence will be brighter. This is Tadros's procedure. He proposes that a previous act of wrongdoing may generate a duty for the offender to compensate, rectify, or make amends to, the victim. Given the existence of this duty, the victim may then be permitted to use the offender in a certain way in order to shield her from further injury or harm. Tadros invites us to imagine that Art has hired a thug to shoot off Bert's arm. Art then owes it to Bert to repair the damage which the hired thug inflicted upon him. Imagine now that the unlucky Bert is exposed to a further attack by Cat, who seeks to shoot off his remaining arm. One way in which Art's duty to Bert could be discharged would be for Bert to use Art to shield him from Cat's attack, thus ensuring that Art absorbs the injury that Bert would otherwise suffer. Now it cannot be denied, in this case, that Art is used by Bert, and Tadros does not deny that it would be normally impermissible for Bert to use Art in this way. However, in this particular case Art is not wronged by Bert, and lacks a complaint against him. Bert's treatment of Art simply constitutes his enforcement of a duty which Art had acquired towards him as a result of the fact that Art had already wronged Bert. This, in outline, is what Tadros calls the *Duty View* of punishment.[2]

[2] For a fuller account, see Victor Tadros, *The Ends of Harm: The Moral Foundations of Criminal Law* (Oxford: Oxford University Press, 2011).

Tadros now inquires whether the Duty View of punishment might be applied to warfare. At least in theory, Tadros thinks that such an extension is possible: if nation A wrongfully attacks nation B, then the fact of that wrongdoing may then allow B to attack A in order to protect itself from a future attack by nation C. As ever, though, matters become more complicated when we ascend from the individual to the collective level. Tadros thinks that the transition from the individual case to the collective level clears some hurdles, but perhaps not others. On his view, the extension from the individual case to the collective case is likely to overcome the complaint that the institutional infrastructure of international law enforcement may be too meagre to permit any punitive actions at all. Tadros is not impressed with this line of argument, because the purpose of institutional infrastructure is primarily to enforce duties whose existence and general character can be discerned prior to the development of institutions whose business is to enforce them. (The duties do not suddenly spring into existence along with the institutions; the institutions arise from the perceived need to discharge the duties which in some sense already exist.) However, punitive wars are likely to involve an intolerable level of disrespect for the lives of the innocent, and for this reason Tadros urges considerable caution in any approach which might wish to award a more central place to punitive wars.

I.3 Self-Defence, Forfeiture, and Mere Resistance

Consider Tadros's treatment of Art and Bert. What might explain the fact that Art has an enforceable duty in respect of Bert? Clearly, the explanation must proceed through facts about what Art has done. The usual way of making this point is to say that Art is now liable to be treated in ways to which he was non-liable prior to his act of wrongdoing. But what exactly accounts for this transition from non-liability to liability? This issue has always been a traditional source of difficulty for the justification of punishment. (How can two wrongs make a right?) But, as Gerald Lang shows in his essay, the very same question also arises in the basic case of self-defence, in which the permissibility of violence has always seemed more intuitively secure.

Lang is concerned to explore certain aspects of what he calls the 'Central Normative Transition' between a victim and an attacker in an ordinary case of self-defence. Intuitively, if the attacker is threatening an innocent victim with injury or death, then the victim is permitted, where necessary, to use a proportionate amount of self-defensive violence to repel the attacker. That permission is also asymmetrical. Finding *himself* under attack, the attacker does not enjoy permission to inflict injury on the victim. In short, the attacker seems to *lose* a right to which he was previously entitled: namely, the right to life, or the right not to be harmed by others. And the victim seems to *gain* a right which she didn't previously have: namely, the right to inflict violence upon the attacker. What explains this transition? How exactly is the normative baton passed from attacker to victim?

One traditional answer to how this transition is achieved appeals to forfeiture. On the 'Forfeiture Account', attackers forfeit their rights not to be attacked, and the fact that they have forfeited their rights dismantles their moral barriers against the victim's self-defensive attack. The Forfeiture Account has generated a long litany of complaints. Many of these complaints, Lang argues, are unconvincing. Much of forfeiture's bad press has been undeserved. But one such complaint, the 'Explanation Problem', does identify a sizeable problem with forfeiture. According to the Explanation Problem, the Forfeiture Account helps itself to a conclusion which needs to be argued for. It does not represent much of an explanatory advance on the claim that the victim is permitted to inflict violence on an attacker to say that the victim is permitted to inflict violence on an attacker because the attacker has forfeited his right not to be attacked. Forfeiture seems to be a place-holder for an explanation, rather than an explanation in its own right. A related complaint about the Forfeiture Account is that it is entirely attacker-focused rather than victim-focused. To make sense of the Central Normative Transition, Lang argues that we should be keeping our eye on the victim as much as on the attacker. A more even-handed description of what unfolds in the normative landscape, Lang suggests, will pay specific attention to what the victim gains, as well as what the attacker loses. But forfeiture is not precluded from playing some role in this more broadly focused explanation of the Central Normative Transition, in which the attacker abuses a relationship which ought to obtain between him and the victim: Lang concludes, on these grounds, that the Forfeiture Account is still half-right, if not wholly right.

Suzanne Uniacke's essay explores a significant contrast between an individual's self-defensive permissions and a state's defensive permissions in war. This is an underexplored contrast which potentially places even greater pressure on the resources of individualism to uphold a recognizable version of just war theory.

Individuals are usually taken to be obliged to meet the conditions of imminence, necessity, and proportionality, in order to take self-defensive action. Each condition enjoys a secure intuitive connection to the basis for self-defence. The imminence condition requires that the attack be imminent. Without this condition, too broad a range of violent actions would get to be justified. (Who's to say what *could* happen in the future? Are we allowed to take preventive action against anyone and everyone who *might* attack us? It would be a recipe for disaster to apply a 'better safe than sorry' principle to the morality of self-defence.) The necessity condition insists that acts of self-defence be necessary in order to avoid harm; if the victim can safely escape the situation without having to deploy violence, she should do so. The proportionality condition instructs the victim not to use violence which is disproportionate to the violence threatened against her by the attacker.

So far, each of these conditions has been stated without any attention to degrees of probability. Since we can be rarely be certain of anything when we act in the real world, how should probability and risk affect these conditions? Neither the necessity nor the proportionality condition is centrally sensitive to the assessment of risk, on Uniacke's view, and acting in self-defence will be permissible just as long as the individual believes that there is *some* chance that the self-defensive action will be successful. But the constraints on war are much more stringent: war is permissible only when there is a reasonable prospect of success. Why the asymmetry? One important consideration involves the risks of collateral damage, the tendency of war to escalate and create wider regional instability, and other such broadly consequential considerations. But Uniacke doesn't want to leave the story at that. She completes her explanation through appeal to a generally under-explored condition in *jus ad bellum*: the legitimate authority condition. The legitimate authority condition, together with the reasonable prospect of success condition, discloses something important about the responsibilities of the state, which as a result endow the state with a very different profile from that of the ordinary defensive actor. The state has a much more extensive set of responsibilities towards its citizens than simply the repulsion of an attack. The state enjoys responsibility for the good of the entire community it governs. It must therefore take a view about whether the peace that would be established after a war successfully fought would be preferable to the peace that must be settled for without going to war, and that decision must be taken in the knowledge that war involves risks, both physical and moral, which are distributed over everyone in the community. These responsibilities entail that war cannot be pursued in the absence of a reasonable prospect of success.

There is a possible difference between Uniacke and F. M. Kamm on the self-defensive victim's rights. Though Uniacke thinks that the barriers to legitimate self-defensive violence are set fairly low, a condition of legitimacy for such violence is that the victim believes her self-defensive act *could* be successful. But the conditions that have already been imposed on self-defence leave us with a puzzle. Imagine that the victim makes a violent response which fails to satisfy Uniacke's conditions: she knows either that it will fail, or that it has a vanishingly low probability of being successful. That would seem to make her response impermissible. If that were so, would an attacker who had already committed a moral offence by attacking the victim now actually have grounds for taking counter-defensive measures against the victim? Having started this episode in morality's bad books, might the attacker complete it with partial restoration of moral honour? That seems implausible, even if the victim has offended against conditions of self-defence for which, as we have seen, there is an important rationale. (Helen Frowe also emphasizes the implausibility of this thought in her essay.) But what can prevent us from reaching this conclusion, if we accept that self-defensive violence is genuinely conditioned by necessity and proportionality?

In her essay, F. M. Kamm explores a category of legitimate violent response which she calls 'mere resistance'. Acts of mere resistance occupy an intermediate place between self-defence and punishment, and can be assimilated to neither of these more familiar categories. On Kamm's view, a failed exercise in self-defence may nonetheless qualify as a successful exercise of mere resistance. Acts of mere resistance may take place, on Kamm's view, when there are no successful escape options available to the victim, and when she is aware of the futility of any attempt of self-defensive violence. Kamm's central example is the 'Taliban Women Case', concerning the domestic confinement of Afghan women prior to 2001. Kamm speculates that these women's violent resistance to their captors may have constituted an 'appropriate response' to the fact that they had been, and were continuing to be, wronged by them. Sometimes acts of mere resistance may be imprudent; there may be no place of greater safety to which a confined woman could flee, and her resistance might lead to her being harmed more severely, or even to her being killed. Even if it was imprudent for such a woman to engage in acts of mere resistance, Kamm thinks the captor wouldn't be *wronged* by such acts. He would lack a complaint against them, and wouldn't be entitled to meet them with violent resistance of his own.

Kamm also puts the notion of mere resistance to other sorts of work, concerning the foreseeable *escalation* of violence. In some cases, the woman may be physically unharmed through continuing confinement, but she may, on Kamm's view, engage in an act of mere resistance which she can foresee would necessitate an increasing level of violence against her captor. Now the morality of self-defence permits the victim to use a proportionate and necessary level of self-defensive violence at each stage of the attacker's resistance, but may instruct a victim not to instigate a violent encounter which foreseeably escalates in violence. That seems to be Uniacke's view. Kamm thinks, by contrast, that the permissibility of mere resistance may permit such an escalation. (Perhaps the victim is in a position to use effective self-defensive violence against only a very high level of violence deployed by the attacker—she has a grenade, say—whereas effective lower levels of self-defensive violence in the cycle of escalation are beyond her means, and such violence as she is capable of producing must be counted as mere resistance instead.) Since mere resistance may entitle the victim to inflict a level of violence on her captor which exceeds the harm currently being inflicted upon her, this category of violence appears to supply moral fuel for the escalation of violence between her and her captor. And that may in turn, as Kamm notes, provide reasons for rethinking some traditional restrictions on the *jus ad bellum* conditions for fighting a just war.

I.4 Infringement, Liability, and Tactical Bombers

Judith Thomson's well-known right-based account of self-defence is exclusively concerned with cases in which the victim's right to life would be violated by the attacker's actions. (As Lang shows, forfeiture might help to provide the rights-based account with the *mechanism* by which the attacker's violation of the victim's right generates the victim's right to defend herself against the attacker.) Because the victim is innocent, and enjoys a right to life, and because the attacker threatens to violate that right to life, the ingredients for the moral asymmetry of self-defensive permissions are securely in place: the victim, but not the attacker, is permitted to use violence which is necessary and proportionate in defence of her life. But there are other situations which challenge the neatness of that asymmetry, and these are explored in the essays by Adam Hosein and Jeff McMahan.

Both Hosein and McMahan are centrally concerned with the 'tactical bomber' case. This case, in McMahan's particular formulation of it, can be described as follows: six just combatants, in a war of humanitarian intervention, destroy a military installation in order to ensure that one hundred innocent civilians will not be killed by unjust combatants. The debris from the bombing stands to kill six villagers who are gathered in a neutral country just across the border from the site of the military installation. May the villagers defend themselves against the bombers, whom McMahan describes as 'justified threateners'? McMahan does not think that the villagers are simply required to sacrifice themselves for the sake of saving the civilians. If they could somehow frustrate the bombers' mission without endangering the lives of the bombers, they would be entitled to do so, even if the civilians died as a result. But what if the villagers are only in a position to avoid being killed by taking violent self-defensive action against the bombers? The villagers are not liable to be killed. But neither are the bombers. By assumption, the bombers have been licensed by morality to carry out this mission. But if they are not liable, then how can it be right for the villagers to kill them? On this issue, Hosein and McMahan return divergent answers.

Hosein recommends a straightforward extension of the rights-based account, where non-liable victims are permitted to use self-defensive force to repel both violations *and* infringements of their rights. This extension is challenged by McMahan's claim that *justification defeats liability*: if the bombers have a justification for destroying the military facility, then they are not liable to be killed by the villagers. To challenge the claim that justification defeats liability, Hosein sketches the *Machine* case. In this case, agent A will be killed by a machine unless agent B suffers a serious but less severe injury: a crushed arm, say. Now B is not under a duty to accept this lesser injury in order to save A from being killed. But is agent C permitted to *impose* that injury upon B in order to save A? Since B is not under a duty to save A, C cannot be described as enforcing B's duty to save A. But, since it would be morally good, if not required, for B to accept a lesser injury to save A's life, C might be justified in *infringing* B's right in order to save A. C would *not* be justified in inflicting such injury upon B, Hosein argues, if she was in a position to suffer the A-saving injury herself. This is because, in shouldering the burden of saving A, C would avoid infringing B's right. (Since it is morally preferable that there be as few infringements as possible, and because C wouldn't be infringing *her own* right, it follows that C should sacrifice herself rather than infringing B's right.) Hosein assumes, importantly, that C is not a position to suffer the injury herself; imagine that B is standing between her and the machine, blocking her access to it. In this case, C's options are either to infringe B's right, or simply allow A to die. Now even if C is justified in imposing the injury on B in order to save A, can B deflect the cost on to C by seizing B's arm and inserting it into the machine? Hosein returns an affirmative answer to this question. But that suggests that B enjoys the right of self-defence against both violations *and* infringements of his right. And that is precisely the lesson Hosein applies to the tactical bomber case. Though the tactical bombers may indeed act with justification, the villagers are not required to refrain from taking self-defensive action against them. The villagers are entitled to act in defence of their rights, without having to pay heed to the larger civilians-saving project which would be served by the infringement of their rights.

One further issue concerns the options available to the tactical bombers for responding to the villagers' self-defensive actions. Can they defend themselves against the villagers' attack? Hosein thinks they can, and that the source of this counter-defensive permission is provided by the impartial justification they have for undertaking the mission in the first place. In short, even though the bombers wrong the villagers, they do not act wrongly, and the combination of these facts comfortably generates two-way defensive permissions: the villagers may defend themselves against the bombers, and the bombers may defend themselves against the villagers' acts of self-defence.

On this particular matter Hosein and McMahan stand in deep disagreement. By contrast with Hosein, McMahan claims that the 'logic of liability' does not allow the generation of this two-way permission. If the bombers are not liable to be killed, then no one else—neither the villagers nor third-parties acting on their behalf—has the right to kill them. Another way of permitting the villagers to defend themselves would proceed through an agent-relative account, where the villagers are entitled to prefer their own lives over the lives of the bombers. This kind of self-concern is perfectly intelligible, and would appear to allow us to break the tie between the villagers, who are non-liable, and the bombers, who are also non-liable. McMahan's central complaint about this strategy is that it *over-generates* defensive permissions: it allows killing in self-preservation, not just killing in self-defence. Assume that the villagers could only repel the bombers' attack by creating an explosion that would destroy the bombers' plane and also destroy all the inhabitants of a further small village which was populated by six other individuals. These further villagers would be designated, in the ethics of self-defence, as 'innocent bystanders'. The further villagers do not themselves constitute any threat to the original villagers. They are clearly innocent, or non-liable. But if the agent-relative account permits the original villagers to kill the non-liable bombers out of concern for their self-preservation, then it will also permit them, out of the very same concern, to take steps which kill the further villagers. That, for McMahan, proves too much. The further villagers cannot be killed in this way.

McMahan concludes that the prospects for finding self-defensive permissions for the villagers are poor. This indicates an important change of position in his thinking. In his earlier work, McMahan noted the tensions created by the bombers' non-liability and the villagers' non-liability, but did not deny that the villagers are morally entitled to act in self-defence.

I.5 Double Effect, Soldiers' Safety, and Non-combatant Immunity

An important theoretical lynchpin in just war theory is provided by the doctrine of double effect, which governs the *jus in bello* rules of war relating to civilians, or non-combatants. (For present purposes, we will use these terms interchangeably.) The doctrine of double effect distinguishes between two types of effect—a good effect and a bad effect—and tells us when the combination of these effects is permitted, and when that combination is prohibited (or at least strongly disfavoured). The combination of good effect and bad effect is permitted when the bad effect is merely foreseen, or when the bad effect is not aimed at either as an end or as a means to the end of achieving the good effect. The combination of good effect and bad effect is prohibited or strongly disfavoured when the bad effect is aimed at either directly, or as a means to the end of realizing the good effect.

In military ethics, the standard illustration of the doctrine of double effect is provided by a pair of cases: the tactical bomber case, which we have already encountered, and the 'terror bomber' case. In the terror bomber case, the bomber deliberately aims to kill civilians in order to demoralize the civilian population so that the war can be brought to an end more quickly. In the tactical bomber case, the killing of the civilians is merely foreseen; it is not aimed at in itself, or as a means to the end of bringing the war to an end more quickly. It is assumed that the civilian death toll is the same in both the tactical bomber case and the terror bomber case. Intuitively, the actions of the terror bomber seem more morally objectionable than those of the tactical bomber, and the doctrine of double effect offers an explanation of these contrasting verdicts. One more important constituent of double effect concerns proportionality: the doctrine insists that the disvalue of the merely foreseen effect should not be disproportionate to the value of the good effect which is directly aimed at.

The doctrine of double effect is a heavily *psychologistic* doctrine: questions of permissibility and impermissibility appear to be settled in large part by the quality of the agent's intentions. The psychologism of the doctrine has exposed it to much criticism, but Kasper Lippert-Rasmussen is not convinced that these criticisms inflict fatal damage on the doctrine. An important recent critic of the doctrine is Thomas Scanlon, and Lippert-Rasmussen devotes most of his essay to a defence of double effect against Scanlon's criticisms.[3]

Scanlon distinguishes between two roles for double effect: as a guide to deliberation, and as critical material for assessing the agent who is engaged in deliberation. Intentions do not matter to the first exercise, and do not determine the permissibility of an action. But intentions can and do matter to our evaluation of the agent. Good agents are well-intentioned agents; they do the right things for the right reasons. But the right reasons for acting are disclosed by principles for acting which, on Scanlon's view, are not themselves constituted by intentions. In war, Scanlon thinks that the permissibility or otherwise of the tactical bomber and terror bomber missions will be settled by principles which establish exceptions to the general prohibition on killing innocents. The tactical bomber mission will be acceptable because it does not make the weakening of the enemy causally downstream from the killing of the civilians, whereas the terror bomber mission makes military weakening a direct causal result of the killing of the civilians.

Lippert-Rasmussen is not convinced that Scanlon has provided a convincing case for these particular exceptions. If a terror bomber mission managed to produce the same results with fewer casualties than a tactical bomber mission, what reason would we really have for preferring the latter over the former? He

[3] See T. M. Scanlon, *Moral Dimensions: Permissibility, Meaning, Blame* (London: Harvard University Press, 2008), esp. chs 1–2.

also thinks that Scanlon's way of accommodating intentions is unreliable: we can imagine a badly intentioned tactical bomber and an honourably intentioned terror bomber. We might still morally prefer the actions of the tactical bomber to the actions of the terror bomber, but the relevance of intentions won't have been accommodated in this pair of cases, which will mean that Scanlon lacks a general explanation of why intentions *seem* relevant to permissibility when in fact they are supposedly irrelevant.

Lippert-Rasmussen also considers a second, somewhat related, objection to the doctrine of double effect, which he calls the 'deliberative perspective objection'. This objection is based on the infelicity, or absurdity, of treating intention as vital to the permissibility of action when viewed from the first-person deliberative standpoint. Imagine the deliberative situation of either the tactical bomber or the terror bomber who has been instructed to carry out his mission. If he is conscientious, the bomber may ask himself whether he will be acting permissibly if he acts on those instructions. But he will surely not ask himself, as a separate question, whether he is acting on the right intentions. That seems back-to-front: from his own point of view, his intentions will surely be morally acceptable if, and only if, what he does is independently permissible. If that is so, the permissibility of his action will not be causally downstream from the quality of his intentions. After all, the bomber may *intend* to act permissibly, but that is no guarantee that whatever he does *is in fact* permissible.

Lippert-Rasmussen counters the deliberative perspective objection with two points. First, it supplies no obvious explanation of why an interest in the character of an agent's intentions is *not* obviously absurd or infelicitous when we take a retrospective view on our own actions, or when, as third-person commentators, we take a view on someone else's actions. Take a statesman's decision to go to war. If the statesman is morally conscientious, then he will be anxious to make the right decision; he will intend to do what is right, and to refrain from doing what is wrong. But we cannot appeal to the statesman's moral anxiety to do what is right in order to establish that whatever he decides will be right. To discover the right course of action, he must look outwards, to the world and the moral principles that apply to it, not to his own intentions. However, and by contrast, it would *not* be obviously absurd for historians and political commentators to pay attention to his intentions, and to amass evidence of what they were, when they undertake an appraisal of the episode. Why the asymmetry between first-person and third-person standpoints?

This brings us to the second point. Lippert-Rasmussen argues that a plausible explanation of why it would be odd for an agent to be concerned with the quality of her intentions in active moral deliberation is that we don't regard our intentions as fixed, or as beyond our control. We regard ourselves as having the capacity to form intentions that conform to our reasons for acting. And, if we embark on deliberation in a morally conscientious way, we will have *already* settled the question of whether what we subsequently do bears the imprint of rightful intention. It would be strange to have to keep checking whether our intentions are keeping up with our deliberations, in order to ensure that they conform to the reasons for acting that we would cite in explanation of what we then do. If Lippert-Rasmussen's suggestions are on the right lines, intentions have not been displaced from the picture. They may still play some legitimate role in establishing permissibility.

For all that, the doctrine of double effect is not always equipped to provide satisfying guidance. Take the problem of how to distribute risk among civilians and combatants, which is the subject of Noam Zohar's essay. Just war theory clearly claims that combatants have duties of protection towards the civilians on whose behalf they fight. But combatants often operate in territory where it is the opposing side's civilians, not their own civilians, who stand in danger. How should the risks of combat be distributed between these groups of individuals? Should soldiers reduce their own safety and military effectiveness by accepting risks in order to increase the safety of the opposing side's civilians? Some writers have campaigned for a 'Soldiers' Safety First' approach to these issues. This approach urges that soldiers' responsibility for the safety of opposing civilians should be lowered, in order to better provide for their own safety.

Zohar is not convinced that double effect reasoning has much of a role to play in resolving these problems. The doctrine of double effect tells us that soldiers will be permitted to launch attacks with merely foreseen but not intended civilian casualties, as long as some other conditions are in place. Even if we ought to agree that the distinction between an effect intended as an end or means to an end and an effect which is merely foreseen is morally significant, the doctrine of double effect does not tell us *why* this distinction is significant. *Why* is less contempt or disrespect shown for civilians when they are killed as a foreseen side-effect, than when they are deliberately targeted?

One way of proceeding here would be to advert to the proportionality condition which governs applications of double effect. But Zohar argues that the proportionality condition, by itself, provides too weak a constraint. Imagine three plans for executing a military operation: plan A, plan B, and plan C. These plans progressively decrease risks to civilians, yet all of them, by assumption, meet the proportionality condition. Zohar suggests that the selection of plan A over plan B or plan C, or plan B over plan C, would plainly reveal disrespect for the civilians. The bare fact that the chosen plan, whichever plan that was, met the proportionality condition even though it had been chosen over another plan which would have reduced civilian casualties still further teaches us that proportionality cannot illuminate the significance of the distinction between the merely foreseen and the directly intended.

The addition of a necessity condition is also incapable of illuminating the distinction. The necessity condition would, it is true, instruct us to choose plan C over plans A and B if the costs of A, B, and C were otherwise equal. However, the necessity condition cannot be applied without taking into consideration the various costs attached to different military plans; and the more complex necessity-plus-cost condition does not tell us very much about the proper distribution of risk among combatants and non-combatants unless those costs reflect the very balance between the proper distribution of risk among combatants and non-combatants that we were seeking to discover in the first place.

Zohar is particularly concerned to expose the fraudulence of one prominent argument for the Soldiers' Safety First approach. This argument describes the choices combatants make among different military plans, with different distributions of risk between combatants and non-combatants, in terms which emphasize soldiers' prevention of harm to civilians. Zohar points out that this emphasis is deeply misleading. Take, as before, the three military plans: A, B, and C. As before, these plans progressively decrease risks to civilians, but now imagine that these risks are inversely correlated with risks to soldiers. Plan A maximizes risks to civilians and minimizes risks to soldiers, plan C minimizes risks to civilians and maximizes risks to soldiers, and plan B takes a middling course for both soldiers and civilians. If B is chosen over A, let's say, then that choice of plan can be described as preventing harms to civilians; civilians are less in danger under B, as compared with A, and soldiers are correspondingly more in danger under B as compared with A. But the death of civilians that will result from the selection of plan B cannot be described as simply a matter of preventing them from being saved, because the deaths are *inflicted* on the civilians by the combatants. The soldiers *kill* the civilians; they do not merely refrain from preventing them from dying. We should therefore avoid the potential confusion, or perhaps the simple dishonesty, that results from conflating a description of the soldiers' choice of a military plan among a set of alternative plans with a description of what the soldiers do when any one of those plans is enacted.

Zohar does not deny that soldiers are already shouldering a large degree of risk by comparison with the risks borne by civilians. That may, in turn, permit them to fight in ways which don't always require them to maximize the level of risk they bear and to minimize the level of risk borne by civilians. However that distribution of risk is to be fixed, though, nothing is gained by a mischaracterization of what soldiers do when civilians die in military operations. Soldiers *kill* civilians, and that potentially uncomfortable fact must be acknowledged.

It is a further matter how morally troubled we should be by the fact that civilians are killed in war. As we have seen, the doctrine of non-combatant immunity erects sizeable barriers against the killing of non-combatants, regardless of the side of the war they are on. (The doctrine in its traditional form held as fully for German civilians as for British civilians in the Second World War, for example.) But how 'innocent' are civilians? Helen Frowe suggests that it all depends. Some civilians may have played quite a substantial role in the generation of the war. They might have agitated for war, or helped in the design or manufacture of weaponry, or supported soldiers in a variety of different ways. If the country is on a war footing, then it will have arranged itself in such a way as to facilitate the fighting of a war. But then it is very difficult to avoid the conclusion that civilians, not just soldiers, contribute to the country's war effort. And, if the cause for which their soldiers fight is unjust, then it is difficult to see how the civilians, any less than the soldiers, escape liability.

However, even if civilians are non-innocent, and make a causal contribution to their country's war effort, it may be possible to reconstitute non-combatant immunity in some other way. Perhaps civilians' causal contributions to their soldiers' efforts is too remote to render them liable to be killed. Or perhaps civilians' causal contribution to their country's war effort is too weak to confer liability upon them.

Frowe is not impressed with these arguments, which have been recently adumbrated by Cécile Fabre and David Rodin. An individual's contribution to a causal chain which leads to a seriously objectionable outcome, such as the undeserved killing of someone who is not liable to be killed, does not have to be proximate in order to render him liable. We do not make discriminations based on degrees of causally proximate contribution to specific threats when we gauge the liability of combatants, so how can this approach be consistently taken towards non-combatant contributors to the war effort? The weakness of each non-combatant's contribution to the war effort is also an unreliable guide to liability. Frowe imagines the following difference between weapons factory production: in one factory, there is a normal assembly line model, where each worker makes only a very small contribution to the production of each gun, and in another factory, there is a tandem system, where each worker produces a whole gun. The output levels for these two factories are the same: two hundred guns per day. Are the workers in the tandem system factory really more liable than the workers in the assembly line factory? Frowe doubts it.

Frowe does not deny that direct attacks on civilians will often fail tests of military necessity. It does not follow from that fact, however, that the civilians are not liable to be attacked, because in her view liability ought to be divorced from the necessity condition. A victim who had the option of fleeing from a murderous attacker would violate the necessity condition if she used violent defensive force instead. But does that mean the attacker would be *wronged* by her defensive attack? Intuition suggests otherwise, and the natural explanation of why we have that intuition, Frowe claims, is that the attacker is still liable to be attacked. (In this respect, Frowe differs from McMahan, Uniacke, and Lang.) Even so, the necessity condition must not be denied its proper place in formulating the rules of war. It will still often be the case that civilians should not be attacked, though they would not be wronged if they were attacked.

Helen Frowe
Gerald Lang
1 September 2013

1

Varieties of Contingent Pacifism in War

Saba Bazargan

1.1 Introduction

According to the most radical prohibition against war, there are no circumstances in which it is morally permissible to wage a war. On this view, which can be called "absolute pacifism," waging war is always morally wrong, not because of what war tends to involve—for example, destruction on a mass scale, the killing of non-combatants, etc.—but rather because war itself is intrinsically wrong. According to a slightly less radical prohibition against war, it is permissible to wage a war provided that no non-combatants are killed. The resulting prohibition, which I will call "conditional pacifism," relegates permissible wars to the realm of conceptual possibility, since all modern wars (aside from nominal ones) ineluctably result in the killing of at least some non-combatants. Robert L. Holmes seems committed to this view, insofar as he both rejects consequentialist arguments in favor of killing innocents, and claims that if the actions necessary for waging war cannot be justified, then neither can the war itself be justified (1989, p. 181). Elizabeth Anscombe is also committed to conditional pacifism, having famously written that anyone who believes that it is ever permissible to kill an innocent displays "a corrupt mind" (1958, p. 17). Both absolute and conditional pacifism are, however, morally untenable. These types of pacifism, though noble, are "dangerously otherworldly in the face of utterly unrestrained oppression or aggression," in the words of Igor Primoratz (2002, p. 221). Recently, a more moderate type of pacifism has emerged—one which is more defensible than absolute or conditional pacifism. This alternative type of war-based pacifism, recently espoused by Larry May (2008, pp. 31–5) and criticized by Jeff McMahan (2010), is called "contingent pacifism."

Contingent pacifists, unlike conditional pacifists, acknowledge that though innocent non-combatants have a right not to be killed by others, this right is not absolute; for instance, this right can be trumped by considerations of proportionality. Nonetheless, contingent pacifists believe that for any given war with just aims, it is very unlikely that it is morally permissible to wage that war. This is not to say that the possibility of a morally permissible war is merely conceptual. Rather, according to contingent pacifists, there have been and in all likelihood will be morally permissible wars. As a result, it might seem that contingent pacifism is not a version of pacifism at all. But contingent pacifism still counts as a version of pacifism insofar as it treats war, at the level of national and international policy, as an activity that cannot be licitly undertaken. On this picture, we ought to treat the prospect of waging a war in roughly the same way we treat the prospect of committing an act of terrorism: as morally reprehensible as terrorism is, there might be, on very rare occasions, circumstances in which it is permissible or even obligatory to commit an act of terrorism. But this does not mean that we should have a Department of Terrorism, or government-funded and trained terrorists standing by to commit acts of terrorism; the same goes for war, if contingent pacifism is correct.

Contingent pacifism, as an account of the morality of war, is still in a nascent stage of development. The purpose of this paper is to advance this topic by distinguishing and developing various versions of it, and by assessing the merits and drawbacks of each. In so doing, I will distinguish the type of contingent pacifism that May and McMahan consider from a significantly different and novel type of contingent pacifism which I introduce. According to the type of contingent pacifism that May espouses and McMahan criticizes, almost all wars with just causes are unjust "tout court" because they violate the constraint of proportionality: the harms they impose on the innocent are too great relative to the relevant evils averted by achieving the war's aims. Accordingly, I call this type of contingent pacifism "proportionality-based" contingent pacifism. There are several ways one might attempt to ground this type of pacifism. I will discuss three of these methods. In doing so, I will argue that if proportionality-based contingent pacifism is indeed mistaken, it is unlikely to be for the reasons that McMahan provides.

I will end by distinguishing proportionality-based contingent pacifism from what I call "epistemic-based" contingent pacifism, according to which the prevalence of false-positive judgments regarding the justness of wars, combined with the devastating harmfulness of unjust wars, requires that we err on the side of caution by adopting strong presumptions against the permissibility of waging wars—even if the presumption disallows, on occasion, waging just wars. I will argue that the strength of this presumption is relative to particular governments, depending specifically on whether the government in question has a history of mistakenly identifying unjust wars as just. This version of contingent pacifism is, I believe, more plausible than proportionality-based contingent pacifism.

1.2 Proportionality-Based Contingent Pacifism

A war with a just cause fails to satisfy the constraint of proportionality, and is thus unjust "tout court" if the war inflicts too much harm on innocents relative to the relevant goods consisting in the achievement of the war's just causes. In calculating whether a war satisfies the constraint of proportionality, the weight that a harm receives depends on how morally bad the harm is. Thus, for example, if killing an innocent is morally worse than allowing an innocent to die, then the harm of killing an innocent would count for more in the proportionality-calculation than the harm of allowing an innocent to die; that is, to satisfy the constraint of proportionality, a greater evil would have to be averted by killing an innocent, than would have to be averted by allowing an innocent to die. According to *proportionality-based contingent pacifism*, the constraint of proportionality is very unlikely to be met in any given war; as a result, it is very unlikely that any given war is just.

In what follows I will investigate in detail three ways that a proportionality-based contingent pacifist might argue that wars are very unlikely to satisfy the constraint of proportionality. The first method involves arguing in favor of a stronger restriction on killing innocents in warfare. According to this argument, the evil which must be averted in order to permissibly kill innocents is significantly greater than generally presumed, which makes satisfying the proportionality-constraint significantly harder. A second method involves arguing that combatants—including those who participate in the furtherance of unjust aims—fail to satisfy a necessary basis for liability to defensive violence; as a result, killing such combatants constitutes a much greater moral harm than typically presumed. This makes satisfying the proportionality-constraint significantly harder. The third method of defending proportionality-based contingent pacifism involves arguing that, in war, some of the harms that the *enemy* commits ought to count in the proportionality-calculation as harms that *we* cause, which makes satisfying the proportionality constraint, again, significantly harder.

Put very roughly, each of these arguments supports varying strengths of proportionality-based contingent pacifism by "raising the bar" on how much evil must be averted in order for a war to be morally permissible. However, no matter how high the bar is raised, there remains the (real) possibility of a war necessary to avert an evil so severe, that the war does indeed satisfy constraints of proportionality. For this reason, arguments in favor of proportionality-based contingent pacifism support varying strengths of *contingent* pacifism at best, rather than conditional or absolute pacifism.

1.2.1 *The strength of the agent-centered restriction on killing non-combatants*

Virtually all modern wars involve killing non-combatants. We nonetheless generally think there is *some* prohibition against killing non-combatants, because typical non-combatants generally do not pose direct threats, and because they do not bear significant responsibility for threats posed by combatants. For these reasons, typical non-combatants are not liable to be attacked in warfare—such non-combatants are, in the relevant sense, "innocents." (I am putting aside for now the much-discussed issue of whether combatants fighting in furtherance of just aims count as "innocent." For the sake of simplicity, in this section my use of the term "innocent" should be taken to refer to innocent *non-combatants* only.) What sort of prohibition against killing innocents is appropriate?

We generally think that there is an agent-centered restriction on killing innocents—a restriction that prohibits killing innocents even to prevent further violations of the same restriction. An *absolute* restriction of this sort is clearly too strong (though, obviously, *conditional* pacifists will believe otherwise). According to an alternative "weighted" agent-centered restriction on killing innocents, it is permissible to kill a given number of innocents if doing so is necessary to save x times as many innocents. A strong enough weighted agent-centered restriction on killing would prevent the proportionality constraint from being satisfied in the vast majority of warfare. On this view, wars with just causes will almost certainly violate the constraint of proportionality by resulting in more innocent deaths than can be justified by the goods the achievement of the just cause consists in—even if these goods consist in preventing further deaths. For example, consider a war with the aim of averting an obvious and tremendous wrong, for example, the widespread massacre of a domestic ethnic minority population by a foreign government. Suppose that achieving this just aim will unavoidably result in some collateral non-combatant casualties. The weighted agent-centered restriction against killing is so strong, the proportionality-based contingent pacifist will argue, that the collateral non-combatant deaths will almost certainly violate the constraint of proportionality, even if these deaths are a necessary side-effect of preventing the massacres. This is not to say, however, that all possible wars are unjust—a *weighted* agent-centered restriction leaves open the possibility of a war which averts a moral harm so catastrophic, that killing some innocents is justified if necessary to avert that harm. For this reason, proportionality-based contingent pacifism counts as a version of contingent pacifism and not conditional pacifism.

As David Rodin points out, most just wars are *not* fought to prevent deaths. Rather, they are fought to protect the civil and political rights of citizenry who are threatened by a foreign or domestic power (Rodin, 2002, pp. 130–132). But if the weighted agent-centered restriction on killing is so strong that it prohibits killing even a few innocents to prevent the unjust murder of many others, then presumably the restriction is strong enough to prohibit killing even a few innocents to prevent the civil rights violations of many others. But *is* the weighted agent-centered restriction on killing so strong that it prohibits killing a few innocents to prevent the murder of many others?

Jeff McMahan argues that the weighted agent-centered restriction against killing is not as strong as the proportionality-based contingent pacifist thinks it is (2010). That is, the restriction does not prohibit killing a few innocents as a necessary means or side-effect of preventing the unjust killings of many others. McMahan's method is to show that, under conditions of uncertainty, the application of a very strong restriction on killing yields absurd results.

Suppose the proportionality-based contingent pacifist claims that it impermissible to kill one innocent person even if doing so is necessary to save one hundred other innocents from being unjustly killed. If this is true, McMahan argues, it follows that it is impermissible to impose a one per cent risk of death on an innocent even if doing so is necessary to save another innocent's life. This restriction on killing under conditions of uncertainty, McMahan argues, would prohibit accepted standards of risk-imposition associated with common practices that impose small but significant risks of death on innocents. For instance, we impose small risks on pedestrians and on children in other cars when we drive. McMahan argues that because the proportionality-based contingent pacifist's restriction on killing is so strong that it prohibits driving and other intuitively acceptable risk-imposing activities, the restriction is too strong.

But I think McMahan's argument is inadequate. Consider the following inference.

If

a. killing one innocent to save the lives of one hundred innocents is impermissible,

then

b. it is impermissible to impose on an innocent a 1 per cent chance of death even if doing so will save the life of some other innocent.

McMahan takes it for granted that (a) entails (b). But there are reasons to doubt this. It is plausible that as a permissibly imposed risk increases in probability, the harm that the permissibly imposed risk must avert increases disproportionately. For example, for it to be permissible to impose a 50 per cent chance of death on an innocent, one must thereby avert *more* than ten times the harm one would avert in permissibly imposing a 5 per cent chance of death on an innocent. On this view, we ought to be risk-averse in circumstances such as those involving imposing risks on innocents, in that we ought to be disproportionally cautious as the probability of killing an innocent approaches certainty. If greater risks must avert disproportionately greater harms, then the proportionality-based contingent pacifist can consistently claim (a) while denying (b). That is, proportionality-based contingent pacifism can plausibly claim that permissibly imposing a 100 per cent chance of death on an innocent must avert *more* than one hundred times the harm that permissibly imposing a 1 per cent chance of death must avert. Likewise, imposing a 1 per cent chance of death on an innocent need not avert one-hundredth the harm that imposing a 100 per cent chance of death must avert. Put more generally, the proportionality-based contingent pacifist can consistently claim that i) killing one innocent is impermissible unless it is necessary to save the lives of at least y other innocents, and ii) it is permissible to impose on an innocent a risk of death greater than 1/y even if doing so does not save any lives.

The upshot is that McMahan cannot presume that the relationship between the degree of risk permissibly imposed and the amount of harm that it must avert, is linear. A proportionality-based contingent pacifist can indeed claim that a weighted restriction on killing is strong enough to disallow all warfare, without claiming that the restriction disallows accepted standards of miniscule risk-imposition.

Where does this leave us? The proportionality-based contingent pacifist claims that a weighted agent-centered restriction on killing is strong enough to prohibit almost all war with just aims, since such wars cause the deaths of too many innocents. The threshold at which it becomes permissible to kill an innocent as a necessary means or side-effect of saving others is so high, on this view, that it is very unlikely that any war will meet it. Like McMahan, I am skeptical of this claim. Intuitively, this restriction on killing seems too strong. At the same time, however, McMahan's argument that this restriction is inconsistent with accepted standards of risk-imposition is too quick. Still, proportionality-based contingent pacifists need an *argument* to show that the weighted agent-centered restriction on killing is as strong as they think it is. That is, contingent pacifists need to provide positive reasons for thinking that we cannot kill one innocent as a side-effect of saving many more. Absent such an argument, we are left, at best, at an impasse. In any case, I turn now to another argument in favor of proportionality-based contingent pacifism.

1.2.2 *The innocence of unjust combatants and their liability to defensive violence*

Typical wars involve killing combatants. In the proportionality-calculation of a war, if the deaths of combatants counted as heavily as the deaths of non-combatants, then virtually no war would satisfy the constraint of proportionality. In contemporary just war theory, the deaths of combatants count for much less in calculations of proportionality than do the deaths of non-combatants. The agent-centered restriction on killing combatants when it is necessary to achieve an aim, is thought to be far more lax than the restrictions against killing non-combatants when it is necessary to achieve an aim. But if unjust combatants are not to blame for their participation in the war, and if blame is a necessary basis for liability to defensive violence, then unjust combatants, like most non-combatants, are not liable to be killed. If this is correct, then killing unjust combatants who are not liable to be killed is as bad or nearly as bad as killing non-combatants who are not liable to be killed. As a result, the deaths of unjust combatants would count as heavily or nearly as heavily in the proportionality-calculation as the deaths of non-combatants. If combatants are typically not to blame for their participation, and blame is a necessary basis for liability to intentional attack, then the evil averted by intentionally killing non-culpable combatants must be very great—nearly as great as the evil that must be averted in order for an attack upon non-combatants to be justified. This makes satisfying the constraint of proportionality virtually impossible in wars that involve killing enemy combatants, even if those combatants are furthering unjust aims.

There is an ongoing debate regarding what the basis of liability to defensive violence is in general, and in the context of warfare specifically. Some believe that combatants fighting in furtherance of a just aim (i.e., just combatants) are morally liable to be attacked by unjust combatants, provided that the attack is necessary for furthering some sufficiently significant military aim.[1] There are those, however, who argue in favor of less permissive conditions for liability to attack; on one such a view, for a combatant to be liable to attack, it is not enough that the attack is necessary to further some military aim—rather, such an attack must further a *just* aim.[2] On this view, unlike the more permissive account, combatants engaged in defensive violence against unjust aggressors intent on conquering their country, are not liable to attack by those aggressors, provided that the defensive violence is

[1] Various arguments in favor of this view can be found in Kutz (2005), Hurka, *Liability and Just Cause* (2007), and Shue (2008).

[2] This view is defended in Rodin (2002), pp. 163–173, McMahan (2006), and McMahan (2009), pp. 104–202.

necessary to stop the aggression. However, even on this more restrictive account, *unjust* combatants are still liable to be attacked, provided that doing so will reduce or eliminate some unjust threat severe enough to justify the degree of preventive harm intentionally imposed on the unjust combatant.

An even less permissive account of the conditions for the basis of liability to attack during warfare is needed to broaden the scope of the proportionality-calculation so that it includes both the deaths of just *and* unjust combatants and weighs them as heavily or nearly as heavily as the deaths of non-combatants. According to one such account of the conditions for the basis of liability to attack during warfare, the target of intentional attack must not only pose an unjust threat, but must do so culpably.[3] That is, a combatant is liable to be attacked only if that combatant poses an unjust threat *and* is to blame for posing that threat. If this is correct, then combatants who are innocent threats—i.e., who pose threats non-culpably—are not liable to attack. That they are not liable to attack does not mean that attacking them is always impermissible; but it does means that the weighted agent-centered restriction against attacking them is much stronger than the weighted agent-centered restriction against attacking those who are indeed liable to be attacked. There are several ways that an unjust threat might be innocent; I will briefly discuss those relevant to warfare.[4]

Imposing certain types of threats can mitigate culpability for unjust actions taken as a result of the coercive threat. It is, however, controversial whether any threat—including a threat of death—can fully eliminate culpability for compliance with a coerced demand to unjustly kill another. Militaries coercively threaten their combatants with a variety of physical and psychological punishments in order to discourage non-compliance with orders. If the only way for a combatant to avoid unjustly killing an enemy combatant is to desert, and if the threat of punishment for desertion is severe enough, then the degree of blame that the combatant bears for unjustly killing is mitigated, and perhaps, in some cases, eliminated. Whether and to what extent blame is mitigated depends, of course, on the type and severity of the punishment with which the combatants are threatened. It is revealing, in this case, to consider the standards of excuse applied in the domestic criminal law. In most jurisdictions, the threat of death—let alone lesser threats—does not provide a fully mitigating legal excuse for killing an innocent. Why should we believe that an analogous threat fully excuses combatants from unjustly killing those who are not liable to be killed? The burden of proof lies on the side of those who claim

[3] For more on the role of culpability in warfare, see Zohar (1993) and Ferzan (2005).

[4] Others have discussed this issue in more detail; see e.g. Rodin (2002), pp. 90–98 and Lichtenberg (2008).

that there is something about war which relaxes the standards of excuse for unjustified killing. While it is safe to say that threats of punishment partially mitigate culpability, it is doubtful that such threats eliminate a combatant's culpability for unjustly killing others.

There are, however, other reasons for believing that a combatant's culpability for killing unjustly is significantly mitigated if not eliminated. Some individuals who kill unjustly are not fully culpable because they are non-culpably ignorant of the relevant moral or non-moral facts. Combatants who voluntarily join the military have or are disposed to have a deferential attitude toward the moral authority of their superiors. This, combined with what Walzer describes as "[t]heir routine habits of law-abidingness, their fear, their patriotism, their moral investment in the state," not to mention the pliability of youth, render them highly susceptible to deception and indoctrination by the state (2000, p. 39). The resulting ignorance regarding the moral and non-moral facts in virtue of which a war is unjust might significantly mitigate their culpability for killing the combatants on the just side in a war.

Mitigated culpability also arises from threats faced during combat. A combatant might not realize the unjustness of participating in a particular combat operation, or even a war, until she is entrenched in combat. Perhaps, given the evidence available prior to combat, she was justified in believing that enemy combatants were liable to attack; only during combat does it become evident that this is not so.

If the combatant realizes during combat that participating is unjust, then she is morally obligated to cease participation. But acting on such a decision during combat operations significantly increases (we can suppose) her likelihood of injury or death (not to mention the injury or death of the combatants who depend upon her participation). In the same way that threats of physical punishment can mitigate responsibility for continued participation in an unjust aim, the threat of injury or death resulting from ceasing participation during combat can mitigate responsibility for a failure to do so.

To justify proportionality-based contingent pacifism, it is not enough to show that some combatants are not liable to be killed some of the time; thus it is not enough to show that some unjust combatants are not to blame for the unjust threats they pose some of the time, even assuming culpability is a necessary basis for liability to intentional attack. But it is safe to say, I think, that even if the mitigating factors I've mentioned do not individually eliminate or significantly mitigate culpability for most combatants most of the time, it is likely that they do so in combination. If this is correct, then to kill such combatants is to kill threats that are largely or significantly non-culpable. If culpability is a necessary basis for liability to defensive violence, and if combatants are typically non-culpable, then combatants are not liable to be attacked, even if they pose an unjust threat. If this is correct, and if all but nominal wars involve killing combatants, then all wars—including those with just aims—will very likely violate constraints of proportionality. This is the upshot of the argument from the innocence of unjust combatants. Of course, there might be wars in which the evil prevented by intentionally killing non-liable combatants is so great, and the number of non-liable combatants killed is so small, that those killings are justified as a necessary means to preventing the great evil. For this reason, the argument from the innocence of unjust combatants entails contingent pacifism and not conditional pacifism.

Though I am sympathetic to the view that combatants are often non-culpable, I believe it is a mistake to think that culpability is a basis of liability to defensive violence.[5] Any combatant (aside from child soldiers) is in a position to recognize that participating in any war is a morally risky activity, in the sense that war always involves imposing *prima facie* wrongs—for example, killing, destruction, etc. They know enough to know that even if the evidence suggests the war is just, there remains a significant chance that the war is unjust, in which case the acts committed in furtherance of the war's aims are egregiously wrong. By participating in a war—even one that seems just—a combatant is participating in a morally risky activity. If the risk actualizes, then she is morally liable to be attacked, in virtue of having courted this risk. The upshot is that combatants can be liable to be killed even if they are non-culpably mistaken in their belief that the war is just.

Of course, this leaves largely unanswered the question of what the basis of liability to defensive killing is—the basis might be that of posing a threat, posing an unjust threat, or responsibility for posing an unjust threat, to name a few contested possibilities.[6] But I am concerned here with a particular defense of proportionality-based contingent pacifism. According to this defense, wars are unjust because they kill too many morally innocent persons, and a reason for thinking that the number killed will always be too many, is that enemy combatants count as morally innocent. This particular defense of proportionality-based contingent pacifism requires a defense of the view that culpability is a necessary basis of liability to defensive violence. And as I have argued, we can plausibly maintain that culpability is not a necessary basis of liability in war.

1.2.3 *Negative responsibility for harms committed by an unjust enemy*

To determine whether a war satisfies the constraint of proportionality, we must assess the various harms we cause in the pursuit of that war's aims. In making

[5] See also McMahan (2005).

[6] See Thomson (1991), Otsuka (1994), Rodin (2002), pp. 79–83, Øverland (2005), and Frowe (2008).

this assessment, ought we to include the harms that the enemy commits—specifically, the harms that the enemy would not have committed had we chosen not to wage the war? If some of the harms that the enemy commits ought to be included in the proportionality-calculation, then the evil that the war must avert, in order to be just, must be severe enough to outweigh not only the harms that we impose upon innocents, but some of the harms that *the enemy* imposes upon innocents as well. This makes satisfying the constraint of proportionality all the more difficult. If the harms that the enemy commits ought to be included in the proportionality-calculation, then should those harms count for less, given that they were committed not by us but by the enemy? Undoubtedly, the answer to these questions will depend in part on the type of harm involved, the purpose (if any) behind committing the harm, who the victims of the harm are, etc. (For instance, if the enemy kills non-combatants that we are using as involuntary human shields, then presumably the harm ought to fully count in the proportionality-calculation, even though it is the enemy, strictly speaking, who kills the human shields.)

If the harms the enemy commits ought to be included in the proportionality-calculation, then this is presumably because we bear a version of what Bernard Williams called "negative responsibility" for those harms; for our purposes here, this is defined as responsibility for what others foreseeably and voluntarily do in response to one's own actions (1973, p. 95). I cannot provide here the conditions determining when and the degree to which we bear negative responsibility. Rather, my purpose is to show how particular stances on this issue can undergird proportionality-based contingent pacifism. In what follows, I lay out an example which shows how the possibility of satisfying the proportionality-constraint is influenced by various stances we might take on the issue of how we ought to count, in proportionality-calculations, the harms that the enemy commits.

Suppose country U launches an *u*njust attack, intentionally targeting non-combatants in country D which cannot effectively *d*efend itself. However, our country is in a position to stop the attacks by country U. The only way to do so is for us to invade and overthrow the government of country U. Because U has minimal defenses, the invasion of U will result in few non-combatant causalities. Suppose that, ultimately, many members of the military in U respond to the overthrow of their government by engaging in acts of terrorism, in which they target *their own* citizens, in order to deter domestic cooperation with the foreign invaders. So though our government prevents the government of U from launching further attacks against non-combatants in D, our invasion, though necessary to stop these attacks, prompts the remnants of U's military to kill a significant number of non-combatants in their own country. Suppose the number of non-combatants in U killed by U's military is greater than the number of non-combatants in D that the government of U would have killed had we not invaded U. And suppose further that U had a despotic government prior to its invasion—the vast majority of non-combatants in U did not consent to, and are not responsible for, their government's attack on D.

By invading U as a necessary means of stopping U's unjustified attacks against D's non-combatants do we violate constraints of proportionality? In assessing the various harms that we cause in the pursuit of our war's aims, if we do not count the acts of terrorism that U's military commits against its own population, then our invasion of U might indeed satisfy constraints of proportionality. But if we do indeed count the deaths that U commits in response to our invasion, then our invasion almost certainly violates the constraint of proportionality. Whether we include in the proportionality-calculation the harms we indirectly cause the enemy to commit, has a tremendous effect on whether the proportionality constraints are satisfied.

Thomas Hurka raises the same sort of issue; he notes that whether the wrongful choices of others can reduce our responsibility for bad outcomes in war is vital in the analysis of the proportionality-constraint. He points out that "the more the proportionality conditions discount resulting evils for others' wrongful agency, the more permissive those conditions are; the less the conditions discount, the more wars and acts they forbid" (2005, p. 50). He rejects the "permissive view" according to which we ought not to include, in the proportionality-calculation, the harms that the enemy commits. Though the permissive view strikes many as untenable, it has its adherents. For example, Holmes argues in favor of the permissive view (ironically in furtherance of a pacifistic argument) when he claims that we are not responsible for what others do, even if their actions are a consequence of decisions we have made (1989, p. 205).

Hurka also rejects "the restrictive view" according to which, in the proportionality-calculation, we ought to include all the harms that the enemy would not have committed were it not for us—on this view, these harms should count just as heavily as the harms that we commit. Advocating the restrictive view is a way to underwrite proportionality-based contingent pacifism. If the restrictive view is correct, then even paradigm examples of just wars might violate the constraint of proportionality. For example, David Rodin, at one point, suggests that the defeat of Nazi Germany ultimately might have caused more harm than it averted (Rodin, 2002, pp. 10–11). This alone certainly does not, he points out, mean that the war is unjust. But if Rodin is correct *and* if the harms Nazi Germany committed in the course of fighting the Allies—harms that the Allies could have avoided by refusing to fight Nazi Germany—ought to be included in the proportionality-calculation partly determining whether the war fought by the Allies is just, then the war seems to violate the constraint of proportionality.

I will briefly argue against the restrictive view by presenting a competing, intermediate view, which addresses the issue of negative responsibility as it applies in the context of warfare specifically. This view, even in its preliminary form, has decisive advantages. According to this intermediate view, we ought to include in the proportionality calculation both the harms that we commit as well as those that the enemy commits in response to what we do. But on this view, unlike the restrictive view, there is a weighted agent-centered restriction only on the deaths that that we directly cause; there is no weighted agent-centered restriction on the deaths that the enemy causes (provided that the enemy kills against our wishes). Put differently, there are deontic constraints on killing directly, but "only" utilitarian constraints on indirectly causing others to kill unjustly, when they do so contrary to our wishes. To better understand this view, let's return to the previous example in which we invade U in order to stop U from attacking non-combatants in D. Recall that, in response to our invasion, U begins targeting its own citizens. Suppose we need to decide whether invading U, thereby indirectly causing U to kill its own citizens, violates the constraint of proportionality. On the intermediate view, the non-combatants that U kills in response to our attack still ought to count in the proportionality calculation that partly determines whether our invasion is just. So if U kills too many non-combatants relative to the number that we save, our invasion violates constraints of proportionality. However, according to the intermediate view, unlike the restrictive view, innocents that U kills in response to our invasion count for less in the proportionality calculation than those that we kill directly, in that there is no weighted agent-centered restriction against indirectly and unintentionally causing U to kill. On this view, it is much easier to satisfy the constraint of proportionality when the enemy is doing the killing than when we are.

The claim that the innocents killed by U count for less might seem callous. But note that in the proportionality-calculation those deaths are given at least as much weight as they would be given from a strictly utilitarian standpoint. By presuming a weighted agent-centered restriction on the killing that we commit, we do not *decrease* the weight of the deaths that U commits—rather, we *increase* the weight of the deaths that we commit. Put simply, it is morally worse to be the ones who are doing the killing. The non-combatants that we kill count for more in our proportionality-calculation than the non-combatants that U kills in response our invasion, not because the non-combatants that they kill are worth less, but rather because there is a weighted agent-centered restriction against killing, but no such restriction on foreseeably, indirectly, and unintentionally causing others to kill. (Note that this formulation forecloses on a "moral loophole" in which we intentionally *outsource* killing to others in order to avoid the agent-centered restriction on killing. Since outsourcing the killing is done intentionally, we bear the same responsibility or nearly the same as we would if we had done the killing ourselves, on the grounds that though the killings were not committed by us, they were nonetheless *willed* by us.)

The plausibility of the intermediate view does not itself defeat the argument from negative responsibility—rather, it serves as a plausible, alternative account of how we ought to factor, in the calculation of proportionality, the harms that the enemy commits because of us. And on this alternative account, bearing some negative responsibility for these harms does not lead to proportionality-based contingent pacifism.

1.3 Epistemic-Based Contingent Pacifism

I will end by considering a novel form of contingent pacifism. According to what I call "epistemic-based" contingent pacifism, it is very unlikely that it is permissible to wage a candidate war, not because it is very unlikely that the war will satisfy all the conditions of a just war, but rather because we cannot reliably determine whether a candidate war is just. More specifically, we too often make false positive judgments regarding whether a war is just. The prevalence of these false positives casts significant doubt on the general reliability of a claim that a war is just. Because going to war when it is impermissible to do so tends to be very wrong, we ought to err on the side of caution by adopting a strong presumption against waging wars.

The strength of this presumption, however, depends on the reliability of a government's judgments regarding the justness of a war. For example, if a government has not in recent history made any false-positive judgements regarding whether a war is just, then the prohibition against waging a given war will be much weaker for that government than it would be for one which has a history of culpable false-positive judgments (especially if the government refuses to take measures significantly reducing the probability that such mistakes will be made again). In such a case, there may very well be just wars that we ought not to fight, because we are subjectively unjustified in believing such wars to be just. The claim here is not that all the candidate wars that such a government proposes to wage are unjust, but rather that culpably mistaken or deceptive judgments in the past preclude a justifiable belief that a candidate war is just.

There remains the possibility, however, of a candidate war the justness of which is luminously obvious, despite the untrustworthiness of the government's claims that the war is just. Suppose a neighboring country embarks on a campaign of extra-territorial genocide against our country; this, if anything, seems to justify a war of self-defense. In this case, past governmental mistakes do not undermine belief in the moral fact that defending against genocide is a just cause for war. In response, it might be argued that even if past governmental mistakes cannot undermine justified belief in the claim that preventing genocide is a just cause for war, past government mistakes—or more likely, outright deception—can indeed undermine justified belief in purported non-moral facts, such as the claim that a genocide is occurring, that it can only be stopped through war, etc. If we know that the government has, for example, falsely accused others of genocide in the past, this casts significant doubt on the government's present claim that a genocide is occurring. But if there are government-independent means to confirm or deny the relevant non-moral facts, and if these means are reliable enough, then supporting the war might be justified, according to the epistemic-based contingent pacifist. In this extreme case, the justness of a candidate war is obvious to an extent that silences skepticism raised by the fact that the government has culpably made false-positive judgements in the past.

The upshot is that it is possible for there to be just wars which we are in a position to recognize as just, despite past deception and mistakes from the government. So according to epistemic-based contingent pacifism, though there is a strong presumption against the permissibility of supporting wars waged by relevantly unreliable governments, such a presumption is, in rare cases, defeasible. This is why epistemic-based contingent pacifism is a version of contingent pacifism, and not conditional pacifism.

It might be argued that abiding by the (defeasible) prohibition imposed by epistemic-based contingent pacifism would allow significant evils to occur, by prohibiting us from waging *just* wars. But epistemic-based contingent pacifism prohibits waging just wars only when we have strong reasons to believe that the war is in fact unjust. That is, it will never be the case that epistemic-based contingent pacifism will prohibit waging a war that we have good reason to believe is just. The fact that the government has made false-positive judgements in the past is precisely what undermines having such a reason. It is true that the cost of avoiding false positives is inviting false negatives—we know that we'll end up failing to wage some just wars, even if we don't know which ones those are. Ideally we would wage wars only when they are just—but this is not an epistemically open option to us. So we are left with either waging just and unjust wars, or with waging no wars at all (except in extremely rare circumstances). And the epistemic-based contingent pacifism will argue that the former option would make things worse overall.

The epistemic contingent pacifist can go further: even if waging no wars at all (except in extremely rare circumstances) does *not* make things go better overall, we *still* ought to be contingent pacifists. The epistemic-based contingent pacifist will argue that we ought to abide by the defeasible prohibition against waging wars, even if this makes things worse from an impartial perspective. This is because, in comparing the consequences of adopting the prohibition with those of the status quo, the costs associated with allowing evil to occur ought to be given disproportionate weight relative to costs associated with actually committing a comparable evil—on the grounds that it is better to allow certain harms to occur than it is to commit those types of harms. So even if epistemic-based contingent pacifism made things impartially worse, we still ought to be contingent pacifists. Of course, if this made things *much* worse from an impartial standpoint, then the moral relevance of the doing/allowing distinction will give way under the sheer weight of the net harms that could be averted by abandoning the prohibition imposed by epistemic-based contingent pacifism. But the point of the argument here is not that epistemic-based contingent pacifism is the morally correct account of war regardless of its consequences—rather, the point is that adopting epistemic-based contingent pacifism need not make things impartially better in order for it to be the morally correct account of war.

Because governments differ in how often they make mistakes or deceive the population regarding the justness of wars, epistemic-based contingent pacifism yields different answers for different governments regarding the strength of the prohibition against waging wars. Very strong prohibitions will apply to some governments, and moderate or mild prohibitions will apply to others. So if epistemic-based contingent pacifism is correct, then pacifism in war is relative to particular governments, in that it is dependent on the reliability of that government's purported judgements regarding the justness of wars. Epistemic-based contingent pacifism is, then, *doubly contingent*—it is contingent in the sense that it admits the possibility of just wars (as all forms of contingent pacifism do), and it is contingent in the additional sense that the strength of the constraint against waging wars is relative to the country in question.

I believe that a doubly contingent form of epistemic-based contingent pacifism is significantly more plausible than proportionality-based contingent pacifism, partly because 1) it is flexible enough to accommodate a permissive stance towards war in some contexts and a restrictive stance in others, and 2) it does not require an implausibly strong agent-centered restriction on killing innocents or a revisionist stance on the basis of liability to lethal defense. This being said, of the forms of contingent pacifism discussed here, a doubly contingent form of epistemic-based contingent pacifism is the weakest form of contingent pacifism, since it allows countries with a history of waging only just wars to continue waging wars. One might think, then, that a doubly contingent form of epistemic-based contingent pacifism does not count as a version of contingent pacifism at all, on the grounds that it denies that a war can be fought only in extremely rare circumstances. But in response, a proponent of epistemic-based contingent pacifism might point out that the countries with a history of waging only just wars are ones that wage wars only in extremely rare circumstances.

Works Cited

Anscombe, E. M. (1958) "Philosophy," *Modern Moral Philosophy* 33: 1–19.

Ferzan, K. (2005) "Justifying Self-Defense," *Law and Philosophy* 24: 711–749.

Frowe, H. (2008) "Equating Innocent Threats and Bystanders," *Journal of Applied Philosophy* 25/4: 277–290.

Holmes, R. L. (1989) *On War and Morality* (Princeton: Princeton University Press).

Hurka, T. (2007) "Liability and Just Cause," *Ethics & International Affairs* 21/2: 199–218.

——(2005) "Proportionality in the Morality of War," *Philosophy & Public Affairs* 33: 34–66.

Kutz, C. (2005) "The Difference Uniforms Make: Collective Violence in Criminal Law and War," *Philosophy & Public Affairs* 33/2: 148–180.

Lichtenberg, J. (2008) "How to Judge Soldiers Whose Cause Is Unjust," in D. Rodin and H. Shue (eds.), *Just and Unjust Warriors: The Moral and Legal Status of Soldiers* (Oxford: Oxford University Press), 112–130.

May, L. (2008) *Aggression & Crimes Against Peace* (New York: Cambridge University Press).

McMahan, J. (2009) *Killing in War* (Oxford: Oxford University Press).

——(2006) "On the Moral Equality of Combatants," *Journal of Political Philosophy* 14: 377.

——(2010) "Pacifism and Moral Theory," *Diametros* 23: 44–68.

——(2005) "The Basis of Moral Liability to Defensive Killing," *Philosophical Issues* 15: 386–405.

Otsuka, M. (1994) "Killing the Innocent in Self-Defense," *Philosophy and Public Affairs* 23/1: 74–94.

Øverland, G. (2005) "Self-Defence Among Innocent People," *Journal of Moral Philosophy* 2/2: 127–46.

Primoratz, I. (2002) "Michael Walzer's Just War Theory: Some Issues of Responsibility," *Ethical Theory and Moral Practice* 5/2: 221–243.

Rodin, D. (2002) *War and Self-Defense* (Oxford; Oxford University Press).

Shue, H. (2008) "Do We Need a 'Morality of War'?," in D. Rodin and H. Shue (eds.), *Just and Unjust Warriors: The Moral and Legal Status of Soldiers* (Oxford: Oxford University Press), 87–111.

Smart, J., and Williams, B. (1973) *Utilitarianism: For and Against* (Cambridge: Cambridge University Press).

Thomson, J. (1991) "Self Defense," *Philosophy and Public Affairs* 20/4: 283–310.

Walzer, M. (2000) *Just and Unjust Wars: A Moral Argument with Historical Illustrations* (New York: Basic Books).

Zohar, N. (1993) "Collective War and Individualistic Ethics," *Political Theory* 21/4: 606–622.

2

Punitive War

Victor Tadros[*]

2.1 Introduction

In modern times, the primary justification that is normally given for going to war is defensive. If one country attacks another country it is permissible for the second country to defend itself against the attack by the first. Other aims of war are normally presented as subsidiary to this main aim. Whilst it is controversial, many people draw a domestic analogy of some kind between defensive war and domestic self-defence. Work on defensive war now probably outstrips work on self-defence in the philosophy of criminal law in sophistication.

In a way, that is not surprising, for many issues that are very important in the context of war, such as whether it is permissible to defend oneself against an innocent or non-responsible attacker, or whether the economic benefits of defending oneself can contribute to the proportionality of defending oneself, only rarely have significance in the context of domestic self-defence. Philosophers of war have, for that reason, been pressed to investigate the philosophical foundations of self-defence in much greater depth than philosophers of the criminal law.

Another rationale that is sometimes given for going to war is punitive. Historically this was the more important justification of war and had a central place in the development of the just war tradition.[1] Whilst the punitive rationale for going to war has recently received some attention from philosophers of war, it is fair to say that work on punishment by those who are primarily interested in domestic criminal law is more advanced than work by those working on war. And again, that is not surprising. The justification of punishment is central to the

* School of Law, University of Warwick. Email: v.tadros@warwick.ac.uk.

[1] See Neff (2005), ch. 2.

criminal justice system. It is only one amongst many other considerations that might justify going to war.

My central question is: to what extent can war be justified as punishment? I hope both to show problems with answers to this question that have been given by philosophers of war and to help to advance debate in the light of my own views about the justification of punishment.

One reason why it is difficult to make progress with my central question is that the justification of punishment is itself very contentious. In line with just war theory I will assume that some range of non-consequentialist principles are valid and that they constrain the permission to harm others. I will not consider the way in which punishment might figure in a consequentialist account of war.

Many non-consequentialists are retributivists. Retributivism, as I will understand it, is composed of two claims:[2]

1) It is intrinsically valuable that offenders suffer in proportion to the gravity of the offence they have committed because that is what they deserve; and
2) It is permissible for the state to ensure that offenders get what they deserve by punishing them.

Whilst retributivism historically played a role in the justification of war, it is unlikely to figure strongly in modern just war theory. Historically, some thought that war was justified in part to punish people for their false religious beliefs.[3] Not many philosophers will think that this idea can contribute to the justification of war.

Some philosophers do believe that wrongdoers deserve to suffer. But even if the first retributivist claim is valid (which I doubt), war is likely to be a very poor way of ensuring that wrongdoers suffer to the degree that they deserve to suffer. Our criminal justice institutions themselves are likely to be poor at promoting just deserts (and some philosophers who are sympathetic to the idea of desert reject retributivism on this basis).[4] War is likely to fare even worse in this regard, given that many of the people who are liable to be harmed in war (on most accounts) are not culpable.[5] As far as giving people what they deserve is concerned war is unlikely to do much good.

Some non-consequentialists are not retributivists. Typically, these theorists have developed accounts of punishment that bear some relationship with self-defence.[6]

[2] This is only one amongst a range of retributivist views. Whilst inadequate, I think that this is the most plausible form of retributivism.

[3] For discussion, see Chesterman (2001), ch. 1.

[4] See, e.g., Ross (1930), pp. 56–64. For further discussion, see Tadros (2011), ch. 4.

[5] See, further, McMahan (2008).

[6] See, e.g., Quinn (1993a), Montague (1995), Farrell (1990), (1995), Otsuka (2003), ch. 3, Ellis (2003), and Tadros (2011).

This, I believe, is the most promising general approach to the justification of punishment. It also, I think, informs the writings of just war theorists who argue that punishment can provide part of the justification, or even a complete justification, for going to war.

2.2 Two Approaches to Punitive War

How has punishment figured in just war theory? The following general strategy has been pursued: deterrence justifies punishment and deterrence helps to justify going to war. I will contrast two ways in which this general strategy has been developed. The first is that of Thomas Hurka. Using Jeff McMahan and Robert McKim's distinction between 'sufficient' and 'contributing' just causes of war, Hurka argues that deterrence can provide a contributing but not a sufficient condition for going to war. Sufficient just causes of war are those conditions that can, on their own, provide sufficient justification for war. Contributing just causes of war can help to further legitimate aims in war, contributing to its justification, but they cannot alone justify going to war.

Here's Hurka:

> Once there is a sufficient just cause, contributing causes can be further legitimate aims in war and can contribute to its justification. They include disarming an enemy and thereby incapacitating it for future aggression, as well as deterring aggression by showing this nation and others that aggression does not pay.[7]

This is said by Hurka to have two implications for war. One is that it may be permissible to continue warmongering against a country that no longer poses any threat. Disarmament and deterrence provide reasons to continue a war that a country was initially justified in engaging in on other grounds. Hurka thinks that the first Gulf War provides an example of this. The war against Iraq was initially justified by Iraq's invasion of Kuwait. But it was permissible to continue the war against Iraq once it had been expelled from Kuwait in order to disarm Iraq. Hurka makes a similar claim about deterrence. Deterrence may contribute to the justice of going to war where it would otherwise be disproportionate to do so. The Falklands War, Hurka thinks, might have been justified on this basis.

Hurka argues that the idea that deterrence can only contribute conditionally to the justification of going to war has an exact parallel in criminal punishment:

> If a person has not yet committed a crime, the fact that he may or even is likely to do so in the future is not a sufficient ground for imprisoning him now. Once he has committed

[7] Hurka (2005), p. 41.

a crime, however, incapacitating him from committing further crimes and deterring other would-be criminals become legitimate aims of punishment, and his sentence can be adjusted to better achieve them.[8]

This idea—that there is a close parallel between the standard view of punishment and Hurka's account of punitive war—is misleading, though. In the case of just war, the sufficient just causes of war aim at preventing the aggressing country from carrying out its aims. Conditional just causes, if they exist, provide a justification for doing more than fulfilling this preventative ambition.

In the case of war, the structure of justification proposed by Hurka is as follows: suppose that country A is attacked by country B. Country A may defend itself to prevent country B completing its attack. Let's call this its primary preventative ambition. If it has sufficient grounds to do this, it might then be permissible for it to prevent future attacks by country B and by other countries by doing things that do not contribute to fulfilling its primary preventative aim. Furthermore, preventing future attacks by country B and by other countries may contribute to the permissibility of fulfilling the primary preventative ambition of country A.

In the case of punishment, in contrast, there is no equivalent of the primary ambition to focus on. The crime has already been committed. The fact that the person has committed a crime is not *itself* a positive reason in favour of punishing the offender in the way that preventing an attack is itself a reason in favour of the use of defensive force. Rather it provides a necessary condition for acting on the reasons that there are to punish offenders—necessary because only the criminal offence renders the offender liable to be punished.

Furthermore, in the case of criminal punishment, the reasons on which we may act in punishing offenders are heavily contested. What seems clearly wrong is to punish offenders more than they are liable to be punished in order better to meet the aims of incapacitation and deterrence. Suppose that an offender commits a minor assault. Suppose also that we could deter him and others more effectively by giving him a heavy sentence. It is nevertheless wrong to give him a heavy sentence. Doing so would be disproportionate. Surely proportionality plays some role in the best account of punishment, in which case we might doubt Hurka's claim.[9]

If that is right, it also calls into question the role of deterrence in just war theory. If we are to draw a parallel with criminal punishment, it would be wrong to harm the attacking country out of proportion to its degree of wrongdoing for reasons of deterrence. Soldiers of the attacking country, it might be argued, are liable to be attacked only in order to avert threats that they pose, or are responsible for posing.

[8] Hurka (2005), p. 42.

[9] For related discussion, see Kamm (2011), pp. 136–140.

What needs to be demonstrated is that the liability of soldiers to be killed is not limited to the threats they currently pose.

Hurka, then, has not demonstrated that punishment can contribute to a just war. He also provides no argument for the claim that punishment can *only* be a contributory just cause of war. In contrast with Hurka, Jeff McMahan thinks that, in principle at least, deterrence can provide an independent just cause of war. On his view, war can be permissible even in the absence of defensive aims.[10] In fact, as McMahan himself indicates, if deterrence provides the justification of punishment this is not quite the right way of putting things, because deterrence is itself a method by which we can defend others and ourselves against threats.

Deterrence is best thought of as a particular way in which we can defend ourselves against threats. It involves showing others that harming us will have bad consequences for them. We might use this method where the person harmed does not now pose any threat herself. They are harmed as a means to avert threats that they might otherwise pose later (in the case of special deterrence) or to avert threats that others might otherwise pose (in the case of general deterrence).

Not all instances in which a person is harmed for reasons of deterrence are punitive. For example, I might harm you in the midst of your attack on me to show that I am capable of harming you to a greater degree if you persist. That would be a form of special deterrence that is used to avert a current threat. Or I might harm an innocent person to show that I am very powerful as a way of deterring attacks against me. Harming the innocent person is not a form of punishment. To be a form of punishment deterrence must be properly related to the conduct which gives rise to the punishment. We can call the conduct the 'punishment basis'.

Normally, the punishment basis will be wrongdoing, but there is no *conceptual* relationship between wrongdoing and punishment. A person can punish another for doing something that is not wrong, and even something that the punisher believes not to be wrong. For example, a gangland boss can punish a henchman for ratting on him whilst at the same time believing that ratting on him was not wrongdoing. Many people believe that wrongdoing is the only legitimate punishment basis. But this needs to be established and cannot be assumed from the outset.

Here is what is required, then, to show that punishment can provide either a sufficient or a contributory just cause for war. Assume that deterrence is central to the justification of punitive war. What needs to be shown is that there can be a proper punishment basis for going to war. To show this, what needs to be shown is that some conduct can render citizens of a state liable to be punished for reasons of

[10] See McMahan (2008).

deterrence and also that war could be an appropriate method of meting out punishment for this reason.

2.3 Deterrence and Harming as a Means

In addressing these questions we will need to be clear on the central objection to harming others for reasons of deterrence and the ways in which that objection can be overcome. The central objection is that deterrence involves harming a person as a means. When I harm you in order to deter you I intentionally harm you as a means to alter your conduct. When I harm you in order to deter others I intentionally harm you as a means to alter their conduct. Special and general deterrence involve harming a person as a means to avert threats.

Many people believe that there is a stringent constraint on harming others as a means.[11] For example, it is wrong to push a person in front of an out-of-control car, killing them, even if that is the only way to prevent the car from running over and killing five people. The constraint, we might think, is not absolute. It is permissible to push the person in front of the car if that is the only way of preventing the car from crashing into a nuclear reactor killing one million people. Nevertheless, the fact that it will do more good than harm is insufficient reason to harm a person as a means to the good of others.

What we need to show is that it is sometimes permissible to harm a person as a means to avert a threat and not simply to destroy their capacity for making the threat. It is controversial whether it is permissible to go to war for preventive reasons. That would involve our going to war to erode the capacity of a country to attack us in the future. Whilst there are difficulties in justifying preventive war in practice, primarily due to the difficulty of establishing that war is required to prevent a future attack, there seems nothing fundamentally problematic about going to war to prevent a future attack.[12]

It might be argued, though, that it is more difficult to justify going to war for punitive reasons. Nevertheless, we might think that going to war for reasons of special deterrence might sometimes be justified on similar grounds to preventive war. Imagine that country A is stockpiling arms with the intention of wrongfully attacking country B. With no good excuse, citizens of A support that policy. B has good grounds for believing (and, indeed, it is true) that if A is successful A will attack B causing massive losses. B will then be unable adequately to defend itself.

[11] There is a voluminous literature on this idea. For my own discussion, see Tadros (2011), chs. 6 and 7.

[12] See, e.g., McMahan (2006) and Buchanan (2007).

However, B could now attack A killing some of the citizens who support the policy of stockpiling arms to attack B. This will deter citizens of A from supporting the policy of stockpiling arms.

This is a case of prevention through deterrence, and perhaps it might be justified. Is this a case of punishment? Subject to what I say here I think that it is. Stockpiling arms with the intention of attacking B provides the punishment basis for B's attack on A. It permits A to attack B for reasons of special deterrence. If punishment of the possession of offensive weapons is justified, and most people think that it is,[13] punishment of a country for stockpiling arms might also seem permissible.[14] A person might be punished for possessing an automatic weapon with the aim of deterring that person from using it in the future. If this is right, it already suggests that McMahan is right and Hurka is wrong to think that deterrence can, in principle at least, provide a sufficient just cause for war.

More controversial is the claim that it is permissible to punish a person for reasons of general deterrence. In the case of special deterrence, the person is harmed to avert a threat that they would otherwise pose. They are responsible for the future threat that would be realized were we not to harm them now. It is often thought easier to justify harming a person to avert a threat that they are responsible for creating than it is to justify harming a person to avert a threat that they bear no responsibility for creating.[15]

Here is a brief argument for why harming a person for reasons of general deterrence might sometimes be permissible. Suppose that Art wrongfully hires a hit man to shoot off Bert's arm. It would be permissible for Bert to use Art as a shield to prevent himself from being killed. This suggests that it is permissible to harm a culpable person as a means to avert a threat that they are responsible for creating.

Now suppose that the hit man is successful and Bert's arm has been shot off. Art owes it to Bert at least to repair the damage that he has done to Bert. How could he do this? Suppose that Cat now attacks Bert. Cat is about to shoot off Bert's other arm. Art, we might think, owes it to Bert to protect Bert from the attack by Cat. After all, he cannot now undo what *he* has done. Preventing Cat from attacking Bert is as close that he can come to doing that.

[13] This is, I should say, a more difficult question than it seems. See, especially, Husak (2004). But no one seriously believes that punishing people for possession of *very* dangerous weapons, such as nuclear weapons, would be wrong.

[14] Oddly, the parallel discussion of preventive war has used the analogy of conspiracy rather than possession of offensive weapons to justify early intervention, distorting the discussion. See, e.g., Buchanan and Keohane (2004) and, in response, Lee (2005).

[15] Some argue that general deterrence can be squared with the idea that a person may only be harmed to avert a threat that they are responsible for. See Farrell (1990), whose view I discuss later. For discussion of the limits of this idea, see Tadros (2011), pp. 272–273.

Furthermore, if Art is unwilling or unable to rescue Bert, Bert might harm Art as a means to avert the threat that Cat poses. Although Art will be harmed as a means, he will be harmed to no greater degree than he would have been required to harm himself in service of the end of protecting Bert. If his duty to protect Bert is enforceable, and there is good reason to think that it is, he lacks a complaint about being harmed as a means. I call this the Duty View of punishment. Punishment is permitted to compel wrongdoers to fulfil the duties that they incur towards victims and others as a result of their wrongdoing.[16]

Now we can see why it might be permissible to go beyond the original just causes of war for punitive reasons. Suppose that country A wrongfully attacks country B and all of the citizens of A support the war effort. B defends itself but suffers great losses in the course of war. It would have been permissible for B to use at least some of the citizens or soldiers of country A as a means to avert the threat (most obviously those who bear the greatest culpability for the attack). We can see that this is permissible from the case of Art and Bert. If B is unable to do this, and B suffers great losses, those citizens of A now owe an enforceable duty to protect B from further harms. They can be harmed as a means to avert threats posed by other countries. So the culpable citizens of A can be harmed to deter C from attacking B.

These conclusions also suggest that punitive wars based on general deterrence may be permissible in principle at least. Suppose that country A attacks country B when B is unable to defend itself. The attack is now over and B has suffered great losses. A no longer poses any threat to B (or to anyone else). Nevertheless, it may be permissible for B, once it is able, to go to war with A for punitive reasons. It can do so in order to deter not only A, but also other countries, from perpetrating future attacks against B.

If this is the only justification of general deterrence, the punishment basis for general deterrence is the culpable causing of harm. If one country attacks another and the attack is repelled without the other country suffering any losses, it will be wrong for the other country to attack the one for reasons of general deterrence. That would imply that general deterrence could not provide a basis for the Falklands War. The losses that were caused by the Falklands War were insufficient, we might think, to justify harming Argentinean citizens as a means to avert threats from other countries.

However, this is not the only justification available for general deterrence. In defending the Falklands War Hurka could appeal to an alternative argument developed by Daniel Farrell.[17] Farrell claims that if one person attacks another she

[16] I defend it at much greater length in Tadros (2011).
[17] Farrell (1990) and (1995).

might make the other person more vulnerable to future attacks by others. It would be permissible to harm the first person to protect the second from future attacks, for to do so would only harm the first person to avert a threat that she is culpably responsible for creating. Perhaps it is true that were the UK to have failed to defend the Falkland Islands the latter would have been vulnerable to future attacks. It could permissibly harm the Argentineans to prevent those attacks. This further supports McMahan's view, contra Hurka that, in principle at least, special deterrence and general deterrence could provide sufficient just causes of war.

I now want to consider two objections to punitive war. The first is that punishment can legitimately be carried out only if there are legitimate institutions to determine who is to be punished and how much. The second is that punitive war will fail adequately to protect the innocent from punishment. The second argument, I suggest, has powerful intuitive support and renders it difficult, but perhaps not impossible, to justify punitive war.

2.4 Punishment and Institutions

I have suggested that it may be permissible in principle to go to war for reasons of special or general deterrence alone. I have also suggested that war on these grounds is properly thought of as punitive war. However, it might be argued that punitive war is wrong not because these principles are not the right principles of punishment but rather because, in the case of war, there is no one who has the authority to mete out punishment.

In his critique of punitive war, David Rodin argues that only someone, or some institution, with legitimate authority, can mete out punishment.[18] A person or institution can have legitimate authority to punish in one of two ways, Rodin believes. One, the relevance of which he quickly dismisses, and rightly so, occurs if the person with authority a) punishes the person punished for their own good; and b) has the capacity to act for the good of the person punished. This arises, he thinks, in the case of parents and children, but obviously enough it cannot apply to states. I should add that even if these conditions are fulfilled we might not think punishment legitimate. For punishing children on paternalistic grounds is easier to justify than punishing adults on these grounds.

The other way arises, Rodin thinks, only if two conditions are fulfilled: a) that the authority is impartial and b) that those who it governs have consented to that authority. In the case of war we have not consented to be governed by an impartial authority, and hence there is no individual or institution with the authority to mete

[18] Rodin (2002), ch. 8.

out punishment. If these conditions must be fulfilled for punishment to be justified, punitive wars are wrong.

I think that a) and b) are each implausibly restrictive. Punishment is sometimes permitted in the absence of impartial individuals or institutions that will do the punishment. We might accept, first, that where they don't exist there are good reasons to create institutions to decide who is to be punished; and, secondly, once those institutions exist individuals are no longer permitted to punish individually.[19] But it is much too strong to claim that there can be no individual right to punish in the absence of such institutions, especially when we have no prospect of creating impartial institutions.

To see this, imagine that you and I are washed up on a desert island. You assault me simply out of spite. If I do nothing I will be at risk of being assaulted again. But if I harm you, you will be deterred from assaulting me again. Surely I am permitted to harm you for deterrence reasons. And that would surely amount to punishing you. Of course, it is hardly ideal that I punish you under these conditions. If I decide whether to punish you it is likely that I will go wrong. If the victims of wrongdoing do the punishing they will likely punish some of the wrong people, or punish some of the right people too much. If my decision to punish you is likely to go horribly awry I may lose the right to punish you altogether.

But the cost that I must bear if I am not permitted to punish you is that you will continue to assault me. I have strong grounds to object to being subject to that fate. In contrast, even if I am permitted to punish you independently, assuming that I am reasonably good at determining what is fair, you will have a decent opportunity to avoid punishment simply by refraining from attacking me. Thus, you lack strong grounds to object to my right to punish you.

Were it possible to create an institution to decide whether you are to be punished and how much, we might well have an obligation to do this. We will have such an obligation if the institution is likely to be fairer and/or more effective than individual punishment; if setting up the institution is not too costly; and if it is likely to generate a reasonable degree of compliance. Once such an institution has been set up, individuals would be required to defer to the institution. This is for the reason that we are more likely to conform to what duty requires of us with respect to not punishing the innocent and not punishing the guilty disproportionately if we do so.

Rodin draws his conception of authority from the Lockean tradition. He thinks that consent is required for political authority because he believes that a set of laws can be just only if they reflect the conception of justice that is held by those who

[19] For further discussion, see Tadros (2011), ch. 13.

are governed by the laws. But it is difficult to believe that an institution has authority over an individual only if that individual has consented to be governed by that institution. They will be required to defer to it if, in doing so, a) they will better comply with their duties than they would were they to act independently and b) there are no other overriding reasons why the individual ought to be permitted to act on his or her own judgement.[20]

This is very important in the context of punishment. Individuals, and indeed states, may be required to defer to punishment institutions simply because they will be more effective and fairer in vindicating that right than the individual or state would be acting independently. It need not be shown, in addition, that the institution is just or impartial. It must be sufficiently just that deferring to the institution is preferable either to acting alone or to doing nothing. Institutions that are well short of the standards of perfect justice or impartiality can fulfil those conditions.[21]

To see this, consider the following. Suppose that you attack me. I now have three options. I can do nothing, I can harm you myself, or I can confer on a third party, Fred, the right to harm you. Fred is willing to do this and he is much more likely than me not to harm you more than is warranted. He is also much more effective than me in deterring others. If he harms you he can achieve the same level of deterrence by harming you less.

If we think that punishment and self-defence are parallels of each other, we will also think that one person is permitted to harm another in punishment only to the minimum degree that is necessary to avert the threat faced.[22] That is true of self-defence and punishment alike. As Fred will do better than me in ensuring that you are not punished more than necessary to achieve the same level of protection for me I will comply with the necessity constraint on punishment more effectively by deferring to Fred than I would by punishing you myself. In that case, if you are to be punished at all, I must defer to Fred's authority. That is so even if Fred is guided by an unjust set of principles or a set of principles that I do not endorse. What matters, with respect to whether I must defer to Fred, is only whether punishment by Fred is likely to be closer to what justice requires than punishment by me.

It might be questioned whether Fred is permitted to punish you. Perhaps it might be argued that the right to punish can never be transferred from me to Fred.

[20] This idea of authority has something in common with Joseph Raz's work. See especially Raz (1986), Part I. It differs from Raz's account in its focus on duties rather than reasons. See Quong (2011) for an excellent defence of this idea. I don't rely on the claim that this is a complete account of authority.

[21] For further discussion, see Wellman (2009).

[22] Retributivists, of course, don't believe this. But, for reasons already outlined, we can leave retributivism aside.

But that is not very plausible. For one thing, you will prefer to be punished by Fred than by me. *You* can hardly complain that it is Fred who punishes you rather than me. For suppose that I, rather than Fred, were to punish you. You would then be exposed to a greater risk of being punished to an unjust degree. For another thing Fred is surely permitted to help me to vindicate my protective rights if I confer on him the right to do so. That this is so is familiar from self-defence. For example, if you wrongfully attack me not only am I permitted to defend myself I am permitted to enlist third parties to help me do so.

Perhaps it might be argued that this latter idea is too permissive. Some people think that the right to defend oneself is at least sometimes grounded in agent-relative permissions. I am permitted to defend myself against some attackers, these people believe, because I am permitted to prefer my own interests to those of my attacker (or those who he will help in attacking me).[23] I don't believe that this is true. But even were it true it would operate only at the margins. For in central cases of self-defence and punishment if I have a right to protect myself by harming you, others are permitted to assist me in protecting myself.

Perhaps it will be argued that I ought to do nothing at all rather than punish you myself or defer to Fred. However, as I have already explained, we often cannot expect people to do nothing when they face the prospect of continued attacks. Even if I cannot expect Fred to be perfectly impartial or just it will often be permissible for him to punish you if that is the only way of averting future threats that I will face from you.

In the context of war, these ideas raise a number of questions. The most important is the question whether we have the obligation to develop our institutions to help us to determine whether punitive wars are just. The idea that institutions to govern defensive force ought to be further developed to ensure that we can have greater confidence in the decisions that they make is familiar. In contrast with personal self-defence, the decision to go to war need not normally occur immediately, and were fair institutions to exist, states could be expected to wait until a determination had been made by those institutions before going to war. If institutions could be expected to do better than individual states in determining whether war is justified, there would be good reason for states to defer to those institutions. That would be so simply on the grounds that in doing so, states would better comply with their duty not to kill others wrongfully. This question has received considerable attention and I do not have much to add.[24]

[23] See, e.g., McMahan (2005), Quong (2009), and Fabre (2009).

[24] See, e.g., Buchanan and Keohane (2004), (2006), Shue (2007), and McMahan (2010), (2012).

The main question is whether we ought to add punishment as an independent ground for going to war at an international level. In the light of my earlier comment, we might think that a world in which punitive war can never be permitted by international institutions is difficult to defend. A state that has been attacked by another state, resulting in severe losses, has the right to go to war with the state that has attacked it in order to deter the latter state from attacking again. Punitive wars are at least permissible with respect to states that have successfully mounted an attack. We are permitted to impose losses on those states to deter them and other states from mounting further attacks on us. In the next section, however, we see some reason to doubt that conclusion.

2.5 War and Punishment of the Innocent

I now want to consider a more powerful objection to punitive war: that through punitive war we will inevitably punish the innocent. We balk at punishment of the innocent. But if punitive war is permissible it might seem that we will necessarily punish the innocent. For many of the people who will be harmed during war are innocent. This might seem a knockdown argument against punitive war.

2.5.1 *Prevention and punishment*

This kind of argument has also been used against preventive war. In the case of preventive war, it has been argued that it is only permissible to harm a person in self-defence if that person is the cause of an imminent threat. The people who will be harmed during a preventive war are not the cause of an imminent threat and they are not liable to be harmed during a war.[25]

This argument is not as powerful against preventive war as it is against punitive war. For in preventive war we do not harm people as a means. We harm them to eliminate a threat that they pose. It is typically easier to justify eliminative harm than it is to justify manipulative harm.[26] Non-consequentialist defenders of just war theory do not always appreciate this point. For example, consider Allen Buchanan's response to the concern that innocent people will be harmed

[25] This kind of argument is sometimes made against the permissibility of preventive war. See Lee (2005). For a response, see A. Buchanan (2007).

[26] See W. Quinn (1993b), p. 186, Quong (2009), Frowe (unpublished), Tadros (2011), ch. 11. It is more familiar to distinguish between 'opportunistic' and 'eliminative' harming, following Quinn. What matters, I think, though, is whether the person is harmed as a means, and not whether her presence creates an opportunity that would otherwise be lacking.

in preventative war. Buchanan defends the permissibility of preventative war by considering the following cases:

The Missile Site. The leaders of country A plan to launch a surprise nuclear attack against country B from a missile base in the interior of country A. If country B waits till the missiles are fully operational it runs a high risk of utter destruction, because once launched the missiles cannot be intercepted. The missiles can be destroyed, and the threat averted, by a missile attack on the site. The personnel at the missile site know that the purpose of the construction is to launch an aggressive attack.

The Underground Missile Site. The same scenario as in Case 1, except that the missile base is deep underground and cannot be destroyed by air attacks. The only way for country B to avert the deadly nuclear attack is to invade country A and destroy the missiles from the ground before they are operational. However to reach the missile site, the troops of country B will have to fight and defeat soldiers of country A. These soldiers are not conspirators—they do not know the conspiracy exists—and they will not be involved in the execution of the conspiracy, that is, the arming and firing of the missiles.

He calls the soldiers of country A 'innocent obstacles.' Buchanan thinks that it is permissible to destroy the missiles in *The Missile Site*. That seems clear enough for three reasons. First, the personnel at the missile site are culpably planning to launch an attack. Secondly, there is no other way to avert the attack. And, thirdly, the deaths of the personnel are a side-effect of destroying the missile site. They are not intentionally killed.

He suggests that it is much more difficult to justify killing the soldiers in *The Underground Missile Site*. That is because, he argues, the soldiers will be killed intentionally rather than as a side-effect of the preventive action. Hence, the Doctrine of Double Effect cannot be invoked. He nevertheless thinks that killing the soldiers of country A might be permitted under the following conditions: a) the attack on the innocent obstacles is necessary to avert the harm; b) conscientious efforts are made to reduce the harm to the 'innocent obstacles,' even if this involves significant costs to country B, and c) a strong proportionality requirement is satisfied, that is, the harm to be averted by the preventive action is not only very great but significantly greater than the harm to the 'innocent obstacles.' He suggests that it would be implausible to think that it wrong to kill the innocent obstacles in that case.

This is not a good argument. Imagine an organ donation scheme that allowed distribution of organs from healthy innocent people to save sick people. Now imagine that such a scheme fulfilled Buchanan's three conditions. First, suppose that all other options to save the sick, even costly options, were considered first, so that killing the one person was necessary to avert the harm. Secondly, suppose that considerable efforts are made to reduce the harm to the one person: they are killed painlessly even though it is very costly to kill them in this way. Thirdly, suppose that a strong proportionality requirement would be satisfied—a person would be killed only if that would lead to at least five others being saved. Surely this organ donation scheme would be wrong even under these conditions. It may well be wrong even if it were agreed to *ex ante*.[27]

A better argument to defend the permissibility of preventive war in *The Underground Missile Site* is that the killing of the innocent obstacles does not involve harming them as a means to a greater good. It is true that the innocent obstacles are harmed intentionally, but not all intentional harming is harming as a means. We can intentionally eliminate a threat or an obstacle without using the threatening person as a means to a further good in a way that harms them. The best understanding of the means principle distinguishes between eliminative and manipulative harm. There is a much stronger constraint on the latter than the former.

That is why punitive war is more difficult to justify than preventative war. Preventative war is eliminative in its aims. It does not involve harming others as a means to a further good. Punitive war, on general deterrence grounds, is clearly manipulative—citizens and soldiers of the country punished are harmed as a means to achieve a further good. For that is just how general deterrence works: it uses the suffering imposed on some people in order to affect the conduct of others.

2.5.2 *Collective liability*

As with preventive war, it is not plausible that punitive war is ruled out because the threat to be averted is not imminent. For we do think that it is permissible to punish a person who is not the cause of an imminent threat; punishment for possession of offensive weapons is a good example of this. Punitive as well as preventative attacks would be permitted for this reason in *The Missile Site*. Those who are harmed are those who stockpile dangerous weapons and they can be punished on the same grounds as those who possess automatic firearms can be punished. They have wrongfully violated a rule that we endorse for reasons of security.

The difficulty with punitive war is rather that many of the people who would be harmed during a punitive war have not committed the relevant kind of wrong that would warrant punishment. *They* are not the possessors of the offensive weapons and they do not pose a threat to us now or in the future. It would seem that only those individuals who are doing the stockpiling are liable to be punished. But they will not be the only people who are harmed during a punitive war.

One possible response to this concern holds that the object of punishment is not those who reside within the state but the state itself. When we punish the state, of course, we harm the individuals within it. But it is the state itself that we aim to punish. We might draw a parallel with the punishment of corporations. When a

[27] See, further, Kamm (1996), ch. 11.

corporation is punished the people who work for the corporation necessarily suffer in consequence. But it is the corporation itself that we aim at punishing.

This argument seems to me unsatisfactory for the following reason. When we consider the problem of punishment we focus on the wrong of intentionally making others suffer. If we vindicate general deterrence as a justification of punishment we conclude that it is sometimes permissible intentionally to harm some people as a means to the good of others. But we will want to restrict the permissibility of doing that in some way. After all, assuming that the means principle is valid, it is not generally permissible to harm an innocent person as a means to the good of others, even the greater good of others.

I have argued that in the case of a culpable attacker we have good reason to endorse an exception to the means principle based on the duty that a culpable attacker has to avert a threat that he has caused. If he fails in this duty he can be held liable to bear a similar cost to avert threats that others caused. When we punish a corporation or a state we cause the suffering of the individuals in that corporation or state. And their suffering is itself essential, for the corporation and the state cannot suffer in themselves. Their suffering is dependent on the suffering of the individuals within them. So if we punish a corporation or a state the individuals within the corporation or the state are harmed as a means to avert future threats. We cannot claim that the individuals within the corporation or the state are not our intended target, for without them our project of making the corporation or the state suffer will necessarily fail.

If we are to justify punishing states or corporations we must show that it is permissible to harm the employees and shareholders as a means to deter future wrongful actions by the corporation, or by other corporations. This strikes me as no easy task. It is especially difficult in this case because we can deter individual wrongful action by punishing the individuals in the corporation. It is easier to justify this in the case of corporations than it is in the case of states, for members of a corporation typically have a better opportunity to avoid liability—they can do so by not joining the corporation—than members of a state would have were we to punish states.

2.5.3 *Indiscriminate harm to the innocent*

A better argument is that whilst it is true that some innocent individuals will suffer if we go to war, it is also true that some innocent individuals will suffer through the operations of our criminal justice institutions. This is so for two reasons. First, some people are harmed as a side-effect of punishment. This includes family members and friends of those who are punished. Secondly, whilst we take steps to protect innocent people against being punished, we also know that the steps that we take are imperfect. Any criminal justice system will punish some innocent people. This fact does not render state punishment wrong.

It is true that if we go to war in order to secure deterrence we will harm some people as a means for the good of others. It is also true that some of the people that we harm will not be culpable. But we need not *intend* the harm to non-culpable people as a means to the good of others, or so it might be argued. We harm a group of people, some of whom are guilty. We intend that the guilty suffer as a means to avert future threats, and the innocent are harmed only as a side-effect of our intention to make the guilty suffer.

Against this, some will say that if we intend to make a group of people suffer we harm all of those people as a means to the good of others. But that may not be true. If it is culpable acts that we wish to deter we might aim to deter culpable acts by making the culpable suffer. Making the innocent suffer will not deter culpable acts, and even if it did we may not intend to deter the commission of culpable acts by making the innocent suffer. So we do not intend to harm the innocent as a means to the good.

Nevertheless, the fact that we will make innocent people suffer, even if we do not make them suffer manipulatively, and the fact that we aim at their being harmed when they do not pose a threat to us, count heavily against the permissibility of punitive war. That is especially so in that the innocent people that we make suffer have not been provided with significant protection by us against being made to suffer in this way. In contrast with criminal justice, we cannot say that we have made considerable efforts to ensure that the innocent don't suffer through war. The fact that we will inevitably harm innocent people, then, makes punitive war difficult for us to justify.

To see this problem sharply, consider two different circumstances in which we might end up punishing innocent people. Suppose there is a group of 100 defendants who are tried and punished for each committing a crime. We make every effort to discover that each defendant is guilty. Inevitably, we make some mistakes and some innocent people are convicted. Let us suppose that 5 per cent of those convicted are innocent. This may not render the scheme wrong.

Now compare the following case. There is a group of 100 people in a stadium. We know that 95 per cent of the people in the stadium have entered illegally. 5 per cent have bought tickets. We cannot discover who has entered illegally and who has bought a ticket. Intuition tells us that it would be wrong to punish all 100 in this case. That is so even though the number and proportion of innocent people punished is the same as in the previous example. It is admittedly difficult to find a justification for distinguishing between these cases and the problem has troubled evidence scholars and epistemologists.[28] I have no systematic argument to offer

[28] For an excellent discussion, see Redmayne (2008).

here, but it does seem difficult to give up the intuition that there is an important difference between these cases.

The case of punitive war, we might think, is more like the second example than the first. We punish a group of people knowing that some of them are innocent and we do not make any attempt to discriminate between the innocent and the guilty. It is much more difficult to justify punishing the group in that case, or so intuition tells us. For this reason, at least if our intuitions about the pair of cases just discussed are warranted, punitive war is very difficult to justify. The problem is not that the innocent will be punished; criminal justice systems also punish the innocent. The problem is rather that we cannot take sufficient steps to discriminate between the guilty and the innocent in the case of war.

2.6 Conclusions

Going to war for punitive reasons has a powerful historical pedigree, but it is difficult to defend. If we reject the idea of the collective liability of citizens to be punished for the actions of their state, as we should, punitive war will involve the punishment of innocent citizens for deterrence reasons. And whilst it is true that punishment institutions will always punish some innocent people, those institutions take considerable efforts to ensure that each person who is punished deserves to be punished. They do not regard it as sufficient that, statistically speaking, a certain threshold is met before punishment is meted out. Rather, the case against each individual must be made out to warrant punishing that individual. Punitive war would not be able to meet this demanding threshold, and for that reason punitive war is also very difficult to defend.

I don't say, though, that it is impossible to defend. One reason why is that in the stadium case discussed earlier, punishing those people within the stadium may not be necessary to avert very significant threats. Refraining from engaging in punitive war, in contrast, may result in the loss of a great deal of innocent life. Abiding by the principle that we only punish on condition that we have taken adequate steps to distinguish the guilty from the innocent may be less plausible in the case of war than it is in the case of domestic punishment. At most, we have seen a good reason to treat punitive war with a greater degree of scepticism than preventive war. The argument presented, I think, is not decisive in ruling it out.

References

Buchanan, A. (2006) 'Institutionalizing the Just War', *Philosophy and Public Affairs* 34: 2–38.

—— (2007) 'Justifying Preventive War', in H. Shue and D. Rodin (eds.), *Preemption: Military Action and Moral Justification* (Oxford: Oxford University Press), pp. 126–142.

Buchanan, A. and Keohane, R. O. (2004) 'The Preventive Use of Force: A Cosmopolitan Institutional Perspective', *Ethics and International Affairs* 18: 1–22.
Chesterman, S. (2001) *Just War or Just Peace?* (Oxford: Oxford University Press).
Ellis, A. (2003) 'A Deterrence Theory of Punishment', *Philosophical Quarterly* 53: 337–351.
Fabre, C. (2009) 'Permissible Rescue Killings', *Proceedings of the Aristotelian Society* 109: 149–164.
Farrell, D. M. (1990) 'The Justification of Deterrent Violence', *Ethics* 100: 301–317.
—— (1995) 'Deterrence and the Just Distribution of Harm', *Social Philosophy and Policy*: 220–240.
Frowe, H. (2008) 'Equating Innocent Threats and Bystanders', *Journal of Applied Philosophy* 25: 277–290.
Hurka, T. (2005) 'Proportionality in the Morality of War', *Philosophy and Public Affairs* 33: 34–66.
Husak, D. N. (2004) 'Guns and Drugs: Case Studies on the Principled Limits of the Criminal Sanction', *Law and Philosophy* 23: 437–493.
Kamm, F. M. (1996) *Morality, Mortality Vol. 2: Rights, Duties and Status* (Oxford: Oxford University Press).
—— (2011) *Ethics for Enemies: Terror, Torture, and War* (Oxford: Oxford University Press).
Lee, S. (2005) 'A Moral Critique of the Cosmopolitan Institutional Proposal', *Ethics and International Affairs* 19: 99–107.
McMahan, J. (2005) 'The Basis of Moral Liability to Defensive Killing', *Philosophical Issues* 15: 386–405.
—— (2006) 'Preventive War and the Killing of the Innocent', in R. Sorabji and D. Rodin (eds), *The Ethics of War: Shared Problems in Different Traditions* (Aldershot: Ashgate), 169–90.
—— (2008) 'Aggression and Punishment', in L. May *War: Essays in Political Philosophy* (Cambridge: Cambridge University Press), 67–84.
—— (2010) 'The Laws of War', in S. Besson and J. Tasioulas *The Philosophy of International Law* (Oxford: Oxford University Press), 493–509.
—— (2012) 'The Prevention of Unjust Wars', in Y. Benbaji and N. Sussman (eds.), *Reading Walzer* (London: Routledge).
Montague, P. (1995) *Punishment as Societal Defense* (New York: Rowman and Littlefield).
Neff, S. C. (2005) *War and the Law of Nations: A General History* (Cambridge: Cambridge University Press).
Otsuka, M. (2003) *Libertarianism without Inequality* (Oxford: Oxford University Press).
Quinn, W. (1993a) 'The Right to Threaten and the Right to Punish', in W. Quinn (ed.), *Morality and Action* (Cambridge: Cambridge University Press), 52–100.
—— (1993b) 'Actions, Intentions, and Consequences: The Doctrine of Double Effect' *Morality and Action* (Cambridge: Cambridge University Press), 175–193.
Quong J. (2009) 'Killing in Self-Defence'. *Ethics* 119: 507–537.
—— (2011) *Liberalism without Perfection* (Oxford: Oxford University Press).
Raz, J. (1986) *The Morality of Freedom* (Oxford: Oxford University Press).
Redmayne, M. (2008) 'Exploring the Proof Paradoxes', *Legal Theory* 14: 281–309.
Rodin, D. (2002) *War and Self-Defense* (Oxford: Oxford University Press).
Ross, W. D. (1930) *The Right and the Good* (Oxford: Oxford University Press).

Shue, H. (2007) 'What Would a Justified Preventive Military Attack Look Like?', in H. Shue and D. Rodin (eds.), *Preemption: Military Action and Moral Justification* (Oxford: Oxford University Press), 222–246.
Tadros, V. (2011) *The Ends of Harm: The Moral Foundations of Criminal Law* (Oxford: Oxford University Press).
Wellman, C. H. (2009) 'Rights and State Punishment', *Journal of Philosophy* 106: 419–439.

3

Why Not Forfeiture?

Gerald Lang

3.1 Introducing Forfeiture

Here is, I hope, an unremarkable description of what happens in standard cases of self-defence: although initially both the Victim and the Attacker have the right not to be killed by the other, and lack the right to kill the other, when the Attacker engages in a potentially lethal attack on the Victim, the Victim *acquires* the right to kill the Attacker and the Attacker *loses* his right not to be killed by the Victim. I am going to refer to this as the *Central Normative Transition of Self-Defence* (or the *Central Normative Transition* for short).

How is the Central Normative Transition to be explained? According to the *Forfeiture Account*, the explanation is approximately this: the Attacker loses his right in virtue of forfeiting his right, and he forfeits his right due to wrongdoing.[1] If the Attacker has lost his right, then the Victim does not act impermissibly in attacking him.

The notion of forfeiture has enjoyed application to two issues: self-defence and punishment. Though some of what I say will have an indirect bearing on the adequacy of forfeiture as a conceptual basis for punishment, and though I will be engaging with some of the literature on forfeiture and punishment, my official business is only with its adequacy as a basis for self-defence.

This essay will be structured as follows. In Section 3.2, I appraise nine objections which have been pressed against the Forfeiture Account, and conclude that the Forfeiture Account emerges unscathed from them. In Section 3.3, I suggest that the Forfeiture Account, just as it stands, is explanatorily underpowered, and, as an addendum to that contention, I say something about Judith Thomson's fluctuating commitments in the area.

[1] See Feinberg (1978).

In response to the 'Explanation Problem' for the Forfeiture Account which emerges in this part of the essay, I will suggest that one of the problems with the Forfeiture Account is that it is entirely Attacker-focused, not Victim-focused, and that we ought to be keeping our eye on both the Victim and the Attacker in arriving at an understanding of the Central Normative Transition. To this end, I attempt, in Sections 3.4 and 3.5, to revive Jan Narveson's well-known argument against the coherence of pacifism, noting objections and amending the argument where necessary. That will allow me, in Section 3.6, to advert to an account of the Central Normative Transition which awards an explanatory role to both the Victim (via a revised version of Narveson's argument) and the Attacker (via the Forfeiture Account). As we shall see, then, the Forfeiture Account is half-right: even if it does not give us the entire story behind the Central Normative Transition, it does give us an indispensable ingredient in the overall story.

3.2 Is Forfeiture a Sitting Duck?

My aim in this lengthy section is to report, and offer replies to, some of the most common recurring problems and difficulties that have been alleged against the Forfeiture Account.[2] I consider nine problems. Though they undoubtedly differ in strength or cogency, they have all managed to exert some influence on the overall standing or reputation of the Forfeiture Account, and for that reason alone it seems sensible to offer replies to all of them. These problems are often held to be fatal to the Forfeiture Account. I think, by contrast, that they are all unsuccessful. If the Forfeiture Account fails, it is not for any of *these* reasons, either alone or in combination with others. It must be conceded, however, that some of these problems cast a rather long shadow over forfeiture; I will be forced to issue a couple of promissory notes along the way.

3.2.1 *The Status Problem*

According to the *Status Problem*, the Forfeiture Account cannot explain why the Attacker *loses* a right, if he still retains the descriptive characteristics which made it appropriate to ascribe a right to him in the first place.

The Status Problem assumes, uncontentiously, that our possession of rights is justified in the first instance by the descriptive characteristics we possess: not just any entity can be a compelling subject for the ascription of rights, and the

[2] Thomson (1976), reprinted in Thomson (1986), outlines a number of charges against the Forfeiture Account; I have also been guided in this section by the discussions in Fletcher (1979), Kadish (1976), Ryan (1983), Montague (2010), and others. (The names of the problems are often mine.)

relevant descriptive characteristics must be the characteristics of, roughly speaking, Lockean personhood. But these descriptive characteristics are not typically lost by the Attacker when he attacks the Victim, so how, in turn, can he be said to have lost any rights, particularly a right as weighty as the right not to be killed?

The most promising reply to the Status Problem is to make the Attacker's right not to be killed *conditional*. On this line of thought, there is no denial that Attacker possesses, all along, the characteristics which make it appropriate to ascribe to him the right not to be killed. However, the Attacker's right not to be killed is held to persist only for as long as he satisfies certain conditions, chief among which is that he does not attempt to kill someone else who has not offended against the same conditions. To put it another way, the Forfeiture Account does not overlook the stability of the descriptive characteristics possessed by the Attacker on each side of the Central Normative Transition, but the rights it gives him will of course be *forfeitable* rights, not *non-forfeitable* rights (cf. Wellman 2012, p. 377).

This reply neuters the force of the Status Problem, though it raises, in turn, two further worries. The first of them is concerned with the basic characterization of the Central Normative Transition. If the Attacker's right is conditional, it can then be claimed that, strictly speaking, the Attacker suffers no *loss* of his right to life when he attacks the Victim; rather, there is simply the *absence* of a right applying to the Attacker when he attacks the Victim. And this means that the Forfeiture Account will be unable to accommodate the Central Normative Transition.

This worry can be easily tackled. Even if we operate with the description of the Attacker's plight according to which his right is absent, rather than lost, an adequate version of the Central Normative Transition can still be stated. For we can still note the contrast between the possession of the Attacker's right not to be killed in circumstances where he poses no deadly threat to the Victim, and the Attacker's non-possession of the right not to be killed in circumstances where he does pose a deadly threat to the Victim. This contrast is really all that matters to the Central Normative Transition, and the contrast can still be stated, without any real loss of accuracy, in the loss-and-acquisition language used to articulate the Central Normative Transition. For it is still the case, when the Attacker poses a deadly attack on the Victim, that the Attacker *loses the protection of the right* not to be killed which he had hitherto enjoyed, and it is still the case that the Victim *acquires* the right to do something she would not otherwise be permitted to do.

The second worry concerns explanatory force: why is the Forfeiture Account entitled to help itself to this conditional structure, without telling us *why* it is so entitled? This is a reasonable question, but it does not undermine my reply to the Status Problem. My reply to the Status Problem did not pretend to give us any *justification* of the Forfeiture Account. It was simply a comment on the *structure* of the

Forfeiture Account. In my view, it would beg the question against the Forfeiture Account to ignore details of this structure, or to deny defenders of the Forfeiture Account the opportunity to articulate it; but defenders of the Forfeiture Account would themselves be open to the charge of question-begging by confusing questions of structure with questions of justification. These issues will be revisited in Section 3.3.

3.2.2 *The Necessity Problem*

The *Necessity Problem* accuses the Forfeiture Account, in effect, of being unable to respect the *necessity condition* on permissible individual self-defence: the condition that lethal self-defensive action is justified only if it is necessary. Thomson illustrates this problem by imagining a malicious Attacker whose deadly intentions against the Victim are frustrated by a fortuitous injury: assume that the Attacker accidentally breaks his ankles, and is thus rendered suddenly harmless, when he leaps out of his tank in order to kill the Victim (Thomson 1986, p. 34; cf. Ryan 1983, p. 512).

Thomson must be assuming that the Forfeiture Account is unable to accommodate the necessity condition because all the material that could possibly matter to forfeiture has already been generated by the Attacker's formation of a deadly and unjustified intention to kill the Victim, together perhaps with the fact that he had already been engaged in the preliminary stages of a serious attack on the Victim up to the point where he leapt out of the tank. But I see no reason to accept this assumption. The difference between a situation in which the Attacker constitutes a credible ongoing threat to the Victim and a situation in which the Attacker does not constitute a credible ongoing threat to the Victim is surely not one which the Forfeiture Account is precluded from being able to register. If that is so, then the Forfeiture Account is not troubled by the Necessity Problem, for it need not be conceded that the broken-ankled Attacker has forfeited his right not to be killed.[3]

3.2.3 *The Proportionality Problem*

According to the *Proportionality Problem*, the Forfeiture Account is unable to accommodate the *proportionality condition* on permissible individual self-defence: though the Attacker is merely *attempting* to take the life of the Victim,

[3] Helen Frowe's 'Non-Combatant Liability in War' (this volume) offers an interesting challenge to the claim that the necessity condition must be accommodated by a theory of liability. Though I cannot offer a full response to Frowe here, it seem to me that the necessity condition plays a fairly deep structuring role in the generation of liability—see my discussion of the other problems in this section, particularly the Shrinking Value Problem in Section 3.2.5—and that it cannot be easily amputated from the Forfeiture Account without causing problems elsewhere.

the Victim is given permission to inflict a *much larger* harm on him, namely, death.[4] In reply to the Proportionality Problem, I will make three points.

First, and perhaps least importantly, there would appear to be an *ad hominem* problem for someone who, like Cheyney Ryan, wishes to recruit both the Necessity Problem and the Proportionality Problem into a single attack on the Forfeiture Account.[5] These problems are mutually inconsistent. The Proportionality Problem invites us to agree that, since the mere attempt to kill someone is much less wrong than actually killing someone, it follows that the Attacker's mere attempt to kill the Victim cannot possibly generate the level of forfeiture which is necessary to license the Victim's killing the Attacker. The Necessity Problem invited us to agree, by contrast, that the Attacker's mere attempt to kill the Victim not only generates a level of forfeiture which licenses the Victim to kill the Attacker, but which actually extends the Victim's license to kill him to a period after the Attacker has lost the ability to sustain a credible attack on her. In response to this tension, however, we clearly need to focus on the Proportionality Problem in isolation from the Necessity Problem (since those who were initially tempted to adumbrate both of them may now elect to surrender the Necessity Problem in order to advance only the Proportionality Problem).

My second point is that the defender of a Forfeiture Account may insist that the Attacker's active attempt to kill the Victim, while not as bad as an actual killing, nonetheless falls above the threshold of harm which can properly trigger a lethal response. But does this not, in turn, undermine my reply to the Necessity Problem? No, for notice that the broken-ankled Attacker in the case Thomson uses to illustrate the Necessity Problem cannot be described as being *actively engaged in a credible attempt* on the Victim's life, though he may still harbour a malicious intention and would resume a credible attack if he possibly could.

A third reply on offer to the Forfeiture Account, and the reply I am inclined to prefer as the most economical, is the claim that the Victim gains only the right to make an attempt on the Attacker's life. This reply ensures a comfortable commensurability between the initial offence and the justified response. Of course, the Victim may succeed in killing the Attacker, but the permission to attempt to kill someone surely cannot be understood as only the permission to submit a *failed* attempt on someone's life. The permission to attempt to kill someone is, rather, a permission to *succeed* in one's attempt to kill him. (After all, the Attacker

[4] There are definite signs of this objection in Thomson (1976), p. 35, though admittedly Thomson does not dawdle over it, and it is embedded in a more complicated dialectic concerning forfeiture and punishment. (I shall address these particular issues later in this chapter, when I discuss the Restoration Dilemma.)

[5] See Ryan (1983), pp. 511–512, who draws explicit inspiration here from Thomson (1976).

is engaged in an attempt to successfully kill the Victim; he is not aiming *not* to succeed in the attempt he is making.) So, if the Victim actually kills the Attacker, there can be no complaint that she has strayed beyond what she was initially given permission to do.

3.2.4 *The Restoration Dilemma*

The fourth problem, which builds upon certain aspects of both the Proportionality Problem and the Necessity Problem, I will call the *Restoration Dilemma* (Montague 2010, pp. 76–79). It can be outlined as follows. Imagine that the Attacker actually kills the Victim. What happens then? Either the Attacker's right to life remains in forfeit, or it is restored. If the Attacker's life remains in forfeit, then he is—counter-intuitively—fair game for anyone else. If the Attacker's right to life is restored, then, paradoxically, his right to life has been restored for severe and successfully completed wrongdoing, whereas his right was forfeited for the lesser offence of merely attempting to kill the Victim. Both horns of this dilemma seem initially uninviting.

In reply, I think we must find ways of occupying the second horn of the dilemma (though I will assuredly be quarrelling with the Restoration Dilemma's *description* of this second horn). The Forfeiture Account does not enjoy any remit to license lethal violence against the Attacker in circumstances where no self-defensive action *can* be taken. This is a simple application of the necessity condition on self-defence. If the Attacker successfully completes his attempt on the Victim's life, then he cannot be said to have forfeited his right not to be attacked *in self-defence*. It is the exigencies of the self-defensive situation which explain why the Attacker can be permissibly killed. So, if the Attacker has *already* killed the Victim, then of course it can no longer be necessary to kill him in order to *prevent* him from killing the Victim.

It does not follow, of course, that withdrawal of a permission to kill the Attacker in self-defence restores the Attacker to a condition of moral unimpeachability. What does follow is that the proper treatment of the Attacker is now answerable to different standards which fall under a separate sub-department of ethics: the area of punishment. The fact that the Attacker *did* forfeit his right to life during the time of the attack on the Victim is, in my view, likely to bear heavily on the question of how he is liable to be treated now, in terms of his proper exposure to punishment and associated moral sanctions. But this is not a line of inquiry which I need to pursue any further here. My present task is only to show that the Attacker's forfeiture of his life whilst he is attacking the Victim does not generate embarrassment for the Forfeiture Account in cases where the Attacker's attempt to kill the Victim has proven successful. The Attacker is not, perversely, *rewarded* by the Forfeiture

Account for success in a project which he was forbidden from undertaking in the first place.

3.2.5 *The Shrinking Value Problem*

It is important to explain the intellectual sources of the temptation to occupy the first horn of the Restoration Dilemma. This takes us to a fifth problem: the *Shrinking Value Problem*.

The Shrinking Value Problem has its origins in Locke's argument in the *Second Treatise on Government* that, in the state of nature which precedes the formation of the state, individuals enjoy the right to punish those who violate their natural rights, and that their permission to punish is explained by the offenders' forfeiture of their rights.[6] But how does Locke characterize forfeiture? Here are three relevant passages:

> [Due to] the crime which consists in violating the laws, and varying from the right rule of reason,...a man...becomes degenerate, and declares himself to quit the principles of human nature and to be a noxious creature... (Locke 1690, 2.10)

> And thus it is that every man in the state of Nature has a power to kill a murderer, both to deter others...and also to secure men from the attempts of a criminal who, having renounced reason, the common rule and measure God hath given to mankind, hath, by the unjust violence and slaughter he hath committed upon one, declared war against all mankind, and therefore may be destroyed as a lion or a tiger, one of those wild savage beasts with whom men can have no society nor security. (Locke 1690, 2.11)

> Indeed, having by his fault forfeited his own life, by some act that deserves death; he, to whom he has forfeited it, may (when he has him in his power) delay to take it, and make use of him to his own service, and he does him no injury by it: for, whenever he finds the hardship of his slavery outweigh the value of his life, it is in his power, by resisting the will of his master, to draw on himself the death he desires. (Locke 1690, 4.23)

Perhaps not surprisingly, commentators have tended to fasten on the pejorative and eye-catching descriptions of offenders which Locke provides. They are variously described as 'wild savage beasts', as 'degenerate', and as 'noxious'; their enslavement is apparently unproblematic, and they appear to be beyond injury. The Lockean influence is alive and well in more recent writings. George Fletcher, for example, thinks that the Forfeiture Account is committed to holding that 'killing an outlaw is like killing a wolf or a fly' (Fletcher 1979, p. 1381; cf. Thomson 1986, p. 34).

All of this may help to suggest the following explanatory picture which the Lockean takes to be at work in the Forfeiture Account: in attacking the Victim, the Attacker forfeits his life; in forfeiting his life, the Attacker has made it the case that his value shrinks to a level at which his fate is morally insignificant; the disvalue of

[6] Locke (1690/1980). For a good discussion of Locke's theory, see Simmons (1991).

the Attacker then explains why it is permissible to kill him. Killing him will generate no disvalue, because *he* no longer has any value. On this picture, it will hardly be surprising if the Attacker's disvalue, which is generated by his initial attack on the Victim, endures after the attack is completed, thus ensuring that the Attacker persists in a permanent condition of moral insignificance.

This picture of the Forfeiture Account, which implies its impalement on the first horn of the Restoration Dilemma, is not one which friends of that account are obliged to uphold. There need be no appeal to the shifting *value* of the Attacker as an explanation for the Victim's permissible use of force against him. Undoubtedly, the Attacker suffers a loss of rights which he used to have. And there must be some *explanation* of that loss of rights. But we are not forced to say, unappealingly, that the community earns its right to inflict sanctions on an offender as a result of the offender's shrunken value.

My earlier treatment of the Restoration Dilemma suggests the proper way of responding to the Shrunken Value Problem. We know, from that discussion, that the treatment of the Attacker is governed throughout by the necessity condition on self-defence. But there could be no plausible explanation of this variability in permissible treatment if permissible treatment was thought to be a response to the Attacker's fluctuating value. This is because we would surely enjoy no independent purchase on the value which was supposedly in a state of flux, and which could explain, in turn, when self-defensive violence was legitimate, and when it was illegitimate. True, the Attacker has done something which makes it permissible for the Victim, or a third party acting on the Victim's behalf, to kill him, but the Forfeiture Account can restrict its concerns with the disvalue of *what he has done*, not the disvalue of *what he is*. In working out what the Victim may permissibly do to the Attacker, we do not have to seek answers in the Attacker's *value*. In the relevant sense, there is nothing here to discover.

3.2.6 The Sitting Duck Problem

The sixth of the problems for the Forfeiture Account will be referred to as the *Sitting Duck Problem*. The Sitting Duck Problem is, in effect, a more temporally restricted version of the first horn of the Restoration Dilemma. The Forfeiture Account tells us that, during his attack on the Victim, the Attacker forfeits his right not to be killed. The Attacker's forfeiture of his right not to be killed explains why the Victim can attack him. But plausibly, given the generous conceptual connections between self-defence and other-defence, the Attacker's forfeiture also seems to explain why *anyone else* might attack him. This is not an embarrassing result when we consider cases of other-defence which are motivated by the aim of protecting the Victim. But we can imagine cases of violence against the Attacker which are motivated by very different considerations. In illustration of the Sitting Duck Problem, David Rodin presents the example of *Bugsey*, a gangster who walks into a bar and kills a rival mobster who just so happens to be engaged in an unjustifiable lethal attack on someone else (Rodin 2002, pp. 73–74). If Bugsey's rival has forfeited his right not to be killed, then it would seem that Bugsey has done nothing wrong. But that is counter-intuitive. Even though the Attacker may be engaged in a lethal and unjust attack on the Victim, he is not a sitting duck for everyone else.

The Sitting Duck Problem accuses the Forfeiture Account, in effect, of sealing us into commitment to an *objective* or *fact-relative* account of self-defence, where the *facts* about the innocence or non-innocence of the Attacker are wholly determining of the permissibility of killing him. Objective accounts contrast with *subjective* accounts, which restrict permissible acts of self-defence or other-defence to acts which exhibit the relevant motives or intentions, or—in stricter versions—to acts which take account of the available evidence.[7] The debate between objective and subjective accounts is, once again, a large one, which I am unable to adjudicate here.[8] But even in the absence of a comprehensive settlement in this debate, a couple of replies to the Sitting Duck Problem can be offered, which should serve to blunt the force of the objection.

First, the Forfeiture Account is not obviously precluded from *supplementing* forfeiture-based considerations with other requirements on agents' motivation. On this view, the Attacker's forfeiture will license legitimate violence against him provided that other conditions are in place as well. Even if the resulting Forfeiture Account must be deemed impure, it need not lose its distinctiveness vis-à-vis other substantive accounts of self-defence. Second, the Forfeiture Account can bite the bullet: the Attacker's forfeiture of his right *does* generate a permission to disarm him in other-defence, which means that Bugsey can kill his rival. So does that mean Bugsey is to be morally commended? No, for his malicious intentions surely generate material for other, separate types of moral criticism. The same point extends to other-defenders whose violent actions against the Attacker may betray recklessness, or negligence, rather than outright malice. True, the Forfeiture Account does imply that any moral charges against these flawed other-defenders cannot be as severe as homicide, but that is not to say that these agents are to be congratulated, or that they escape moral censure.

We can perhaps think of other-defenders such as Bugsey as beneficiaries of moral luck. While their character and intentions may mark them out for serious

[7] See Parfit (2011), pp. 150–151, for further discussion of the contrasts between the 'fact-relative', 'belief-relative', and 'evidence-relative' senses of wrongness.

[8] For some further discussions, see Christopher (1998), Ferzan (2005), and McMahan (2005b).

moral criticism, they have not, in fact, performed actions which can be deemed homicidal. But I do not think that should disturb us any more than we were disturbed by the cases illustrating the Necessity Problem. What makes homicide the terrible crime it is cannot be stated independently of the fact that it involves the *killing* of an innocent person—a person who is wronged by being killed. If the person Bugsey has targeted for death is in the process of attempting to kill another innocent person, then Bugsey's victim is not, in the relevant sense, innocent, and the malicious intentions which lie behind Bugsey's attack on him will simply not possess the full moral toxicity that they would have otherwise possessed.

3.2.7 The Scope Problem

The seventh problem I shall call the *Scope Problem*. According to the Scope Problem, the Forfeiture Account supports an unacceptably limited set of permissions in respect of the Victim's right to engage in self-defence. To see why, we need briefly to consider the different specimens of Attacker. The canonical case of the Attacker is often referred to as the *Culpable Attacker*. The Culpable Attacker is typically taken to meet at least the following conditions: he is deliberately and culpably engaged in an attack on the Victim that is unjustified, but is not misinformed. Next, there are the *Innocent Attacker* and the *Innocent Threat*. The Innocent Attacker is an agent whose agency is being lethally deployed against the Victim, but who has diminished responsibility, or no responsibility at all, for the deployment of that agency. The conditions which Innocent Attackers labour under may be highly varied: they include false belief, hypnosis, brainwashing, psychosis, an under-developed capacity for responsibility (think of child soldiers), and other conditions which may impair agency either locally or globally. The Innocent Threat is an agent who poses a threat to the Victim, but not through any deployment of his agency: think of an agent, caught by a gust of wind, who is falling through the air towards the Victim.

According to the Scope Problem, Innocent Attackers and Innocent Threats cannot be said to have forfeited their right not to be killed if they are not responsible for what they have done. (Innocent Threats do not even *act*, so they cannot be reasonably accused of acting *wrongly*.) But that is an unwelcome implication, because Innocent Attackers and Innocent Threats may be legitimately killed in self-defence.[9]

[9] For this type of argument, see Thomson (1976), Fletcher (1979), and Kadish (1976). Thomson's commitments with respect to this issue are preserved in Thomson (1991).

There is an extensive debate about the scope of self-defensive permissions.[10] Some writers who are sympathetic to the Forfeiture Account agree with the implication that the account cannot license self-defensive violence against Innocent Attackers and Innocent Threats, but actually see this as an advantage of the Forfeiture Account, rather than anything which needs to be apologized for. This is because, on their view, the Victim may *not* attack (certain types of) Innocent Attackers or Innocent Threats.[11] Other defenders of the Forfeiture Account, who think that Innocent Attackers and Innocent Threats can be legitimately attacked in self-defence, may insist that the notion of forfeiture is not out of place even when we are dealing with Attackers whose agency has been compromised: perhaps there can be non-culpable or even non-responsible rights-violators, and perhaps it makes sense to say of moral agents, even those agents whose agency has been compromised or entirely silenced, that they may be in morally inappropriate, rights-violating places (Kamm 1992, p. 47).

I cannot go into any further details here about the scope of self-defensive permissions. This is because, happily, the Scope Problem is unlikely to enjoy any decisive implications for the fate of the Forfeiture Account. Why is that? It is because the conceptual resources on offer to the Forfeiture Account for responding to the scope issue are likely to be informed by the broader arguments which decide how the scope of permissible self-defence is going to be fixed. Let us imagine that the scope of permissible self-defensive action should be fixed broadly, such as to encompass violent action against Innocent Attackers and Innocent Threats. If that account is defensible, it may then furnish us with resources which show that these types of attacker have forfeited, albeit in a non-responsible way, the right not to be killed.[12]

Now let us imagine, by contrast, that the scope of permissible self-defensive action should be fixed much more narrowly, as encompassing only Culpable Attackers. If this narrower account is correct, then once again the Forfeiture Account risks no embarrassment, as it will surely be capable of restraining its ascriptions of forfeiture in ways which are governed by the truth of that

[10] For those who think the scope is broad, see Thomson (1991); for those who defend an account of narrower scope, see McMahan (2005a), Otsuka (1994), and Rodin (2002), ch. 4. (Some writers, such as Quong 2009, Frowe 2008, and Benbaji 2005, offer a hybrid account according to which it is permissible for both the Victim to kill the Innocent Attacker and Innocent Threat, and for the Innocent Attacker and Innocent Threat to kill the Victim.)

[11] See, e.g., Rodin (2002), ch. 4.

[12] Another possibility is that, even if forfeiture cannot be plausibly assigned to Innocent Attackers and Innocent Threats, it may continue to be assigned to Culpable Attackers. Perhaps we cannot have a one-size-fits-all grounding account of self-defence. That need not impugn the Forfeiture Account as a defensible solution to paradigm instances of the Central Normative Transition.

independent account about scope. Questions of scope are plausibly prior to ascriptions of forfeiture, and we should not expect the Forfeiture Account to issue verdicts which are at odds with the line favoured by whichever account in the debate about scope is ultimately to be preferred.

3.2.8 *The Suitability Problem*

The eighth problem is the *Suitability Problem*, which is concerned with the Old Testament-style 'eye for an eye' reasoning popularly associated with theories of forfeiture. Imagine highly unusual circumstances in which an Attacker's imminent threats to rape or torture the Victim can only be avoided by inflicting rape or torture on the Attacker. Does it follow from the Forfeiture Account that the Attacker forfeits, in such circumstances, the right not to be raped, or tortured? That will seem highly resistible to those who hold that there are secure moral constraints against rape, torture, and other particularly distressing violent acts, even when these acts are inflicted upon agents who would otherwise inflict them upon other, innocent agents.

A number of replies are available to defenders of the Forfeiture Account. First, they may be inclined to bite the bullet: perhaps the infliction of rape and torture in situations of self-defence, *genuinely* restrained by the application of the necessity condition, is more tolerable than the infliction of such penalties *as punishments*, which would surely strike most of us as cruel and unusual. But this reply may encounter difficulties when aspects of the Sitting Duck Problem are taken into consideration. If one is inclined to take a lax approach to motivating attitudes in cases of other-defence, then it may take more than an acceptance of the existence of moral luck to make it seem permissible for other-defenders to engage in acts of rape and torture. Of course, the response to the Sitting Duck Problem might have already pre-empted this particular difficulty (not least because the preferred response to the Sitting Duck Problem might understandably have been shaped by an awareness of the Suitability Problem).

But there is another reply, adumbrated by Christopher Heath Wellman, which may be tempting to defenders of the Forfeiture Account, and which is of independent theoretical interest in any case. According to this reply, and contrary to a common understanding of what the very idea of forfeiture consists in, the Forfeiture Account is *not* committed to saying that, if an Attacker is threatening to violate rights *X*, *Y*, and *Z* in the Victim, then his own rights to *X*, *Y*, and *Z* have been forfeited (Wellman 2012, p. 385).[13] For Wellman, forfeiture can take a more inexact

[13] This like-for-like construal of forfeiture is initially upheld, e.g., by Boonin (2008), p. 105. He is later prepared to entertain a weakening of it, but at the cost of generating another problem for the Forfeiture Account: see Section 3.2.9 in this chapter.

form, where the Attacker forfeits rights which are roughly commensurate with, or equivalent to, the rights he violates, or threatens to violate.[14] For example, rather than saying that the Attacker forfeits his right not to be raped, we can say instead that the Attacker forfeits the right not to have (perhaps extraordinary) levels of 'ordinary' or garden-variety violence inflicted upon him. If Wellman's proposal is on the right lines, the Forfeiture Account can sidestep the Suitability Problem.

3.2.9 *The Equivalence Problem*

But is Wellman's proposal sound? David Boonin suggests not, and argues that this sort of response to the Suitability Problem suffers from a fatal flaw (Boonin 2008, p. 111). I will call this the *Equivalence Problem*.

The Equivalence Problem takes the form of a dilemma: either we uncover a genuine equivalence between the Attacker's right to *X* (which he is held not to have forfeited) and his right to *T* (which he is held to have forfeited), or we do not. If we do, then all the advantages which are gained in the denial that the Attacker has forfeited his right to *X* will surely be lost in the affirmation that the Attacker has forfeited his right to *T*. If the right to *T* really is equivalent to the right to *X*, then why won't forfeiture of either one of these rights cause as much consternation as forfeiture of the other? Now this problem can be evaded if it is denied that there is equivalence between the Attacker's right to *X* and his right to *T*. But that simply takes us to the second horn of the dilemma. If there is non-equivalence between the right to *X* and the right to *T*, then the Wellman-flavoured proposal fails by its own lights, and there will be a class of rights to which the Forfeiture Account will not be applicable.

The dilemma can be broken by quarrelling with its second horn: we should be content to settle for only *rough* equivalence between non-forfeitable rights (such as the right to *X*) and forfeitable rights (such as the right to *T*). There *may* be acts which, by their very nature, are never permissible to perform: rape and torture, perhaps. If such acts exist, they will be plausibly be impermissible in every circumstance because of the indignity they inflict upon, or lack of respect they express for, their victims. Neither should we expect these impermissibility-generating characteristics to be successfully analyzable in terms of the *harm* or *expected* harm caused by the acts in question. Killing someone might actually be more harmful than torturing him: in support of this contention, a prospective victim of torture

[14] Since Wellman is concerned with punishment, not self-defence, it is actual violations of rights, rather than threats of rights violations, which matter to him. But this distinction between actual violations and threats of violation should cease to be distracting just as soon as the Proportionality Problem has been laid to rest.

might, without delusion, prefer to be tortured than to be killed. The fact that this individual may prefer to be tortured than to be killed is consistent with the permissibility of killing him (in some circumstances) and the impermissibility of torturing him (under any circumstances).

Though these issues certainly invite more scrutiny from those who hold that torture is absolutely impermissible,[15] the *prima facie* coherence of this position is a gift to defenders of the Forfeiture Account. This is because the characteristics of acts which would offend against non-forfeitable rights need not be understood in terms which make the prospect of violations of those rights more *harmful* to their holders than the forfeiture of the forfeitable rights which are roughly equivalent to them. In terms of *harmfulness*, then, forfeitable rights and non-forfeitable rights may indeed be equivalent. This is an encouraging result for friends of forfeiture.

3.3 The Explanation Problem

None of the nine objections I have considered inflicts fatal damage on the Forfeiture Account, but trouble of a recognizable sort still lies ahead.

Consider Thomson's summary of her later views on self-defence:

> [W]hat makes it permissible for you to kill [Attackers] is that they will otherwise violate your rights that they not kill you, and *therefore* lack rights that you not kill them. (Thomson 1991, p. 302; emphasis added)

It seems entirely legitimate to ask: what is the force of this 'therefore'? What is the connection supposed to be between the *impermissibility* of an Attacker's actions and the *permissibility* of the Victim's self-defensive actions against them? The transition seems mysterious, or at least under-explained. I will refer to this problem as the *Explanation Problem*.

The Explanation Problem infects earlier descriptions of forfeiture, applying to punishment. Here, for example, is W. D. Ross's well-known description of the relationship between forfeiture and punishment:

> The essential duty of the state is to protect the most fundamental rights of individuals. Now, rights of any human being are correlative to duties incumbent on the owner of rights, or . . . to rights owned by those against whom he has rights; and the main element in any one's right to life or liberty or property is *extinguished* by his failure to respect the corresponding rights in others. (Ross 1930, p. 60; emphasis added)

[15] For further discussions of these issues, see Steinhoff (2006), McMahan (2008), and Kamm (2011), ch. 1.

Though Ross does not mention forfeiture by name in this passage, it is plainly forfeiture he has in mind. But *why* are rights extinguished in the way Ross suggests, at least in cases where we are not dealing with contractual obligations which plainly lapse upon breach of duties in the party with whom one has contracted?[16]

Let us cast about for answers. Some writers appear to have been tempted by the conditional structure of the rights ascribed to the Attacker by the Forfeiture Account.[17] But, as I explained earlier, this does not constitute an *argument* for the Forfeiture Account. The Forfeiture Account still owes us an explanation of *why* the rights ascribed to the Attacker take this conditional form.[18] Neither can the first-order Hohfeldian structure of rights deliver any argument for forfeiture. Before the events which create the circumstances of the Central Normative Transition, both the agent who turns out to be the Victim and the agent who turns out to be the Attacker have a claim on each other not to be attacked. When the Attacker launches his attack on the Victim, he is in breach of the duty not to attack her, but that by itself does not explain why *her* duty not to attack *him* has now been suspended.

One potential explanation of why the Explanation Problem persists as a problem for the Forfeiture Account is that the need to account for the mysterious mechanisms of forfeiture has not always been honestly confronted. In this connection, it might be useful to distinguish between two possible roles that forfeiture might play in its contribution to the Central Normative Transition. In one sense, the Forfeiture Account could be construed as a *substantive rival* to all the other accounts that have been offered for the permissibility of self-defence. These rival accounts come in different shapes and sizes. One might propose, for example, that the Central Normative Transition is to be explained in terms of a just distribution of harm, or by appealing to the Victim's legitimate self-concern. But in a second sense, the notion of forfeiture might be operating in a more *formal* sense, as little more than a synonym for loss. In this more formal sense, the Attacker's forfeiture of his right not to be killed is simply what you arrive at when you have supplied some *other* explanation of the Central Normative Transition.[19]

[16] For insightful commentary on Ross's argument, see Sher (1987), pp. 72–74.

[17] See, e.g., Goldman (1979).

[18] Other rights-schemas explored in Thomson (1976), involving the violation of rights *versus* the infringement of rights, or rights differing in their degrees of stringency, will suffer from the same basic problem: namely, the need to say more to explain the Central Normative Transition.

[19] Morris (1991) argues that the Forfeiture Account is dependent on other, substantive explanatory resources, and suggests that this actually counts as an advantage of the Forfeiture Account, since it permits the case for punishment to be grounded in the wider social purposes served by the institution of punishment. This strikes me as a potentially more useful advantage to theories of punishment than to theories of self-defence.

It is not always easy to pinpoint which use of 'forfeiture' writers have in mind. Judith Thomson's work is a prime example of this elusiveness. Though it includes no explicit revocation of her earlier criticisms, Thomson's later work on self-defence does not betray anything like the hostility to the Forfeiture Account which was so prominently on display in 'Self-Defense and Rights'. Indeed, the term 'forfeiture' and its cognates are used fairly liberally throughout her discussion of self-defence in *The Realm of Rights* (Thomson 1990, esp. pp. 361ff.). Now is that because Thomson had abandoned her earlier criticisms of forfeiture, or it is because she was operating with a different understanding of forfeiture which was supposedly invulnerable to those earlier criticisms? It is not easy to say; Thomson pays no concerted attention to forfeiture in these later discussions.

One possible suggestion is that, in *The Realm of Rights*, Thomson saw no reason to abjure the notion of forfeiture because she using the term in a less committed, formal way, rather than in a more committed, substantive way. That suggestion, however, is not helped by the following reference to forfeiture in her article 'Self-Defense':

> What is in question is not whether the innocent aggressor *forfeits* his right but whether he *lacks* it. (Thomson 1991, p. 301; emphases added)[20]

This sentence definitely suggests that Thomson was not simply equating 'forfeiture' with 'loss'. But it raises, in turn, the question of why she did not completely steer clear of 'forfeiture' and its cognates in these later discussions.

I have two suggestions. First, Thomson is principally concerned, in 'Self-Defense', with the *scope* of self-defence: she is anxious to show that the Victim enjoys the right of self-defence against Innocent Attackers and Innocent Threats, as well as Culpable Attackers. To say that the Attacker forfeits his right to life may suggest (at least to Thomson) that the Attacker must have done something minimally intentional in order to forfeit his right to life. As Thomson thinks that even Innocent Threats may be killed, she is most likely anxious to avoid any hostages to fortune that may emerge through a dependence on the notion of forfeiture. It seems to me, however, that forfeiture need not be restrained in these ways.[21] A second suggestion is that Thomson was, in effect, oscillating between thinking of forfeiture in a substantive way and forfeiture in a formal way.

[20] The analysis Thomson offers in her 1991 article is an expanded, or at least complementary, version of the analysis offered in Thomson (1990).

[21] This is what I tried to suggest in my discussion of the Scope Problem in Section 3.2.7.

Thomson should perhaps not be chided too much for this oscillation (if, as I suspect, she is prone to it); for both versions of forfeiture appear to face the Explanation Problem, which now needs to be unpacked.

Consider the formal sense of forfeiture. If we are interested in the Central Normative Transition, then we will not be paying any attention to forfeiture until we have reached an explanation of the Central Normative Transition. Forfeiture cannot be part of the explanation of the Central Normative Transition; it is wheeled out simply to announce that an explanation has been reached on *other* grounds. Perhaps we might think that there is nothing wrong with that: it is precisely what we would expect if we are thinking about forfeiture in a formal sense.

However—perhaps more surprisingly—when we examine forfeiture in the substantive sense, a rather similar problem emerges. For the Forfeiture Account *still* seems to suffer from a kind of explanatory reticence. Compare the Forfeiture Account with an account such as the 'Forced Choice of Lives' Account advanced by Philip Montague (Montague 1981, 2000, 2010). According to the Forced Choice of Lives Account, the Victim's permission to kill the Attacker emerges as the just or fair distribution of harms in cases where the Attacker's actions have made it the case that not everyone can live. It is no part of my remit here to discuss in detail the merits of the Forced Choice of Lives Account. The only point I want to make about it is that, even in outline, it seems more explanatorily *ambitious* than the Forfeiture Account. It sets out to explain *why* the Attacker loses his right and *why* the Victim acquires a right to kill the Attacker. The Forfeiture Account, by contrast, appears to short-circuit that explanatory project by simply declaring *that* the Attacker's right has been lost due to his morally problematic actions (or movements, in case we are dealing with Innocent Threats and the Forfeiture Account has seen fit to embrace a wider account of the scope of self-defensive permissions).[22]

In my view, it is a bad idea to separate the role of the Attacker and the role of the Victim in the overall explanatory story. But that is arguably the offence of which the Forfeiture Account is guilty. The Forfeiture Account seems Attacker-focused, not Victim-focused: it is the loss of the Attacker's right which explains why the Victim acquires the right to kill him. But further reflection should confirm that this cannot be the whole story. We should not expect the Attacker to lose the right to life without keeping in mind what he would otherwise do the Victim. These things should fit together in the overall substantive explanation of the Central Normative Transition; the reason why the Victim is permitted to do something she

[22] Simmons (1991) argues that considerations of fairness can underpin theories of forfeiture. My preferred description of Simmons's argument is to say that the fairness argument is doing the substantive work for him, which then entitles him to appeal to forfeiture in a formal sense.

would not otherwise be permitted to do cannot be separated for very long from the reason why the Attacker is no longer protected by a right which he would otherwise enjoy. These facts plausibly stand or fall together.[23] That does not mean that the notion of forfeiture is destined to play no role in that overall explanation. But it does mean we cannot expect it to shoulder the entire explanatory burden.

3.4 Supplementing Forfeiture: Narveson on the 'Logic of Rights'

The Forfeiture Account is Attacker-based. To fill out the explanatory picture, we need to pay more attention to the Victim. In my view, a promising place to start is with a fairly old, well-known, and—in the considered view of many—discredited argument proposed by Jan Narveson against pacifism.

Narveson argued that pacifism is 'actually incoherent because self-contradictory' (Narveson 1965, p. 259). His conclusion is delivered, in effect, by the following argument:

(1) *Red*'s right (or claim-right) 'just *is* a status justifying preventive action', or 'an entitlement to protection' for *Red*. (Narveson 1965, p. 266; Narveson 1968, p. 150)

It supposedly follows that:

(2) If Red has a claim-right against *Blue*, then Red enjoys a liberty to take whatever necessary means are called for in order to prevent Blue's violation of Red's right.

And so, as a particular substitution instance of (2):

(3) In case Red's right not to be attacked by Blue can only be upheld by Red's violent counter-attack against Blue, then Red has the right to engage in a violent counter-attack against Blue.

Narveson's *Anti-Pacifism Argument*, as I shall refer to it, has generated severe criticism. I shall briefly state two problems with it.[24] Though these problems are

[23] This is a point well made by Rodin (2002), p. 75, who describes the lost right of the Attacker and the acquired right of the Victim as simply different sides of the same conceptual coin. Other writers, such as Ryan (1983), p. 512, have tended to proceed as though these normative facts come apart. On Ryan's view, we can convince ourselves that the Attacker has lost his right not to be killed, but still stand in need of a *further* explanation of why the Victim has acquired the right to kill the Attacker. This seems wrong-headed to me. What Ryan might be getting right, however, is the need to pay attention to both the Attacker and the Victim in a single explanatory story we construct for the Central Normative Transition.

[24] A form of the Suitability Problem has also been pressed against Narveson by Teichman (1986), esp. pp. 33–34 and Ryan (1983), pp. 514–515. Since I have already addressed the Suitability Problem in

indeed weighty, I believe that the argument can be largely patched up, and that it remains powerful.

First, the Anti-Pacifism Argument seems insensitive to the distinction between self-defence and self-preservation. To see why, consider an *Innocent Onlooker*, an agent who is standing near the Victim, and who could be used, at the cost of his life, to deflect or absorb the lethal injury which will otherwise be visited upon the Victim. Intuitively—and certainly for non-consequentialists—it is wrong to use the Innocent Onlooker in this way. The wrongness would persist even if there were a number of Victims, so that the killing of the Innocent Onlooker would at least achieve a net saving of innocent lives. Now the problem with the Anti-Pacifism Argument is that (2) does not offer any materials for distinguishing between Attackers and Onlookers. Though (3) is a particular substitution instance of (2), (2) would also support (4):

(4) In case Red's right not to be attacked by Blue can only be upheld by Red's violent counter-attack against *Green*, where Green is an Innocent Onlooker, then Red has the right to engage in a violent counter-attack against Green.

But (4) is intuitively unacceptable.

A second problem with the Anti-Pacifism Argument—and this problem also helps to explain its exposure to the first problem—is that it is entirely Victim-focused, not Attacker-focused. Its mistakes are therefore a mirror image of the mistakes made by the Forfeiture Account, which is entirely Attacker-focused, not Victim-focused. Once again, I think we need to be keeping our eye on both the Attacker and the Victim in our attempt to explain the Central Normative Transition. Our task is to construct a single account which provides gainful employment for both the Attacker and the Victim.

3.5 The Revised Anti-Pacifism Argument

The *Revised Anti-Pacifism Argument* consists of two claims. The first claim is shared with the original Anti-Pacifism Argument. It seems to me that Narveson is quite right to insist that:

(1) Red's right (or claim-right) 'just *is* a status justifying preventive action', or 'an entitlement to protection' for Red.

Section 3.2.8, I will not discuss it here. Teichman, in particular, provides a number of further trenchant criticisms of Narveson's argument as it is actually articulated, such as his linkage between wrongness and rights-violation. To avoid engaging with these particular problems, I have offered a deliberately stripped-down version of Narveson's argument. (The colour-coded agents are also my addition.)

This claim would appear to be a conceptual truth.[25] Why is that? Compare the outcome where the Attacker's attempt is successful with the outcome where the Attacker's attempt is thwarted: it cannot be a matter of moral indifference which of these two outcomes is realized. Clearly, morality must favour or prefer the outcome in which the Attacker's attempt is thwarted. Nor can this be just a matter of morality's bequeathing upon the outcome in which the Attacker's attempt is thwarted a special *description*: a description which states 'MORALITY FAVOURS THIS OUTCOME'. If it is true that morality favours this outcome over the outcome in which the Attacker's attempt is successful, then it must follow, I think, that morality affords us *permissible effective means* to bring about the preferred outcome.[26]

So far, so good. Still, and as we have seen, the 'whatever it takes' condition asserted by Narveson is far too strong. The condition therefore needs to be finessed. Rather than (2), I propose that the Revised Anti-Pacifism Argument consists in the combination of (1) and (5):

(5) If Red has a claim-right against Blue, then Red enjoys a presumptive liberty to take whatever necessary and proportionate means, including violent means, are called for against Blue in order to prevent Blue's violation of Red's right.

We need, of course, to unpack (5) at greater length. Let us consider the first problem, concerning the Anti-Pacifism Argument's failure to distinguish between self-defence and self-preservation. The right to engage in self-defensive action is generated in response to an attempted rights violation, and the Victim's right to take countervailing measures is thus, I submit, properly restricted to the use of force against the would-be rights-violator. Attackers, but not Onlookers, may be attacked by the Victim (or by others acting in other-defence of the Victim). That means that Red can attack Blue, but not Green. But what is the difference between Blue and Green, such that Red can permissibly kill Blue, but not Green? Forfeiture is about to re-enter the story.

3.6 Conclusion: Where Does Forfeiture Fit In?

The Revised Anti-Pacifism Argument pays proper attention to both the Attacker and the Victim in the overall explanatory story of the Central Normative

[25] Rodin (2002), p. 37, concurs, though without any argument.

[26] Even Ryan (1983), p. 514, who takes pacifism very seriously, concedes that the 'logic of rights' establishes at least this much.

Transition. In one important sense, the explanatory story ought to start with the Victim. It is the Victim's rights-protected interests which trigger her right to attack the agent who poses the threat to those interests. The Victim's counter-attack is properly directed at the Attacker, rather than at Onlookers, because of the particular role played by the Attacker in the generation of the threat. And here it must be the morally problematic actions or movements of the Attacker which select him—and only him—as the appropriate target of self-defensive violence, which in turn re-introduces the notion of forfeiture.[27] So forfeiture does, after all, play a distinctive role in the overall story of how the Central Normative Transition is to be explained. It is not the whole story, but it is an irreducible part of the whole story. The Forfeiture Account is half-right.

It may be complained that the invocation of forfeiture is still explanatorily reticent: the claim that the Attacker (but not the Onlooker) has forfeited his rights is not much of an improvement on the claim that, because the Attacker (but not the Onlooker) threatens the Victim's rights, he may be killed in self-defence.[28] But that complaint would, I think, be ungenerous. We can say, not inaccurately, that the claim that the Attacker forfeits his rights is *made* true by the claim that the Attacker threatens to violate the Victim's rights. But we can also say more to display the *significance* of the fact that the Attacker threatens to violate the Victim's rights; we can therefore supply more commentary on the content of the claim that the Attacker has forfeited his right.

The moral relationship between the Victim and the Attacker is immensely important to this story, and explains the ultimate relevance of forfeiture. It allows us to explain both why the Victim's interest in her self-preservation properly triggers her right to use violence to uphold those interests, and to explain why her right to deploy violence is properly restricted to the agent, or agents, whose actions or movements threaten her. The Attacker's attack on the Victim disturbs a moral relationship which ought to obtain between them; a relationship which is committed, minimally, to the non-violation of their respective vital interests.[29] When the Attacker attacks the Victim, he breaches that relationship, which thus releases the Victim from her duty not to violate the interests of the Attacker, and at the same time permits her to take steps to protect her own interests.

The disturbance of this relationship should also be of concern to other agents. I favour an account of self-defence which ties it closely to other-defence: the very

[27] The reference to 'actions or movements' is meant to provide for the possibility that Innocent Attackers and Innocent Threats forfeit their rights; but, again, my stance on this issue (in this essay, at least) is agnostic.

[28] Massimo Renzo, in particular, has made me see the force of this objection.

[29] For suggestive discussions, see also Nagel (1972) and Rodin (2002), ch. 4.

same considerations which permit self-defence also typically or presumptively favour other-defence.[30] But is that really plausible, if the Victim's activation of self-defensive violence is triggered by the Attacker's disturbance of the relationship which obtains between them? Other agents are not parties to *that* relationship, so what justifies their involvement?

It is true that other agents are not *in* the particular relationship which obtains between the Victim and the Attacker, but that fact alone does not prevent these other agents from legitimately taking an interest in the preservation of that relationship, or in intervening when that relationship is disturbed in order to protect the threatened party. It should be a familiar point that the disturbance of at least some relationships generates agent-neutral reasons for third parties to intervene on behalf of the violated party in those relationships. (As a relatively easy case, think of the relationship between a parent or a guardian and a child he is abusing.) The relationship I envisage between the Victim and the Attacker is not, after all, one of intimacy or friendship, where loss or diminution in the relationship simply cannot be restored by third parties. It is, rather, a relationship which each of us bears to everyone else. When those relationships are in good repair, we are doing all we can to uphold morality's demands on us; when they fall into disrepair, there are moral deficits to account for, and to be corrected. The good standing of our mutual moral relationships does not, of course, eliminate our vulnerability to natural evils, but it helps to eliminate our vulnerability to wrongdoing, which should at least allow us to be reconciled to our place in the social world.[31]

References

Benbaji, Y. (2008) 'A Defense of the Traditional War Convention', *Ethics* 118: 464–495.

—— (2005) 'Culpable Bystanders, Innocent Threats, and the Ethics of Self-Defense', *Canadian Journal of Philosophy* 35: 623–640.

[30] I do not deny that there are complicated cases, particularly in conditions of war, or when Innocent Attackers and Innocent Threats are involved, which challenge or complicate the conceptual connections between self-defence and other-defence. See McMahan (2009), pp. 45ff., and Benbaji (2008), for a discussion of some of the problems. It still seems to me, however, that the considerations which license self-defensive violence are the same considerations which normally or presumptively license other-defensive violence.

[31] I thank the participants at the Conference on War and Self-Defence, University of Sheffield, August 2010, for their helpful comments on a more rudimentary version of this material, and the audiences at two seminars in Leeds for further helpful comments on later versions. For particularly influential comments or exchanges, I thank, in particular, James Dempsey, Jamie Dow, Daniel Elstein, Greville Healey, Ulrike Heuer, Wouter Kalf, Frances Kamm, Megan Kime, Rob Lawlor, Jeff McMahan, Massimo Renzo, Georgia Testa, and Tim Taylor. I also thank David Mapel and two anonymous readers for Oxford University Press for their useful comments on an earlier version. I'm especially grateful to Helen Frowe for her detailed and probing comments on earlier drafts.

Boonin, D. (2008) *The Problem of Punishment* (Cambridge: Cambridge University Press).

Christopher, R. (1998) 'Self-Defense and Defense of Others', *Philosophy and Public Affairs* 15: 123–141.

Feinberg, J. (1978) 'Voluntary Euthanasia and the Inalienable Right to Life', *Philosophy and Public Affairs* 7: 93–123.

Ferzan, K. (2005) 'Justifying Self-Defense', *Law and Philosophy* 24: 711–749.

Fletcher, G. (1979) 'The Right to Life', *Georgia Law Review* 13: 1371–1394.

Frowe, H. (2008) 'Threats, Bystanders, and Obstructors', *Proceedings of the Aristotelian Society* 108, Part 3: 365–372.

Goldman, A. (1979) 'The Paradox of Punishment', *Philosophy & Public Affairs* 9: 42–58.

Kadish, S. (1976) 'Respect for Life and Regard for Rights in the Criminal Law', *California Law Review* 64: 871–901.

Kamm, F. M. (2011) *Ethics for Enemies: Terror, Torture, and War* (Oxford: Oxford University Press).

——(1992) *Creation and Abortion* (Oxford: Oxford University Press).

Locke, J. (1690/1980) *Second Treatise on Government*, edited by C. B. Macpherson (Indianopolis: Hackett).

McMahan, J. (2009) *Killing in War* (Oxford: Clarendon Press).

——(2008) 'Torture in Principle and in Practice', *Public Affairs Quarterly* 22: 111–128.

——(2005a) 'The Basis of Moral Liability to Defensive Killing', *Philosophical Issues* 15: 386–405.

——(2005b) 'Self-Defense and Culpability', *Law and Philosophy* 24: 751–774.

Montague, P. (2010) 'Self-Defense, Culpability, and Distributive Justice', *Law and Philosophy* 29: 75–91.

——(2000) 'Self-Defence and Innocence: Aggressors and Innocent Threats', *Utilitas* 12: 62–78.

——(1981) 'Self-Defense and Choosing Between Lives', *Philosophical Studies* 40: 207–219.

Morris, C. W. (1991) 'Punishment and Loss of Moral Standing', *Canadian Journal of Philosophy* 21: 53–79.

Nagel, T. (1972) 'War and Massacre', *Philosophy and Public Affairs* 1 (1972): 123–144.

Narveson, J. (1968) 'Is Pacifism Consistent?', *Ethics* 78: 148–150.

——(1965) 'Pacifism: A Philosophical Analysis', *Ethics* 75: 259–271.

Otsuka, M. (1994) 'Killing the Innocent in Self-Defense', *Philosophy and Public Affairs* 23: 74–94.

Parfit, D. (2011) *On What Matters*, Volume One (Oxford: Oxford University Press).

Quong, J. (2009) 'Killing in Self-Defense', *Ethics* 119: 507–537.

Rodin, D. (2002) *War and Self-Defense* (Oxford: Clarendon Press).

Ross, W. D. (1930) *The Right and the Good* (Oxford: Clarendon Press).

Ryan, C. (1983) 'Self-Defense, Pacifism, and the Possibility of Killing', *Ethics* 93: 508–524.

Sher, G. (1987) *Desert* (Princeton: Princeton University Press).

Simmons, A. J. (1991) 'Locke and the Right to Punish', *Philosophy & Public Affairs* 20: 311–349.

Steinhoff, U. (2006) 'Torture—the Case for Dirty Harry and against Alan Dershowitz', *Journal of Applied Philosophy* 23: 337–353.

Teichman, J. (1986) *Pacifism and the Just War* (Oxford: Basil Blackwell).

Thomson, J. J. (1991) 'Self-Defense', *Philosophy and Public Affairs* 20: 283–310.
——(1990) *The Realm of Rights* (London: Harvard University Press).
——(1986) *Rights, Restitution, and Risk: Essays in Moral Theory*, edited by W. Parent (London: University of Harvard Press).
——(1976) 'Self-Defence and Rights', Lindley Lecture, University of Kansas; reprinted in Thomson 1986. (Page references are to the reprinted 1986 version.)
Wellman, C. H. (2012) 'The Rights Forfeiture Theory of Punishment', *Ethics* 122: 371–393.

4

Self-Defence, Just War, and a Reasonable Prospect of Success*

Suzanne Uniacke

It is widely accepted that the use of force in self-defence against an unjust threat is justified only if the force is necessary and proportionate.[1] These two conditions of justified self-defence do not require that the actor has or believes that he has a reasonable prospect of fending off the threat. On the contrary, it is generally accepted that a person can be justified in acting in self-defence even if he is unlikely to succeed. This can be contrasted with what the Just War Doctrine requires of defensive war. The principle of *jus ad bellum* that governs recourse to war stipulates a reasonable prospect of success. In practice this means that a political authority is justified in waging a defensive war only if it believes on good grounds that the 'success condition' is met.

This chapter has two related aims. The first is to defend the existence of this particular divergence between *jus ad bellum* as opposed to personal self-defence. This might seem a surprising aim, since the conditions of *jus ad bellum* explicitly include a reasonable prospect of success whereas the prevailing view about personal self-defence is that it can be justified even if the prospect of success is low. However, prominent contemporary theorists who regard the principles of defensive war as closely aligned to those of personal self-defence tend to ignore or side-line this difference.[2] At least one author claims that the self-defence

* For helpful comments on issues discussed in this chapter I would like to thank Helen Frowe, Antony Hatzistavrou, Matthew Kramer, Ingmar Persson, participants in the UK Analytic Legal and Political Philosophy Conference (2009), and philosophical audiences at Hull, Sheffield, and Stirling.

[1] Since a person might act on the basis of false beliefs or evaluative misjudgement, I should say more accurately that self-defence or purported self-defence is widely believed to be morally justified only if, at the time of action, the actor believes on reasonable grounds (allowing for the exigency of the situation) that what he is doing is both necessary and proportionate in relation to an unjust threat that he aims to fend off.

[2] For instance: 'The difference between war and other forms of conflict is a difference only of degree and thus the moral principles that govern killing in lesser forms of conflict [such as self-defense] govern killing in war as well' (McMahan 2009, p. 156).

conditions of necessary and proportionate force imply a reasonable prospect of success.[3] I argue in the next section that this claim is mistaken.

My second aim is to examine the basis of this particular difference between personal self-defence and *jus ad bellum*. If justified self-defence does not require a reasonable prospect of success, why should defensive war require it? The sheer difference of scale between the two types of conflict might seem the obvious answer. Personal self-defence typically involves a relatively small number of people and may result in harm only to one. War, by contrast, usually involves extensive loss of life and injury and destruction and disruption on both sides. War is more likely adversely to affect many people who are not direct parties to the conflict; war is also more liable to escalate and to develop in unpredictable ways than are acts of personal self-defence. (Thus it might be far more difficult to assess the likelihood of success with war than it is with self-defence.) These differences are certainly important and it is easy to see why the scope and extent of the harm involved in war could generate stricter justificatory conditions than those of personal self-defence. I shall argue, however, that this explanation misses the deeper significance of the *jus ad bellum* 'success condition'.

The 'success condition' warrants more critical attention than it usually receives in contemporary discussions of Just War principles. For instance, arguably this condition is morally too restrictive: perhaps some threats are so dreadful that a nation could be justified in resisting them against terrible odds; there could be threats that it would be ignoble, even wrongful for a nation not to resist at great cost and when the chance of success is small. A satisfactory critique of the 'success condition' along these lines would need to address what I shall take to be basic to the condition's rationale, namely, the essentially political nature of a decision to wage war.

In the next section I argue that necessary and proportionate self-defence does not require a reasonable prospect of success. The following section addresses aspects of the wider relevance of a reasonable prospect of success to justified personal self-defence. The final section presents an interpretation of the *jus ad bellum* 'success condition' within Just War thinking, as grounded in important assumptions about the nature of political authority and responsibility that do not apply to personal self-defence.

Permissible Self-Defence: Necessary and Proportionate Force

The claim that necessary and proportionate self-defence requires a reasonable prospect of success can seem intuitively plausible, especially in relation to the

[3] Statman (2008), pp. 663–664.

proportionality condition. How could it be proportionate to use harmful force in self-defence if there is little chance of fending off the threat or reducing its effects? This might sound like a rhetorical question, but on the contrary it invokes a more encompassing notion of proportionality than that included in the proportionality condition of self-defence. The use of proportionate force in self-defence involves a comparison between the harm inflicted on the attacker in relation to the threat fended off/interest protected.[4] If, for example, the force that would be necessary to fend off a threat to your life will inflict serious injury on the attacker, this is proportionate even if the odds are against your being able to fend off the attack. The likelihood of successfully fending off a threat is a distinguishable, further consideration (which I discuss later); it is not internal to or implied by the condition of proportionate force.

A more complex and interesting argument might be based on the necessity condition, which requires that force be indispensable if the threatened injury is to be avoided either completely or to some extent. Can force be necessary in this sense only if there is a reasonable prospect of success? We need to look closely at the necessity condition to see why the answer to this question is no.

The necessity condition applies to particular acts of self-defence and it involves two steps. The first step establishes that it is necessary for a particular actor in a particular set of circumstances *to use force* in self-defence; the second establishes that it is necessary for the actor to use *this degree* of force. An example will help explain these two steps and also why it is important to distinguish them. Say *A* threatens to shoot *B*. It might be unnecessary for *B* to use self-defensive force if *B* could escape *A*'s threat by taking cover. The likelihood of success is relevant to this judgement in the following way. It could be risky for *B* to take cover if, say, *B* does not know what *A* will do next and taking cover could significantly compromise *B*'s ability to defend himself should this become necessary; *B* might be more likely to avoid being shot if he uses force against *A* straight away. The first step must allow for the relevance of considerations of risk and cost to *B* in judging whether it is necessary for *B* to use force, as opposed to taking other possible action to avoid *A*'s threat. *B*'s using force could pass the first step if taking cover is too risky. It would be different if we change the probable outcomes of *B*'s options so that *B* has an equal or a better chance of avoiding being shot if *B* takes cover than if he uses force against *A*. In these altered circumstances, and more generally, it is unnecessary for *B* to use force if

[4] For convenience I shall refer to a person against whom defensive force is directed as an attacker, although not all such persons are strictly-speaking attackers. I discuss the proportionality condition more fully in Uniacke (2010).

there is a non-harmful, alternative course of action that is equally or more likely to succeed. *B*'s use of force would not be unnecessary, however, simply in virtue of being unlikely to succeed in fending off *A*'s threat, since this could nonetheless be *B*'s best or only option if he is to avoid being shot.

It could also be necessary for *B* to use force against *A* where *A*'s threat has a low chance of success independent of any self-defensive measures by *B*. Say *B* knows that *A* is a poor shot. Here again considerations of risk and cost to *B* are relevant to whether it is necessary for *B* to use self-defensive force. Even if *B* believes that *A* will probably miss his target, it may be that *B* cannot reasonably be expected to rely on this. All the same, in such a case the necessity condition's first step requires that (*B* believes that) *A*'s actions could inflict injury. (Otherwise in using force against *A*, *B* is not acting to fend off (what *B* believes is) a threat.)

If it is necessary for *B* to use self-defensive force against *A*, the question then becomes the degree of force that *B* needs to use. The second step can be stated in the following way: It is necessary for *B* in circumstances *y* to use force of degree *x* in order to fend off threat *z* if (*B* reasonably believes that) it is unlikely in circumstances *y* that *B* will fend off *z* unless *B* uses force *x*. This second step is consistent with: (i) (*B*'s recognizing) the possibility that *B* could actually fend off *z* by using less force than *x*; (ii) (*B*'s recognizing) the possibility that by using force *x*, *B* will not actually fend off *z*; and, significantly, (iii) (*B*'s recognizing) a low probability that by using force *x*, *B* will fend off *z*.[5]

Neither step of the necessity condition requires a reasonable prospect of success. But before we can confidently say that the necessity condition does not carry this implication we need to address a counter claim that appeals to the rationale of the condition itself. The use of unnecessary force falls outside the self-defence justification because it causes *needless* harm. Harm inflicted in self-defence can be needless because it is *excessive* in going beyond what would be sufficient to avoid or to fend off the threat. It is the infliction of excessive harm that the condition of necessary force most commonly disallows. However, perhaps harm inflicted in self-defence can be needless for another reason, namely that it *fails* in what it aims to achieve.

Would the harm *B* inflicts on *A* be needless if *B* is unsuccessful in fending off *A*'s attack? The answer to this question needs to take into account that there are degrees of success and also that what counts as successful self-defence can be

[5] The second step concerns the degree of force that *B* needs to use if he is to *fend off* the threat. This does not settle the prior question of whether it is necessary for *B* to use force, as opposed to avoiding the threat some other way.

relative to the threat itself or to an intended outcome, to the actor's aim under a particular description. Self-defence that does not fend off a threat completely might reduce the injury that a victim would otherwise have suffered; for example, *B* might deflect *A*'s knife so that it slashes *B*'s arm instead of stabbing him in the chest. Here we might regard *B*'s self-defence as only partially successful if he intended to fend off injury altogether. Nonetheless, *B* successfully fended off a threat to his life and he might also have succeeded in minimizing injury to himself as much as he could do in the circumstances. For these reasons, the harm that *B* inflicted on *A* was not needless. But what if *B* doesn't manage to reduce the injury that he would have suffered had he not used force; what if the harmful force *B* inflicts on *A* is completely ineffective as self-defence? In this case the harm *B* inflicts on *A* is not needless in relation to *B*'s attempted self-defence, provided that in using force against *A*, *B* intends to fend off the threat to some extent and might succeed in doing so.

Although harm inflicted in self-defence is not needless simply in virtue of its being unlikely to succeed, as an instrumental aspect of the justification of self-defence the condition of necessary force does require *some* prospect of success. In practice this means that *B* must believe both that the force he uses is capable of fending off *A*'s threat to some extent and also that the degree of force he uses is not excessive.[6] *B* can believe the former even if he thinks the prospect of success is low. (*B* can consistently believe: It is unlikely that I can fend off *z* unless I use force *x*; and there is only a small chance that if I use force *x* I will fend off *z*.) But if *B* does not believe at the time of action that the force he uses is capable of fending off *A*'s threat to some extent, then he cannot justify it as self-defence or attempted self-defence.[7] (This is true of instrumental justification more generally. For example, a doctor cannot justify administering painful treatment as necessary to relieve a patient's medical condition unless she believes when she administers the treatment that it could have this effect. Similarly, I cannot justify driving at high speed

[6] This can be person specific in cases of collective attack. Say *B* is attacked by five people, each of whom he would need to shoot in order to fend off being killed; *B* has only two bullets and he shoots two of the attackers. Although *B* cannot defend himself from the threat posed by all of the attackers, in shooting two, he is defending himself from being killed *by them*.

[7] Irrespective of whether a person can attempt something that is objectively impossible, she cannot attempt something that at the time of action she believes is impossible. This might be disputed by appeal to examples like the following: *A* believes that it is impossible for her to move a rock; she decides to prove this by attempting to move the rock. But in this example *A* attempts to prove that she cannot move the rock, and she attempts this by exerting maximum force in the belief that it cannot be sufficient to move the rock. If, contrary to what *A* believes possible, she does in fact move the rock, then *A* has failed in what she attempted to do, namely prove that she cannot move the rock.

as an attempt to get an injured person to hospital in time unless I believe that there is a chance that my driving at this speed could achieve this.)

The unavailability of the self-defence justification might seem unduly harsh in some instances in which a person uses force against an unjust threat that she knows she cannot fend off or reduce and where we would consider that the attacker is not wronged by the harm inflicted. Consider an example in which *C* is incapable of fending off a rape by *D* but during the attack *C* manages to inject *D* with a substance that (*C* knows) will paralyze *D* in twelve hours' time. We might regard this as an instance of 'gestural' or symbolic self-defence and consider that although it lies outside the realm of genuine self-defence it can be justified in terms of values close to those that justify self-defence or attempted self-defence. Alternatively, what *C* does might be characterized in other terms; for example, as an attempt to pre-empt or to deter further such attacks by *D* on *C* or on others, or as a punitive act against *D* that might or might not be justified in terms of a somewhat wider right of direct retaliation against an unjust attacker.[8]

As far as the conditions of necessary and proportionate force are concerned, a person can permissibly use force directly to fend off an unjust attack against odds that mean that although (she believes that) there is some prospect of success, there is no reasonable prospect. However, this does not settle the question of whether a reasonable prospect of success is relevant to the justification of acting in self-defence all things considered. I address aspects of this further question in the next section, where I highlight considerations that bear upon the particular contrast between personal self-defence and defensive war that I shall discuss in the final section.

Permissible Self-Defence: The Moral Relevance of a Reasonable Prospect of Success

Across varying recent philosophical accounts of the justification of self-defence there is widespread agreement that use of necessary and proportionate force in self-defence does not wrong an unjust attacker: that is to say, it does him no

[8] Statman argues that this type of example can meet a 'success condition' because *A* succeeds in protecting her honour. However, the right of self-defence is a right to *fend off* unjust harm, which is precisely what the victim in this example is unable to do. (Although *A* is powerless to *defend* herself against *B*'s attack, she is able to inflict delayed harm on *B*.) Whether the self-defence justification can incorporate defence of one's honour depends on the sense of 'self' that we can legitimately defend by using harmful force against another person.

injustice, it does not violate his rights.[9] If we accept, as I do, that in defending himself against *A*, *B* can be acting within his rights and not violating *A*'s rights, the likelihood of success could nevertheless be relevant to whether *B* is justified in exercising his right of self-defence against *A* all things considered.[10] For instance, the likelihood of successfully fending off an attack is relevant to the justification of infringing the rights of any uninvolved bystanders who would be injured as a foreseen incidental effect of *B*'s self-defence.[11] In some circumstances, perhaps benevolence towards an attacker is morally the better course where self-defensive force is extremely unlikely to succeed and will inflict serious harm on the attacker. I do not wish to downplay the relevance of these two types of considerations to the justification of acting in self-defence all things considered. However, given the chapter's central concerns I shall focus my discussion of the relevance of the likelihood of success on the situation the self-defending actor in particular.

A person who acts in self-defence aims to fend off injury or reduce its severity. The injury that the victim of an unjust attack would fend off is not simply, for example, wounding, kidnap or death, but also the violation of his corresponding right to bodily integrity, liberty or life. If self-defensive force is unlikely to succeed, the actor might have nothing to lose by the attempt: if he does not try to fend off the threat, then he will suffer whatever injury is coming; if he resists, there is a chance that he can avoid or reduce it. There will, however, be cases in which by acting in self-defence a person potentially *increases* the injury that he may suffer. (A victim of rape or abduction, for example, might be killed because she struggles to resist or escape, whereas she might have survived had she submitted. If *B* shoots at *A* in self-defence and misses, *A* might then come after *B* with a greater purpose.)

Is a person justified in increasing the threat he faces by engaging in self-defence only if there is a reasonable prospect that the defence will succeed? The claim that there are unjust injuries that a person can legitimately try to fend off at very significant risk of suffering a greater injury himself will be relatively uncontroversial where the interest being defended is itself a grave wrong, such as rape or

[9] On some accounts (e.g., Otsuka 1994 and McMahan 2005 and 2009) an attacker is liable to suffer defensive harm only if he is also responsible for posing an objectively unjust threat. Alternative accounts (e.g., Thomson 1991) hold that self-defence against, e.g., a deranged attacker need not infringe or violate his rights. This issue can remain moot for the purposes of thischapter.

[10] More generally, a person can have a right to do *x* in circumstances in which, all things considered, she ought not to do *x*. I might have a right to call in a debt, for instance, that I ought to waive on compassionate grounds.

[11] McMahan includes harm to bystanders as relevant to a notion of *wide* proportionality, as opposed to narrow proportionality which refers to harm inflicted on the attacker (McMahan 2009, pp. 20–24). As far as narrow proportionality is concerned, self-defence can clearly be proportionate if success is unlikely.

abduction.[12] However, disagreement will arise about the legitimacy of acting in self-defence that is unlikely to succeed against a threat, for example, a minor blow, that is clearly 'not worth' the greater risk incurred, for example, death or serious bodily harm. In a case such as this, some people will regard self-defence as not simply imprudent but wrongful; on this view, a right of self-defence notwithstanding, the victim ought to suffer the lesser injury and it is a moral failing on his part not to see this. Many others, however, will regard the significant risk of greater injury that the self-defending actor takes in such cases as irrational but not wrongful.[13] In incurring a significant risk of suffering a greater injury by acting in self-defence that is unlikely to succeed, the defender acts on a judgement of comparative value. Whether or not this judgement itself is defensible, the fact that the defender makes it in relation to *his own* life or safety is important to the legitimacy of acting in self-defence in any such case.

The escalation of defensive harm against the attacker is also relevant to the justification of acting in self-defence in such cases. Consider an example in which *B* wrongfully threatens *A* with a minor blow. *A* is holding a gun and could effectively fend off the immediate threat by shooting *B*; this would inflict disproportionate harm on *B*, however. *A* attempts to fend off the minor blow by struggling with *B*. This has little chance of success and increases the risk to *A* to the point that *B* threatens *A*'s life. *A* then shoots *B* in self-defence. In this example, the force *A* uses against *B* at each stage of the conflict is proportionate in relation to the particular threat that *A* is fending off at that stage. Nonetheless, while *A* has a right to struggle against *B*, *A* acts wrongfully in exercising this right in the circumstances if *A* foresees that struggling with *B* is unlikely to succeed as self-defence and will result in *A*'s inflicting defensive harm on *B* that is very disproportionate in relation to *B*'s original threat.[14]

Where a person knowingly significantly increases the risk by engaging in self-defence that is unlikely to succeed, it is morally important that the additional risk he incurs or greater injury he suffers, together with any moral risks involved in escalating the force needed for self-defence, he takes on his own behalf. As I outline

[12] Victims of rape or abduction are often also killed, of course.

[13] It might be wrongful for other reasons of course; e.g., if the person has obligations towards dependants.

[14] We can be morally required to suffer an unjust injury if the force necessary to fend it off would be very disproportionate in relation to either a current threat or a foreseeable escalation. All the same, there is a threshold above which proportionate self-defence could be justified even if the victim foresees that the threat will thereby escalate significantly; for example, an attacker who threatens to break your arm shouldn't get immunity from your proportionate self-defence by threatening to kill you if you put up a fight. However, people are likely to disagree about the degree of unjust harm someone is morally required to suffer rather than escalate the threat by defending himself.

in the final section, in two important respects the *jus ad bellum* 'success condition' is unlike this. First, it limits a nation's right to wage war, as opposed to being a moral constraint on the justified exercise of that right all things considered; second, its rationale invokes assumptions about the nature of political authority and responsibility that are inapplicable to acting in self-defence.

Defensive War: The *Jus Ad Bellum* 'Success Condition'

The principle of *jus ad bellum* requires that war be a 'last resort': waging war must be necessary to achieve a just cause for which the war is fought. And just as the necessity condition of self-defence requires the *possibility* of successfully fending off the threat, so too the *jus ad bellum* condition of 'last resort' requires that fighting a war must stand a chance of achieving the just cause. The principle of *jus ad bellum* also stipulates that there be a *reasonable prospect* of success. This additional, more demanding 'success condition' raises obvious questions: To what standard does it appeal: what is a reasonable prospect of success in this context? Why does *jus ad bellum* require a reasonable prospect of success? Should *jus ad bellum* (invariably) require this? My discussion of the first and second of these questions will identify differences of principle between defensive war and personal self-defence that are relevant to addressing the third question.

What is a reasonable prospect of success? Clearly what we regard as success in a particular context has an important bearing on whether there is a reasonable prospect of achieving it. However, irrespective of what we take success to be, a reasonable prospect of achieving any outcome, *x*, requires that *x* is a reasonable expectation at the time of action. An actor has a reasonable expectation of *x* if he believes on reasonable grounds that *x* is more likely than not; but not only if he believes this: an actor can have a reasonable expectation of *x* even if he believes that the probability of achieving *x* is less than fifty percent, provided the odds of achieving *x* are not too low. The hard question at this point is, of course, what is too low? 'Reasonable prospect of success' is not a precise standard and no doubt the *jus ad bellum* 'success condition' is intended to allow prudent judgement about how low an expectation is too low. Nonetheless, on any plausible reading the 'success condition' holds that a political authority can be justified in resorting to war only if it believes on reasonable grounds that success is significantly more than an outside chance. This does not tell us why the principle of *jus ad bellum* includes the 'success condition' or what is to count as success in this context.

One answer to the question of why *jus ad bellum* includes the 'success condition' is that it simply reiterates the *jus ad bellum* condition of proportionality. This interpretation will be congenial to those who maintain a close alignment between the principles of justified self-defence and those of defensive war, but the *jus ad bellum* 'success condition' is not substantively redundant in this way. The proportionality condition and the 'success condition' express distinguishable *jus ad bellum* requirements; thus, resort to war might be proportionate in relation to fending off a threat of something truly terrible when the likelihood of successful defence is relatively low. Moreover, as I will go on to outline, within the Just War tradition the 'success condition' requires far more than successfully fending off a threat.

An alternative explanation is that the 'success condition' is necessary to the justified exercise of a right of national defence, as opposed to being a condition of the right itself. On this view, while a nation has a right to fend off an unjust external threat, akin to right of personal self-defence, the scale of harm unleashed by war, including the probability of collateral harm on both sides, means that it can be justified in exercising this right only if there is a reasonable prospect of success. This interpretation takes the 'success condition' seriously but nonetheless falls short. As an explicit element of *jus ad bellum* the 'success condition' is more plausibly taken to imply that a political authority has no right to initiate the evils of war in a cause that is very unlikely to succeed. In explaining why this is so it will be instructive to consider the rationale of the condition within the Just War tradition. Even if we consider the 'success condition' morally too restrictive in relation to some threats, the condition's Just War rationale points up an essential difference between fighting a defensive war, as opposed to acting in personal self-defence that bears on the justification of both of these actions. The rationale of the 'success condition' also reveals that what the Just War Doctrine regards as *success* in the case of defensive war goes far beyond what would constitute (analogous) success in a case of personal self-defence.

A satisfactory interpretation of the *jus ad bellum* 'success condition' needs to appreciate the reason why the principle of *jus ad bellum* also explicitly requires that war be declared by a legitimate authority. This latter condition is not simply a matter of procedural legitimacy. On the contrary, it stems from the view that the right to wage war is grounded in the duty of a political authority to protect the community. This is part of its wider duty to act for the good of the community for whose welfare it is responsible, a duty on which its authority depends and on the basis of which it has a right to commit the nation to war. We can note here that if indeed the right of a political authority to resort to war is based on its duty to protect the community, then under the combined conditions of *jus ad bellum* a political authority would also have a duty to resort to war.[15] Personal self-defence, on the other hand, is discretionary: individuals have a right but no equivalent duty to defend themselves against unjust attack. Our obligations to other people, towards our dependants for instance, might give us a duty to exercise our right of self-defence in some circumstances, but the right of personal self-defence is not itself also a duty.

This particular contrast between defensive war and personal self-defence might prompt the suggestion that a decision by a political authority to wage a defensive war is more like a case of one person going to the defence of another person who comes under attack and for whose protection she is responsible, as opposed to self-defence in the strict sense in which a person defends his or her own life or safety. That suggestion is unsatisfactory, however. Defensive war is not really akin to third-party defence, since in declaring war a political authority acts on behalf of the whole community and the nation itself subsequently fights the war.[16] The closest analogy in the personal sphere is not that of personal self-defence or even third-party defence, but rather the situation of an individual who is in a position of authority and responsible for the welfare of a group, who commits the whole group to fighting against an attack, with all that brings in its train.

Unlike a person who acts in self-defence on his own behalf, a legitimate authority declares war on behalf of the whole community. This includes those who will be fighting under its command as well as all those who are thereby collectively at war. In declaring war a political authority thereby commits the nation itself to war with exposure to all of the risks, including the moral risks that such a commitment entails.[17] A declaration of war includes not only commanding or committing citizens to expose themselves to greater injury than they might otherwise suffer if the war is not fought, but also commanding or committing them to engage in or to support widespread acts of killing and destruction.

In the context of the Just War Doctrine, the duty of a legitimate authority to act for the welfare of the community grounds its *jus ad bellum* right to declare war on behalf of the community; at the same time it also significantly restricts the scope of this right in terms of a corresponding responsibility to act for the good of the community. The significant difference between the principles of defensive

[15] See Uniacke (2002).

[16] Wars of humanitarian intervention, or wars in defence of an ally, are more like cases of third-party defence.

[17] The moral risks include, but are not confined to, the possibility of acting on mistaken beliefs about the facts that support waging the war and the creation of opportunities for acts that violate the principle of *jus in bello* that governs conduct within war.

war and those of personal self-defence that these considerations bring to the fore is that in declaring war a political authority acts on behalf of others for whom it is responsible, thereby committing them to a common purpose that implies significant costs and risks for them as agents as well as potential victims. Within the Just War Doctrine, this insight is closely associated with the view that the legitimacy of political leaders, including their authority to declare war, depends on their acting for the good of the community.[18] What constitutes 'the good of a community' is open to interpretation of course. As explained thus far, the *jus ad bellum* 'success condition' might be thought to be consistent with a decision to run a significant risk of defeat at very great cost, as opposed to surrendering to a threat of something truly dreadful. However, Just War principles are also clear that the aim of political leaders must be peace with justice: the goal of fighting a war must be to re-establish a peace that is preferable to the peace that would have prevailed if the war had not been fought.[19] This is a very tall order. Significantly, the right of personal self-defence carries no comparable requirement. Legitimate self-defence implies no intention on the part of the self-defending actor beyond the limited, direct aim of fending off the attack, and an act of self-defence will be successful if it achieves that aim. Moreover, unlike the 'success' of *jus ad bellum*, self-defence admits of partial success where an external threat is fended off to some extent but not completely.

Because the *jus ad bellum* 'success condition' reflects assumptions about political authority and responsibility, its application to defensive war encompasses considerably more than fending off an attack. Within the Just War tradition the right of a legitimate authority to wage war invokes duties on the part of political leaders that mean that the aims of war (and thus also the 'right intentions' of those who declare war) extend well beyond an immediate just cause. These wider aims explicitly include the promotion of the common good and the securing of a lasting peace, which are held to be the over-arching responsibilities of a political authority who declares war on behalf of the nation that subsequently wages war.

On the interpretation offered here, the *jus ad bellum* 'success condition' is far-reaching and very demanding both in terms of what it takes the duties of a political

[18] The model of political authority that this view invokes is relevant to whether the principle of *jus ad bellum* should (invariably) include the 'success condition'. However, it would be wrong simply to assume that the Just War rationale of the 'success condition' necessarily implies government by a paternalistic elite or that it is alien to communitarian conceptions of political legitimacy. A decision to wage war by the government of a representative democracy is arguably subject to this rationale. Even in a direct democracy, citizens must take responsibility for acting in the interests of the nation as a whole and for committing others, their fellow citizens to war.

[19] Contemporary statements of these principles include essays in Coppieters, Bruno and Nick Fotin (eds) (2002).

authority to entail and also in what it takes success in war to include. Perhaps these purported duties are too extensive, and the corresponding conception of success in war too broad. Nonetheless, even if we were to favour a much narrower conception of what can legitimately count as success in waging a defensive war, namely simply fending off an enemy attack, the rationale of the *jus ad bellum* 'success condition' would continue to recognize the essentially political nature of waging war in virtue of which the *jus ad bellum* conditions are not simply those of personal self-defence writ large.

References

Coppieters, Bruno and Nick Foton (eds.) (2002) *Moral Constraints on War: Principles and Cases* (Lanham, Md: Lexington Books).

McMahan, Jeff (2005) 'The Basis of Moral Liability to Defensive Killing', *Philosophical Issues* 15: 386–405.

——(2009) *Killing in War* (Oxford: Clarendon Press).

Otsuka, Michael (1994) 'Killing the Innocent in Self-Defense', *Philosophy and Public Affairs* 23: 74–94.

Statman, Daniel (2008) 'On the Success Condition for Legitimate Self-Defense', *Ethics* 118, 4: 659–686.

Thomson, Judith Jarvis (1991) 'Self-Defense', *Philosophy and Public Affairs* 20: 283–310.

Uniacke, Suzanne (2002) 'Self-Defence and Just War', in Janssen, Dieter and Michael Quante (eds.) *Gerechte Kriege* (Hrsg.) (Paderborn: Mentis-Verlag) 64–78.

——(2010) 'Proportionality and Self-Defense', *Law and Philosophy* DOI 10.1007/s10982-010-9090-x. Published on-line 17 December 2010.

5

Self-Defense, Resistance, and Suicide

The Taliban Women*

F. M. Kamm

Suppose it is asked "How should we address the greatest evils and injustices of our time?"

5.1 Harming and Injustices

The first thing that might occur to one in response is how to determine whether some injustice or evil is greater than another. One approach is to think how many people are going to be affected and to what degree they will be badly affected. One considers how badly off each individual will be and how many individuals will be so affected. But part of our question is to consider whether injustices and evils make a difference to how we should react by contrast to how we would react to a natural disaster where as many people are each harmed as badly. An example bearing on this issue is owed to Thomas Scanlon. Suppose you see an individual in one pool who is drowning and you know he was wrongfully pushed in the water by a person trying to murder him. In another pool, farther away, there is another person who just fell in because a lightning bolt struck him. Should you decide whom to save based on the fact that in one case the person would die as the result of an

* This essay was not delivered at the Self-Defense and War Conference. The paper delivered there, "Reasons for War: Goals, Conditions and Proportionality," appears in my Uehiro lectures volume, *Ethics for Enemies: Terror, Torture, and War* (Oxford: Oxford University Press, 2011). This essay is a revised version of a short (15-minute) unpublished talk given at Princeton University Center for Human Values as part of a panel on the topic "How Should We Address the Greatest Evils and Injustices of Our Time?" 27–28 April 2000. In revising it, I have tried to retain its character as a talk given to nonphilosophers. The topic pertains to the issues of the conference and has renewed relevance in the light of recent events in Afghanistan in 2010. The essay was also given as a Popper Seminar paper at the London School of Economics in March 2011. I am grateful to the audience and to Prof. Alex Voorhoeve for their comments on that occasion and to Gerald Lang for additional comments.

injustice and in the other the person would die as a result of a natural disaster? Scanlon said no, that fact is irrelevant. You should decide on the basis of the probabilities of saving the individuals, assuming other factors are equal.[1]

I think I agree with Scanlon in this case, but I do not think it shows that a victim's dying of injustice never contributes to our choice of whom to save. Certainly, if one has oneself pushed the person in the pool, one should take care of one's own victim before taking care of the other person. However, this will be true whether the latter is the victim of a natural disaster or of *someone else's* injustice. Consider another case: In one place, five people are being threatened with death by a group of terrorists. Elsewhere, there are five people being threatened with death by a volcano. I think the fact that we would stop an injustice in the process of happening if we went to the first place could matter to what we should do. (Notice that, in Scanlon's case, the act of the villain is over, and we can prevent only the unjust harm due to it.) Indeed, I think it could be reasonable to prevent an indignity or unjust acts to one set of people rather than prevent even greater material harm, but due to natural causes, to another set of people. (We do this on a mass scale, e.g., if we invest more money in a police force rather than in health care.)[2] We could reasonably be concerned with preventing unjust acts and indignity and not only harm.

5.2 Permissible Responses to Injustice

With this as background, I want to discuss some other questions about only those people who are victims of injustice and moral evil (and not of natural disasters). If the rights of innocent persons are being seriously violated, we might first ask what it would be permissible for the victim himself to do, and then what it might be permissible for others to do on his behalf. I shall be concerned with the outer limits of permissible action, that is, the most one could permissibly do. It certainly may not be permissible to do everything that is physically necessary in order to stop injustices, as doing so may actually produce more injustice by being a disproportionate response. On the other hand, for reasons of prudence we may often choose not to do what is at the limit of what is permissible. However, knowing what the outer limits of permissibility are can help us see just how serious an injustice or moral evil is and why doing less than the most that is permissible would also be justified.

[1] See reference to Scanlon's example in Samuel Scheffler, *The Rejection of Consequentialism* (New York: Oxford University Press, 1994).

[2] I touch on this issue in my *Intricate Ethics* (New York: Oxford University Press, 2007) ch. 9 "Conflicts of Rights".

What is it permissible for a potential victim to do to a perpetrator? One factor we should recognize in answering this question may help us to distinguish between morally evil and unjust acts. I shall here consider such an evil act to be an unjust act that is done by a perpetrator who has as his *final goal* to cause such things as pain, suffering, death, or humiliation to others.[3] Those who cause such things merely as means to another goal or those who cause such things as side effects need not do evil acts in this sense. Nevertheless, they may still act unjustly because, *prima facie*, we owe it to people not to treat them in these ways even though we do not seek bad effects per se.

An unjust agent who does not do evil acts may be acting under false beliefs. Suppose he thinks that, when he causes his victims harm, he is carrying out the plans of God and this makes his act just. If this is actually a false belief, then his treatment of their victims is a violation of their victims' rights and his act is unjust. Suppose an agent is in fact acting unjustly, though he himself does not recognize this. I think he can liable to his victim's acts of self-defense just as if the agent's final goal were to cause pain, suffering, death, or humiliation. By saying he is liable, I mean at least that, in virtue of what he has done, he has no complaints and is not wronged by his victims' response if it is necessary to stop the harm to them.[4] So I do not think that an evil act—or knowledge by an agent of his injustice as I have identified it—is necessary in order to respond in self-defense to an unjust act in the most forceful way possible, at least if this stops the act or harm from it. Perpetrators of unjust acts, evil or not, can be liable to certain harmful acts being done to them in order to stop their unjust acts.

Sometimes, however, the victim's resistance would not succeed as self-defense; that is, it would not stop the wrong act or the harm from it, and in some cases a victim can know this. (I shall call this "mere resistance.") Even in these cases, resistance that harms a perpetrator, though it does not help the victim, might be permissible, I think. Mere resistance might be justified only as an appropriate response to what the perpetrator is doing independently of its further useful consequences.[5] I shall return to this issue later.

Furthermore, I think that a victim may sometimes impose greater harm on a perpetrator than the latter would impose on his potential victim. Consider a

[3] In other work, I have not restricted the use of "evils" to moral evils; it has included mere harms.

[4] I here follow Jeff McMahan's use of the term in his *Killing in War* (New York: Oxford University Press, 2009). A deluded child who aims a loaded gun or someone who mistakenly attacks an innocent person can be permissibly forcibly stopped.

[5] Barbara Herman might be interpreted as sayinging something similar in her "Murder and Mayhem," reprinted in her collection, *The Practice of Moral Judgment* (Cambridge, Mass.: Harvard University Press), pp. 113–131: "I must not assent to be the victim of aggression. This gives more than permission for an act of self-defense when that is necessary to resist the aggression; it imposes a requirement that aggression be resisted. Though I may not be able to prevent the aggressor's success,

hypothetical case called Locked in the House: Somebody will keep you (an innocent person) locked up in a house permanently. (He thinks God commands this as the appropriate way to treat you.) He is not going to kill you or physically harm you so long as you stay in the house and you know that this is so. In one variant of this case, if you leave, he will attack you, and even kill you. It seems to me that if the *only* way you could escape is by killing the perpetrator, it would be permissible to kill him. This is so even if we assume that what you do to him would be worse than what he would do to you if you did not try to escape. He is committing a serious injustice in keeping you in the house against your will, whether or not under threat of death if you leave, and that is going to count in determining what response is permissible.

Now suppose a gang of perpetrators, rather than one, will keep you locked up. They each act unjustly, and *they are all* liable to attack. Hence, you may kill *many* perpetrators just so that you escape unjust confinement that itself will not cause your death.

In most places in the world, locking an innocent person in a house, as in Locked in the House, is prohibited by law. Hence, in these places, the perpetrator would commit a *legal* injustice, acting contrary to law. However, suppose there were no law barring innocent people from being permanently locked up against their will in a house, under threat of death if they leave. Would this imply that it was morally wrong of the victim to kill the perpetrator in order to prevent or end his being locked up? I do not think so, for being locked up in this way when it is not a legal injustice is still a serious moral injustice, and it *should* be legally prohibited even if it is not. What if there is a law that actually makes it permissible or required to permanently lock up innocent people against their will in a house? Such a state-sponsored moral injustice seems to be grounds for morally justified rebellion if this is necessary to stop the injustice. It is not always morally wrong to disobey morally unjust laws. (It was not morally wrong of slaves to escape slavery in pre-Civil War America. If slaveholders tried to prevent this, a slave who resisted in self-defense in a manner proportionate to avoiding slavery would have done no moral wrong.)

Nevertheless, I think that victims ought to try to defend themselves with as little harm to those who are perpetrators as possible, as long as reducing the harm to the perpetrator is not likely to impose great costs on the victim. Subsequent

I may not be passive in the face of aggression. Passivity is here like complicity" (p. 129). However, I do not argue for a requirement and I do not think nonresistance constitutes complicity. A possible alternate account of mere resistance (that I do not accept) sees it as carrying out a deterrent threat that has failed to deter.

punishment of perpetrators may impose additional harm on them when this is no longer needed to resist their injustice. But self-defensive harm is not punishment; it is needed to resist a perpetrator and to help a victim. However, a victim's causing harm to a perpetrator while resisting him seems to be permissible even if it is not reasonable to expect that it will improve the victim's condition and it will, in fact, not improve his condition. Such mere resistance to unjust action as an appropriate response to it when it is occurring is also different from punishment. The latter could occur if acting during an unjust act is intended to produce harm to the perpetrator only after his act and its bad effects are over. Mere resistance, however, can raise special moral problems because there is no obvious goal whose attainment signals the end of permissible harm to a perpetrator the way a successful escape signals the end to permissible self-defensive harm. For this reason, mere resistance can be more harmful to a perpetrator than successful self-defense. It should not be engaged in when successful self-defense is possible, in part because escaping harm to oneself is a way of resisting the *effects* of a wrongful act while showing appropriate concerns for the good of freedom whose importance helps account for the wrongfulness of the perpetrator's act. (This is so even if an unsuccessful attempt to harm the victim were to continue.)

Finally, I think that, in the cases that I have described, it would be permissible for third parties to act on behalf of the victim, doing what the victim himself could permissibly do in self-defense and even in "mere resistance," at least if (but not only if) the victim would approve of such intervention. Of course, third parties might choose not to act because of the cost to themselves, and I think that is also a permissible response if the cost is great enough.

(In these remarks, I have spoken only of action against a perpetrator. I shall here not deal with the problem of innocent bystanders who might be hurt in the course of a victim's self-defense or resistance, or in the course of acts by others. This is a very complicated issue, though I think that innocent bystanders might sometimes permissibly be endangered in this way, though they, unlike perpetrators, would have their rights infringed and might be owed compensation.)

5.3 Taliban Women

5.3.1 Self-defense and mere resistance

In order to consider possible implications of what I have said for an actual injustice in our time, I shall take the example of the Taliban women prior to 2001 (Taliban Women Case). Suppose the Taliban women were kept essentially under "house arrest," as described in my previous hypothetical case. Suppose that they would be physically attacked, raped, or killed only if they left the houses on their own.[6] And suppose they were sequestered because the Taliban believed truly that the word of God required this control of women. Furthermore, we can assume that those who do this to women represent the views of the group that controls the state, so their actions are not contrary to state law and may actually enforce it. Does what I have said in Section 5.2, using the Locked in the House Case, imply that nothing about the perpetrators would stand in the way of these women being morally justified in killing the perpetrators if this were necessary in order to free themselves?

It might be said that there is a morally important difference between the two cases. In Locked in the House, we might have been imagining that if you escaped the perpetrator's house and his physical attacks upon you once you left, you would rejoin a society in which you would be safe from attack and further attempts to restrict your liberty. That is, your self-defense would have improved your condition not just with respect to the perpetrator's control over you but overall as well. In the Taliban Women Case, a woman who escaped from the house and her perpetrator's power would enter into perhaps a more hostile environment populated with other potential perpetrators. (This might not be true if her escape were part of a group uprising strong enough to ward off further threats, but I shall assume this will not occur.) If a woman who successfully defends herself against one perpetrator realizes that she gains little, if anything, for herself in terms of overall improved conditions or even makes her fate worse, does this imply that it is morally wrong of her to attack and even kill those who keep her in the house and may physically harm her if she leaves? I do not think it does.

If someone commits the serious moral injustice we are considering, it seems to me that he is liable to being attacked if this is necessary to stop the wrong he does even though others will step in to take his place and commit even more serious wrongs to the same victim. The perpetrator is not wronged, and he has no complaint if this is done to him rather than allowing him and not others to harm the victim. It is for the victim to choose whether she will act contrary to prudence (i.e., making herself worse off) in order to react against an injustice to her. After all, would we say that those who rose up in the Warsaw ghetto during the Second World War

[6] Apparently, there is an expression in Afghani, voiced by some Afghani, whether Taliban or not, that translates as "a wife should be in the home—or in the grave" (quoted by Nicholas Kristof, in *New York Times*, 25 October 2010). However, the supposition (for the sake of argument) that women would not be harmed if they stay at home is unlikely to be true. A recent *New York Times* article describes the beatings and abuse within marriage of Afghan women, who subsequently burned themselves to death. These are not described as specifically Taliban marriages. See Alissa J. Rubin, "For Afghan Wives, a Desperate, Fiery Way Out," *New York Times*, 7 November 2010. Derek Parfit has suggested that if the women were treated well in captivity, this would make a difference to the permissibility of killing their captors. I disagree.

had no right to kill some Nazis who were oppressing them when they knew their fate would not improve because other Nazis would take the place of those they successfully killed in self-defense?[7]

What if only a severe nonlethal attack by the Taliban woman on the present perpetrator is possible but she knows it is not sufficient to free her from that perpetrator? This is a case of mere resistance to an injustice, which cannot stop any part of the injustice but only harm the perpetrator. It seems to me that the perpetrator is liable to being harmed by his victim simply as an appropriate response to the wrongful act he is doing even if it is known that it will not be effective in stopping or reducing the bad effect of what he is doing. Analogously, suppose a victim knows that a perpetrator will certainly succeed in raping her. The rapist is not immune to being attacked by the victim during the course of the rapist's successful act. The victim may even resist (if it is an appropriate nonpunitive response to what is being done to her) what she foresees will lead to the death of the rapist following the successful rape.

I conclude that it would be morally permissible, even if not wise, for Taliban women sometimes even to kill God-fearing people who would not kill the women if they remained in the house. The women would also be justified in mere resistance to the perpetrators as it is an appropriate response to wrongdoing independent of good consequences. What I have said also implies that third parties could appropriately respond to wrongdoing with mere resistance, in addition to being permitted to do on behalf of the women what the women would be permitted to do in self-defense.[8]

I emphasize that there may be prudential reasons why neither third parties nor the women should do these things because the consequences would be worse for the women or the third parties. In addition, side effect harm to innocent bystanders, including harsher treatment of other women, could be a moral reason for

[7] I first discussed the case of the Warsaw Ghetto in "Harming Some to Save Others from the Nazis" in E. Garrard and G. Scarre (eds.) *Moral Philosophy and the Holocaust* (London: Ashgate, 2003). Even if Nazi plans had not been extermination but only confinement in "model" camps, a doomed uprising would have been permissible, I believe. In this regard, it is interesting to consider cases where an agent is liable to being killed to stop his attack, even though what he does is not unjust. In these cases, it does seem impermissible for a victim to resist such an agent when this would do the victim no good. For example, a pilot may be justified in attacking a military facility despite collateral harm to civilians. Nevertheless, he may be liable to being killed by those civilians if this is necessary and sufficient to stop the collateral harm to themselves. (Jeff McMahan discusses this issue in his *Killing in War.*) However, suppose his being killed is not sufficient to save the civilians from collateral harm because they will certainly soon be harmed to the same extent by another pilot. Then it does seem that the first pilot's being justified in his act implies that the civilians would be morally wrong to kill him as resistance to his act.

[8] Acting on behalf of the women—rather than just in resistance to wrongdoing—may have to assume their consent to this. Suppose that no individual suffers an injustice great enough to be permitted to kill in self-defense, but each of *many* individuals is oppressed in the same way. Is it also

not killing perpetrators. The important point is that if it were unwise or morally impermissible for anyone to react in the extreme way I have described, when killing would be necessary in order to free the women or even merely to resist unjust acts against them, it would not be because the perpetrators have a right not to be harmed to this extent.

Of course, an additional important question is whether killing perpetrators would really be necessary in order for the women to escape (or even to appropriately resist) being kept in the house. If not, then in these circumstances, *out of concern for the rights of perpetrators*, killing might become impermissible.[9] For example, suppose several women in a household could overpower those guarding them or a woman could use nonlethal means of escape. Suppose communication was possible between women in different households so that nonviolent group resistance would be effective. Then killing might be impermissible. (However, if such resistance would be put down violently, killing might again become necessary as a means of self-defense or mere resistance.) If alternative means besides killing were possible, but the cost of using them were too high—e.g., alternatives made it more likely that women would be recaptured—then violence might again be permissible. This is not to deny that supererogatory continuation of nonviolent resistance by particular women might be more effective in ultimately altering the status of all women in the country.

5.3.2 *Cause for war?*

Jeff McMahan and Thomas Hurka have said that war by an outside nation merely in order to free Taliban women would not have been justified.[10] McMahan gave as his justification that third parties would be permitted to kill in defense of others *only* if those others would be permitted to kill in their own defense. However, victims who lack equal legal rights to employment and political participation are not justified in killing those who denied them legal equality in order to achieve legal equality.

possible that so many people being treated improperly is a sufficient condition for *any individual* to kill to stop the oppression of these many women? This possibility seems to raise the problem of aggregation; that is, whether for moral purposes, it is correct to add up small losses wrongfully imposed on separate individuals in order to create a large loss, albeit only in aggregate. Is there something about many people, not just one, being treated unjustly that allows us to add up the small losses even if in the absence of injustice it would be wrong to aggregate smaller losses? This is a topic that deserves discussion it will not get here.

[9] This issue was especially important in 2010, when the Afghani government was not controlled by the Taliban and had some commitment to the rights of women. There was a responsibility on the part of victims to take advantage of alternative legal means provided to protect themselves.

[10] Comments in response to questions at the Conference on War, University of Calgary in October 2006.

Neither McMahan nor Hurka dealt with whether being sequestered at home, with or without threat of death if one left, was a sufficient ground for killing those who kept one sequestered. Suppose it was a sufficient ground at least sometimes and only those perpetrators would be killed in a self-defensive action. Then McMahan might agree that third parties could permissibly kill the perpetrators, at least if the women consented to this. But would this be sufficient to show that a nation-state could permissibly declare war (or even engage in "targeted assassinations") to free the Taliban women from "house arrest"? If not, then there must be some reason other than that women themselves and third-party individuals may not kill the Taliban that stands in the way of a just war by a nation state. It may be issues of state sovereignty that impede intervention. (Currently, exceptions are made only in cases of genocide.) Also, war may involve out-of-proportion amounts of side-effect killing of innocent bystanders or greater side-effect harm to the women themselves than they choose to risk. Suppose the women would be permitted to kill their perpetrators in self-defense or resistance, but they choose not to in order to avoid greater harm to themselves. If they would be harmed to the same degree in a war (or by the acts of any third parties), then it seems impermissible for others to attack perpetrators whom it is permissible for women to attack. For various reasons, a victim's being permitted to kill may not be a sufficient condition for a state (or even individual third parties) being permitted to kill the perpetrator even if it is a necessary condition.

In addition, it is also not clear that it *is* a necessary condition (i.e., it is not clear that *only if* it is permissible for the women to kill is it permissible for others to do so on their behalf). There might be factors other than the relation between perpetrator and victim that affect whether a victim herself is permitted to kill the perpetrator. For example, suppose the women had duties to family members that would make it wrong for them to engage in resistance that would otherwise be justified. They might then lack permission to kill perpetrators on grounds that did not undermine the permission of third parties to kill the perpetrators on their behalf.[11]

5.4 Suicide Bombers

Now consider a further possible implication of what has been said. Reports by Amnesty International and the Red Cross say that many women ruled by the Taliban prior to 2001 killed themselves instead of killing the perpetrators of injustice to them. They committed suicide by swallowing acids that burned

[11] Of course, women may be mistaken in thinking that their duties to care for others (such as children) override their right to act for their legitimate self-interest and to oppose wrongdoing.

the esophagus (a slow and painful death) in order to avoid the type of life they were living.[12] Suicide seems to have been a needed escape for these women. It may have given them the sense that they, not others, controlled their lives, and it may have been used to psychologically punish or create guilt in their oppressors. Nevertheless, it also suggests that the women had no hope of reprieve and, perhaps, that they were deeply depressed by their circumstances. Such depression would have made it unlikely that these women, at least, could have used other violent or nonviolent means of escape and resistance, even had this been physically possible. But let us now consider the issue of permissibility of such alternatives to suicide, not the physical or mental possibility of their use.

Suicide is not a means of escape from house arrest that is a morally required alternative to harming a perpetrator of house arrest. It involves a cost to the victim that is too great just to avoid harming the perpetrator for the sake of escape. Might this imply that even those who felt the need to escape by suicide could *also*, were they capable of it, permissibly have killed perpetrators? In other words, instead of *only* killing herself, could a woman committed to killing *herself* also have permissibly killed the perpetrators?

At least two grounds might be suggested to justify a suicidal Taliban woman's also killing a perpetrator. The first ground is defense of others. That is, given that the person committed to suicide need not kill a perpetrator in order to escape injustice to herself, she might still permissibly kill a perpetrator if this were necessary and useful to help other victims. (Here, a victim takes on the role of a third party toward other victims.) The second justification is related to the permissibility of attacking someone while he oppresses as mere resistance even if this does nothing to stop the injustice. In this case, a victim plans suicide as the means to escape her oppression, and killing the perpetrator is merely a response to his unjust action. The second ground implies that if one must escape a grave injustice by suicide, it is permissible to take the perpetrator along in an act of mere resistance. One might even think of this as a form of "suicide bombing," very different from the form with which we are acquainted.

These two justifications for killing a perpetrator when the victim's suicide will otherwise occur anyway may seem inadequate. First, how could a woman permissibly kill perpetrators even if this would help other women, given that she runs no risk of costly consequences to herself in using nonlethal means of helping others, as she will shortly commit suicide anyway? This objection, however, would not

[12] See Jan Goodwin, "Buried Alive: Afghan Women under the Taliban," OTI Online (27 February 1998), <http://www.freerepublic.com/focus/f-news/524499/posts>. In 2010, there were reports of Afghani women (not necessarily under the Taliban) setting themselves afire. See n. 7.

apply when killing the perpetrator is truly necessary to help other victims or when using alternative means to help others would interfere with her suicide. A second objection is to attacking a perpetrator as mere resistance. If one will successfully avoid oppressive acts by suicide, it seems there is no personal oppression to resist by killing a perpetrator. And it does not seem that the fact that someone is driven to use self-harming means of escape licenses her to *punish* the perpetrator with death.[13]

However, suicide (which involves intending one's death) is not the only response to no longer caring to live if one is required to live in a certain way. A woman who no longer cares that she will die in escaping from the perpetrator could also engage in mere resistance to the perpetrator, perhaps foreseeing with certainty but not intending that she will die. For example, she may foresee that others will kill her for her resistance. If she wishes not to fall under the control of those who might recapture her, however, she may secondarily have tools ready with which to commit suicide. Such a two-step course of action seems both permissible and better than leaving perpetrators unresisted by choosing suicide as a first step. People ideally should become stronger and more resolute in their resistance once they are willing to forego the life that acquiescing to oppression would bring.

5.5 Actual Third-Party Approaches

In conclusion, I want to analyze two actual approaches that were taken by non-state agents in dealing with the crisis of the Taliban women prior to 2001. One approach was to combine condemning the Taliban with isolating them. Oxfam, e.g., stopped operations on an important project redirecting water to a certain area in Afghanistan because, it said, "We concluded that our core principles are not negotiable. Oxfam will work with women in Kabul, or not at all."[14] Oxfam was not allowed to work with women because that would have involved the women's being in public. The nature of this statement—Oxfam will work with women in the area or not at all—might suggest that Oxfam thought it would be engaging in invidiously discriminatory behavior if it worked in the area in accord with Taliban rules.

[13] Killing a perpetrator to rescue some other victims may not be permissible if using it will make the situation become worse overall for yet other victims. By contrast, even if the situation will become worse for other women if one woman commits suicide—greater controls are introduced on them—I do not think this is sufficient reason to rule out her escape by suicide. A victim need not stay in a very bad situation, sacrificing herself personally in an important way, just because perpetrators will respond to her escape by maltreating others. However, if she decides to act to help others (by killing a perpetrator), it seems reasonable for her to consider the interests of all others and not just some others (with the possible exception of loved ones).

[14] See Goodwin, "Buried Alive" (n. 13).

For example, it would have had to abide by the policies of the regime and employ only men in the area.

Perhaps this may be a misleading description of what would have been involved in Oxfam's continuing to redirect the water. After all, redirecting water would not require Oxfam actually to discriminate against women if it did not employ any Afghanis to do the job or if women would not have applied for work on the project even had they been free. And the women would also have benefited by redirection of the water. Hence, it is possible that the underlying principle of the Oxfam action is better described as noninvolvement with others who are perpetrators of injustice. After all, given what they are doing to the women, the perpetrators may lose a right to have Oxfam assistance to redirect water. Even at the cost of not providing water to innocent bystanders and victims of the Taliban, Oxfam's first aim was noninvolvement with perpetrators of the injustice. Oxfam might also be interpreted as putting concern with the dignity of the Taliban's victims ahead of their short-term material interests in water. I think that this is a morally permissible approach to the problem.

Ultimately, however, Oxfam may have thought that threatening noninvolvement was a means of winning concessions for women's legal rights. This approach was explicitly taken by the UN World Food Program.[15] During a food crisis in Afghanistan, Oxfam had the opportunity to distribute wheat through the efforts of Afghanis. It insisted that it would work with Afghani people in distributing the wheat only if Afghani women were allowed to work in the distribution process. At first, the government refused, as it believed women were supposed to stay at home, but, apparently, they eventually let the women work on the project. This suggests that the rulers were willing to sacrifice their own religious principles for the sake of their interests. Whether one thinks that laudable or not, that is what they appear to have done.

The underlying principle suggested by these approaches to dealing with the injustice is that, without involving oneself in a discriminatory policy, one may offer a benefit to perpetrators of injustice who no longer have a right to the benefit given their unjust conduct, in exchange for some improvement in the de facto status—not just the short-term material interests—of the victims of injustice. I think this approach to dealing with injustice is morally acceptable even though women in the society who are not involved in the immediate project will continue to be required to stay at home. But it is important that such policies be used with an eye to the status and fate of all the victims, not just the small group who may immediately and directly benefit.

[15] See UN Economic and Social Council, "Discrimination against Women and Girls in Afghanistan," *Report of the Secretary-General*, 28 January 2002, p. 6.

6

Are Justified Aggressors a Threat to the Rights Theory of Self-Defense?*

Adam Hosein

6.1

It is normally wrong to harm or kill other people. This is because they normally have rights that you not harm or kill them. But there are important special cases where people lack these rights and so it is permissible to harm or kill them. Cases of legitimate self-defense are among these. Suppose that on your way out of the bar someone tells you they are about to break your leg, just for the amusement it will bring them. Morality permits you to prevent this by inflicting harm on them first, as long as the harm is necessary to prevent it and not disproportionate. For instance, you could permissibly prevent their assault with a kick in the shins.

According to what I'll call "Rights Theorists" of self-defense, such as Judith Jarvis Thomson, the explanation for why you may kick the thug is that he would otherwise violate your rights.[1] More specifically, the explanation goes like this. When people act in ways that will violate your rights, they lose their rights to not be harmed by you, just to the extent that harming them is necessary to protect your rights, and within a constraint of proportionality.[2] I will say, in terminology borrowed from Jeff McMahan, that people who lack rights that you not harm them in a certain way are "liable" to be harmed by you in that way. Thus, people who are

* For extremely helpful comments on this chapter, many thanks to Mahrad Almotahari, Tyler Dogget, Helen Frowe, Gerald Lang, and Jeff McMahan.

[1] See Thomson (1991) for the classic statement of this view. I draw heavily on her discussion there and her work more generally.

[2] In the rest of this chapter I will largely drop the qualifications of necessity and proportionality but they should be assumed throughout.

going to violate your rights become liable to be harmed by you. Their liability to be harmed is what makes it permissible for you to harm them.

In the case at hand, the bar thug is going to violate one of your rights, namely your right to not have your leg broken. Given this, he is liable to be harmed by you as a means of preventing your right being violated and thus it is permissible for you to kick him. Or so argues the Rights Theorist.

6.2

We have seen that the Rights Theory of self-defense is very attractive because it provides a simple and plausible explanation of why and when you may defend yourself from attackers. We should thus hang on to it if we can. In what follows I shall consider an important challenge to the theory presented by Jeff McMahan. I shall argue that McMahan's objection can be defused, but first I will need to introduce a distinction.

The violence of the bar thug is just pointless violence which lacks any rationale and this makes it relatively obvious that defense is permissible in this case. Most Rights Theorists focus on cases of this kind, where there is an attacker who has no justification for the wrongful threat he is imposing. We can easily imagine, and are familiar with, a different kind of case where an attacker imposes a threat that will wrong someone and does possess a good justification for imposing it. The justification he might have is that by imposing the harm he can bring about a substantial good, such as benefits to himself or others. We are morally permitted to wrong people when we have a good justification for doing so. For instance, suppose that to get my friend to hospital I must trespass on your lawn. Surely this is permissible, even though in doing so I will wrong you.[3]

So, we need a distinction between permissibly and impermissibly wronging someone and there is some standard terminology to mark this distinction. Whenever someone permissibly wrongs another they "infringe" a right. But when they impermissibly wrong someone they "violate" a right.[4]

Now, we can further distinguish two types of rights infringers, two types of attackers acting with justification. Suppose there are three parties, Attacker, Victim

[3] The assumption that one can wrong someone whilst still having a good justification is one I share with McMahan and so I don't spend much time defending it. But here is another kind of case that motivates it. Suppose that I have made conflicting contracts: I have a deal with both you and Naim to provide 100 widgets. Presumably I would be justified in giving the widgets to Naim if he needs them more urgently but I would still have to compensate you. Why? Plausibly, because I have still *wronged* you. So my action was an instance of justified wronging. See Thomson (1992) for examples of this kind and further discussion.

[4] I have followed McMahan's terminology here in treating rights infringements and violations as mutually exclusive. Others, including Thomson, treat violations as a species of infringements.

and Beneficiary, and Attacker can secure a significant benefit for Beneficiary by imposing a (comparatively small) cost on Victim. Attacker would merely infringe Victim's rights by imposing the cost on her. In the first sort of case it would be morally *good*, or praiseworthy, of Victim to voluntarily help Beneficiary herself (if she can) but not morally *required*. In the second sort of case, Victim is morally *required* to help Beneficiary (if she can).

The distinction between things that it would merely be good of us to do for others and things that we are morally required to do for them is a familiar one.[5] For instance, suppose we are leaving a meeting and I can either offer to drive you home, going some distance out of my way, or I can let you walk there, safely but more slowly. It would be good of me to offer you a lift but I'm not morally required to do so. I wouldn't do anything wrong by not taking you home. By contrast, if you collapse in the meeting and need to be driven to the hospital immediately I may not complain that the hospital is out of my way—I am morally required to take you there and would commit a serious wrong otherwise.

McMahan has suggested that cases of mere infringement, where people are permissibly wronged, present a serious problem for the Rights Theory. The cases of infringement that he discusses are of the first kind I just mentioned: cases where the victim of the threat is not morally required to bear the cost that will be imposed on her. Since I am replying to McMahan I will focus initially on cases of that kind too but later in the paper I'll discuss cases of the second sort and what the Rights Theory has to say about them.[6] For the time being when I speak of "rights infringers," or of "justified threats", I will have in mind only threats of the first kind.

McMahan asks us to consider the following case:

Tactical Bomber: A tactical bomber fighting in a just war has been ordered to bomb a military facility located on the border of the enemy country. He knows that if he bombs the factory, the explosion will kill innocent non-combatants living just across the border in a neutral country. But this would be a side effect of his action and would be proportionate to the contribution that the destruction of the facility would make to the achievement of the just cause. As he approaches, the non-combatants learn of his mission. They cannot flee in time but they have access to an anti- aircraft gun.[7]

[5] See, for instance, Thomson (1971)'s distinction between being a "Minimally Decent Samaritan," which is morally required, and being a "Good Samaritan," which is not.

[6] Some readers may wonder whether there really are any infringement cases of the first kind, where it is permissible to inflict a cost on someone that they aren't morally required to bear. I will consider this possibility later on the paper also, though for the time being I'll follow McMahan in supposing that there are.

[7] This case, and the argument that follows, are found in McMahan (2005). For a revised argument and some important new suggestions see McMahan, "Self-Defense Against Justified Threateners" (in this volume)

He suggests that since the bombing is for a just cause, proportionate in the damage it will produce and so on, it is permissible, even though it would kill some non-combatants. I will follow him in assuming this. Since the cause is just, significant benefits will be produced by the attack. Yet, we do not typically think non-combatants are morally required to lay down their own lives, even for the sake of the just cause.[8] So, the tactical bomber is a rights infringer of the first sort just discussed: the victims of his attack, the non-combatants, are not morally required to bring about the benefit that will result from his attack.[9]

McMahan asks: is it permissible for the non-combatants to defend themselves from the bombing using their anti-aircraft gun? The intuitive answer, as he says, is "yes," it does seem permissible for them to protect themselves from the bombing.

McMahan claims that the Rights Theorist cannot explain this intuitive response to Tactical Bomber. Why? Thomson, in developing the Rights Theory, considered only cases of self-defense against people who threaten to impermissibly wrong you (cases of rights *violations*). According to her central statements of the theory you are permitted to defend yourself against someone if they are going to violate one of your rights. So, the Rights Theory as developed by Thomson says nothing about whether you can defend yourself against a justified threat because a justified threat will not violate any of your rights (they will merely *infringe* them). The tactical bomber presents a justified threat and so is not going to violate the rights of non-combatants. So, the Rights Theory is silent on the question of whether the non-combatants may defend themselves (though not in conflict with the intuition that they can defend themselves).

Thomson, as I said, simply didn't consider cases of rights infringement when developing her theory, so it is not surprising that the resulting theory is silent about them. I will argue that the Rights Theory can plausibly be extended to cover them. I propose that we adopt a Rights Theory that says that people become liable to harm when they are going to either violate *or* infringe a right.

I think this is a very plausible extension of the Rights Theory. To see why, consider what it is that makes a would-be rights violator liable to harm. I suggest that what makes this person liable to be harmed is that he threatens to *wrong* someone. It is very plausible to think that it is not unjust to use force against someone to stop them wronging yourself or others. If this is true, then people become liable to be

[8] McMahan (2005) also assumes that in the normal case that bomber's mission is of sufficient importance that the non-combatants are required to commit suicide to ensure its success.

[9] Furthermore, it follows from the fact that the non-combatants are permitted to defend themselves that they are not required to commit suicide for the sake of the just cause.

harmed when they threaten to wrong others. Thus, a good explanation for why would-be rights violators are liable to be harmed is that they threaten to wrong others. But would-be rights infringers also threaten to wrong others. So, they too must be liable to be harmed. Hence my proposal: people become liable to be harmed when they are going to either violate *or* infringe a right.

If we extend the Rights Theory in the way I have proposed then, on the face of it, the Rights Theorist has a perfectly good explanation for the intuitive response to Tactical Bomber. We want to know why the fact that the bomber is threatening to inflict harm on them permits the non-combatants to inflict harm on him. The Rights Theory, as I have reformulated it, says that people become liable to be harmed when they are either going to infringe or violate the rights of others. The bomber is going to infringe the rights of the non-combatants and so, on the Rights Theory, he is liable to be harmed. Thus, it is permissible to harm him since he lacks a right not to be harmed.

McMahan denies that the Rights Theorist can give the quick explanation I just suggested. In particular, he suggests that it is implausible to think that the bomber becomes liable to be harmed just because of the threat he poses to the non-combatants. This is implausible, McMahan claims, because the tactical bomber acts with justification. The bomber poses a threat, but a threat that is justified by substantial moral reasons. This justification, McMahan says, should surely exempt him from liability to be killed. Why should it exempt him? There are good moral reasons for the tactical bomber to perform the bombing. It is true that in performing it he will infringe some people's rights, but his moral reasons are strong enough to outweigh the existence of those rights. It seems strange, then, to say to him "there are strong moral reasons in favour of your action, but all the same if you perform it you will have to accept the loss of some of your rights." Why should he have to bear the heavy cost of liability to harm when he is performing an action that is morally good?

More generally, McMahan's suggestion is that, in his slogan, "justification defeats liability". A little more precisely, the principle he proposes is this.

Justification Defeats Liability (JDL): An attacker who imposes a threat of harm that will wrong another person does not thereby become liable to harm if the threat he poses is justified.[10]

If this principle is correct, then the Rights Theorist's explanation for why the non-combatants can defend themselves is wrong. According to that explanation,

[10] This is a version of McMahan's gloss on the "justification defeats liability" slogan in McMahan (2008) p. 5.

the non-combatants may permissibly impose harm on the tactical bomber because his threat makes him liable to harm. But if JDL is correct, then the tactical bomber's threat cannot make him liable to harm because the threat he poses is justified.

6.3

So, is JDL correct? We have seen some reasons for thinking that it is *prima facie* quite plausible. All the same, it is false, which we can see by considering the following case.

Machine: Suppose a car crusher machine malfunctions and a person, A, is trapped in its jaws. If the machine is not stopped, A will be crushed and die. The only way the machine will stop is if B's arm (which is especially large) is placed in the gears. But this will cause B's arm to be seriously damaged. A third person, C, is standing close by and realises that all of this is the case.

May person C jam B's arm into the gears? Doing so will infringe B's right to not have his arm damaged, but it will also produce a very substantial benefit, namely preserving A's life. I think we should therefore say that it is permissible for C to make use of B in this way; we should say that such a threat would be justified.[11] Suppose C goes ahead and puts B's arm in the works. The gears are turning and will soon damage B's arm. C has created a threat to B but, I have suggested, a justified threat: one backed by substantial moral reasons.

Suppose now that it is possible for C to save A *without* harming B. B's arm must be put in the machine but it will not be harmed if C's arm is put in the machine also. C's arm would provide a cushion so that B does not suffer harm but C does instead and A would still be saved. Surely in this case if C decides to save A by putting B's arm in the machine then she must voluntarily put her arm in with B's. Intuitively, if C decides to help save A's life and she can bear the costs of doing so, then she must bear those costs rather than passing them on to B.

This intuition is not surprising since we generally think that if you are going to do something to help others, and you are not morally required to help them, then you must bear the costs of helping them yourself rather than passing those costs on to others. For instance, if you want to do something to help a person that needs a kidney transplant, then you must donate one of your own kidneys rather than appropriating some third party's kidney.[12] There is a good explanation for these intuitions. The explanation is that it would be more *just* for you to bear the relevant

[11] If you disagree with my intuition here, decrease the harm to B in the case just to the point where the action becomes permissible by your lights.

[12] Thomson (2008) emphasizes this fact also and with similar examples.

costs rather than some third party and the reason it would be more just is that it would involve less *wronging*: you would wrong the third party if you were to impose the costs on them, whereas you would wrong no one if you bore those costs yourself. Similarly, justice requires that C volunteer her own arm for harm rather than B's in the case at hand because otherwise C would wrong B.

Now suppose that C has put B's arm in the machine but is unable to put her own arm in the machine with B's (perhaps she lacks the strength to squeeze it in). As before, A will be saved whether or not it is B or C's arm that gets mangled. May B now grab C's arm and squeeze it in the machine with his? It seems to me plainly permissible for B to do this, effectively transferring the harm from himself to C. Also, it does not seem to me permissible for C to prevent B from doing this by fending him off. These claims about B and C's permissions seem especially plausible when we remember that if C has the choice she should save A by damaging her own arm rather than B's.

Thus, there is an asymmetry between B and C in the case we are considering: B may defend himself from C but C may not defend herself from B. And a very plausible explanation of this asymmetry is that B has a right that C lacks. B may defend himself from C's attack because he has a right that C not harm him. C, however, does not have a right that B not harm her and so is not permitted to defend herself from B's attack.

It thus seems that C has become liable to be harmed by B because of the wrong she will have done to B if B's arm is damaged (namely, the wrong of causing B to have a mangled arm). C incurs this liability despite the fact that her threat to B had a sound moral justification (saving A's life). Thus, Machine presents a counter-example to McMahan's JDL principle. According to that principle, if an attacker creates a justified threat, then their threat will not make them liable to harm. C's threat is justified but it all the same makes her liable to harm. Here justification does not "defeat" liability.

6.4

Let me briefly consider a potential objection to my argument against JDL. Some people might resist my premise that if C decides to save A and has the option of bearing the costs of saving A herself then she must do so.[13] Accepting it might seem to commit us to a set of claims that are incompatible. If the only way to save A were for C to bring harm onto herself of a mangled arm, she would not be

[13] I'm grateful to Jeff McMahan for raising this concern in correspondence (though I present it in a slightly different form here).

morally *required* to do this. She would be permitted to stand back and allow A to die. Furthermore, if the only way to save A were to harm B, then, I have accepted, it would be permissible for C to harm B. Now suppose that C discovers that she is faced with all three of these options at once: she can do nothing, harm herself for A's sake or harm B for A's sake. The following line of reasoning seems available to her: Harming B is permissible if it's the only means of saving A. As it happens, there is another way of saving A, namely by harming myself. But I'm not required to do that, so the availability of this option shouldn't affect what else I am permitted to do. So, I am permitted to harm B for A's sake.

According to my earlier argument, harming B in this case is actually not permissible, because C has the option of harming herself instead. Yet the reasoning I just outlined seems compelling. How can it be that when we add an option that it is otherwise permissible to take (harming B for A's sake) to an option that it is permissible not to take (harming C for A's sake) it becomes impermissible to take the former option?

To see how this can be possible consider the following variant cases. I have said that C would be permitted to mangle B's arm if this was only way to save A's life. Suppose C's options were instead to do nothing or to save A by merely mangling one of B's fingers (a lesser harm than a mangled arm). Faced with these two options C would be permitted to mangle the finger but also to do nothing. Now suppose these three options are combined: C can either mangle B's arm to save A, mangle B's finger to save A, or do nothing. It would be impermissible, I take it, for C to mangle B's arm in this situation. We have thus found a case where when we combine an option that it is otherwise permissible to take (mangling B's arm) with an option that it is permissible to not take (mangling B's finger) we find that the former option becomes impermissible. This is just the kind of situation that earlier seemed very puzzling.

How is this situation possible? Why does adding the possibility of merely mangling B's finger to save A rather than mangling B's arm make the latter impermissible? In all the cases we have considered so far being beneficent, or acting to help others, is permitted but not required.[14] However, the following principle, which I briefly appealed to earlier, plausibly applies to these cases: if you are going to be beneficent you must do the beneficent action that best conforms to what justice requires. I'll call this "the principle of just beneficence." This principle makes sense of the situation we just considered. It is permissible for C to not be beneficent, to do nothing for A. However, if C is going to do something to help A she must do the

[14] I'm using "beneficent" in perhaps a broad sense here to mean any action done to benefit those in need.

beneficent action that best conforms to the requirements of justice. In the scenario at hand, it is preferable as a matter of justice for C to merely mangle B's finger rather than his arm because the former would involve doing a lesser wrong to B and it is more just to do someone a lesser wrong rather than a greater wrong. Thus, if C is going to help A, then she must do so by mangling B's finger and not by mangling his arm. So, the principle I proposed explains why C may not mangle B's arm.

The same principle may be used to explain the combination of claims that we began with and found initially puzzling: that C may not harm B to save A if she has the option of harming herself for the same purpose, even though she is not required to harm herself and is permitted to harm B if that is the only means of saving A. According to the principle of just beneficence, if you are going to be beneficent you must do the beneficent action that best conforms to what justice requires. So, if C is going to save A she must do the action that best conforms to what justice requires. If C harms B she will wrong him, whereas if she harms herself no-one will be wronged. It is more just to do the action that involves less wronging. Thus, if C is going to save A she must do so by harming herself not by harming B. Once we recognize the relevant, very plausible, beneficence principle, there is no problem in understanding why C must be prepared to bear the costs of saving A herself.

Furthermore, as I said earlier, we ordinarily expect that people should bear the costs of their own beneficence rather than displacing these costs onto others. For instance, as I said, if one wants to help someone in need of a kidney transplant, one must give one's own kidney rather than appropriating someone else's. The principle of just beneficence explains not only the machine case but also this broader array of cases: you may not take someone else's kidney because this would wrong them and so you would better conform with the requirements of justice by giving your own kidney.

6.5

So, JDL is false and thus cannot be used to undermine the Rights Theory in the manner I discussed earlier. Still, the reader will have noticed that there is an important difference between Machine as I've described it and McMahan's Tactical Bomber case. In both Machine and Tactical Bomber, an attacker creates a threat which is justified by the good outcome it would produce. Now for the difference. In Machine, the defender, B, can defend himself from the attacker, C, without preventing the good outcome from obtaining. A's life will still be saved even if B defends himself. By contrast, if the non-combatants in Tactical Bomber strike at the bomber, the good he could otherwise create will not obtain. If the bomber is shot down he will not be able to destroy the munitions dump and thereby further the cause of justice.

The reader may thus wonder whether there is a plausible modified version of JDL which entails that justified attackers of the Tactical Bomber kind do not incur liability whereas justified attackers of the Machine kind do. The revised principle might look like this:

Justification Defeats Liability* (JDL*): An attacker who imposes a threat of harm that will wrong another person does not thereby become liable to harm if (a) the threat he poses is justified and (b) harming him would prevent him from doing the good he would otherwise do.

JDL* is, on the face of it, ad hoc and thus doesn't have the intuitive pull that JDL perhaps has. There is also, I'll now argue, a much deeper problem with JDL*.

According to JDL*, person C in the Machine case is liable to be harmed by B, just as we intuitively judge. But JDL* entails that if this case were different, such that B's defensive action would prevent A's life from being saved, then C would not be liable to harm from B. So, if we accept JDL*, then whether C posseses a right not to be harmed by B turns on whether harming C would be bad for a third person A. This seems to me to be highly implausible because it conflicts with fundamental ideas about rights and their grounds.

Sometimes we have rights that seem to be established by convention. For instance, my right to use the cricket club facilities is of this kind. These rights seem to depend on the existence of various institutions or agreements for their existence. But other rights, such as the right to not be kidnapped, do not seem to be like this. Let's call these non-conventional rights "basic rights." When we argue that a person X should be accorded something because she has a basic right to it, we appeal to some fact about X to justify the claim that she has a right.[15] Philosophers disagree about what exactly the relevant facts about X are.[16] Some say that we should just appeal to X's interests. For instance, to justify X's right not to be harmed they would appeal to X's interest in not being harmed. Other philosophers focus on X's will. But they all focus on facts about X. By contrast, if we think X should be accorded something for reasons that are not primarily to do with X's own interests and so on, then we do not say that X has a right to it. For instance, perhaps I should give my guitar to Euan because everyone will enjoy hearing him play it but we wouldn't say that he has a right to the guitar.

It thus seems to be a central fact about our concept of a right that the grounds on which an individual has a basic right are facts about that individual. Now, people's

[15] I draw here on Hart's (1982) discussion.

[16] See Wenar (2011) for a useful summary of the main views.

rights are not the only factor that affects what we ought to do. As we saw earlier, it is sometimes permissible to do an action even though someone has a right that we not do it, because there are other strong considerations unrelated to rights that tell in favour of the action. And these other considerations may have nothing to do with the rights holder. So, whether a basic right may be *infringed* depends on facts about people other than the rights holder. My point is just that whether someone *has* a basic right in the first place seems to depend only on facts about that person.

If this is so, then JDL* must be false. The right not to be harmed seems to be plainly a basic right. But, as we have seen, JDL* entails that whether an individual has a right not to be harmed can depend on facts about whether harming her would benefit other people. Rather than giving up on some of our fundamental notions about rights we should give up on JDL*.

6.6

JDL, then, appears to be false and cannot be rescued through revision. Still, though, it might seem that we are left with a puzzle. I said earlier that there is a plausible *prima facie* case in favour of JDL and yet we have seen that JDL turns out to be false. To be really satisfied with rejecting JDL we should be able to identify the problem with that *prima facie* case. I have some suggestions about what that problem is but first let us remind ourselves of why JDL seemed attractive.

JDL seems attractive, I said, because it reflects the idea that morality should not require you to suffer for doing a morally good action. So, for instance, acting in ways that are charitable, which is morally good, should be met with encouragement and praise, whereas the infliction of gratuitous harm, which is morally bad, should be met with condemnation and sanction. But, according to this line of reasoning, to say that a justified attacker becomes liable to be harmed because of their attack is to say that they should suffer a penalty despite the fact that they are acting in a morally good manner. So, liability to harm should not be incurred by justified attackers.

This line of reasoning in favour of JDL sounds plausible, but the Rights Theorist has good reason to reject it. The reasoning assumes that the only reason why an attacker could incur liability to harm is that they should suffer a penalty for performing a morally bad action. But the Rights Theorist can, and should, deny this. On the Rights Theory, an attacker becomes liable to be harmed by their victim when, and because, their attack will wrong their victim. Furthermore, as I have emphasized throughout, the question of whether one is performing an action that is morally wrong is distinct from the question of whether one's action will wrong any particular individual. According to the Rights Theory, the reason self-defense against an attacker is permitted is not that the attacker is doing something morally wrong and thus should be penalized but, rather, that his attack will otherwise wrong the victim and so it is not unjust for the victim to use force to prevent this. The mistake in the reasoning for JDL that I outlined is that it ignores an explanation of liability that isn't grounded in the importance of penalizing people for wrongdoing.

So much for the initial intuitive case for JDL. However, in later work Jeff McMahan has suggested a subtler version of the reasoning in favour of JDL that may seem immune to the criticism I just made and which I will now consider (McMahan, 2008, p. 8). His suggestion goes like this. In self-defense cases we are confronted with a victim who, in the status quo, is going to suffer harm. They can prevent this harm to themselves by inflicting harm on someone else, usually the attacker. Whatever the victim does someone will suffer a harm: either the victim themselves, if the status quo is maintained, or someone else if the victim chooses to inflict harm themselves. There is thus, McMahan says, some inevitable harm to be suffered and the moral question is who should suffer it. What we should ask then, McMahan suggests, is who we should prefer to suffer the harm, as a matter of justice: Does justice require that the victim suffer the harm or that someone else, such as the attacker, suffer the harm? If justice requires that an agent be harmed then, McMahan proposes, they are liable to be harmed.

Turning to cases of justified attacks, McMahan claims that justice no more requires that a justified attacker suffer the inevitable harm than it requires that the victims of his attack suffer it. So, for instance, he writes: "given that just combatants who pose a threat of wrongful harm have positive moral justification for their action, there is no reason why justice would demand that unavoidable harm be distributed to them, for acting out of respect for morality, rather than to innocent bystanders."[17] Why does justice not favour harm to such attackers over their victims? Viewing the situation impartially, McMahan claims, there is no reason to prefer that someone who is acting in a morally good way suffer harm than someone who is completely innocent. This means, McMahan argues, that justified combatants are no more liable to be harmed than their innocent victims. Hence, he endorses JDL.

The Rights Theorist has good reason to reject this more subtle argument too. Suppose we go with McMahan's suggestion that we should think about liability by first thinking about where it would be most just for a harm to fall (I don't think we should do this, but let's do so for the sake of argument). The issue is: how do we decide where it would be most just for the harm to fall in cases of justified attack?

[17] Wenar (2011).

One option is to say that it would be equally just for the innocent non-combatants to bear the inevitable harm as it would be for the tactical bomber because the bomber is acting with moral justification. A second option is to say that justice requires the bomber rather than the non-combatants to bear the inevitable harm because he is going to wrong someone whereas as they are not. If we take the first option, we should accept JDL and if we take the second we should reject it. Which should we take? McMahan, as we saw, directs us to the first option. But he doesn't offer any justification for this. The only line of reasoning I can see for taking the first option is the intuitive idea I discussed earlier that morality should not require you to suffer for doing a morally good action. But, we've seen already, there is every reason for the Rights Theorist to reject this idea and so the Rights Theorist is free to take the second option and reject JDL.

6.7

I would now like to consider another objection to the Rights Theory involving Tactical Bomber. If my argument so far has been correct, then the reason why the non-combatants in Tactical Bomber are permitted to defend themselves by imposing harm on the bomber is that the bomber is liable to be harmed in this way or, equivalently, the he lacks a right not to be harmed in this way. The reason he lacks this right is that he presents a wrongful threat to the non-combatants.

McMahan objects that if this account is correct, then it should not be permissible for the bomber to defend himself from attack by the non-combatants (McMahan 2005). For, McMahan reasons, if the bomber is liable to be harmed by them, then they are not wronging him by attacking him. And if they are not wronging him, then it should be impermissible for him to defend himself from attack. But, McMahan suggests, surely the bomber is permitted to defend himself. Therefore, he cannot be liable to attack by the non-combatants.

We have assumed from the outset that the bomber's mission is of sufficient impartial importance to justify his carrying it out even though it will kill the non-combatants. Now, suppose that as the bomber flies into enemy airspace to carry out his mission the non-combatants start to attack him. If the importance of his mission is sufficient to justify killing the non-combatants then it is surely of sufficient importance to justify repelling their attacks with whatever force is needed along with, eventually, killing them.

This shows that the Rights Theorist has a perfectly good response to McMahan's objection. It is true, she can say, that the bomber is permitted to repel the attacks, but this is just because of the impartial good his mission will produce. The fact that he is liable to attack from the non-combatants does not take away this justification for repelling their attack. We can thus both say that he is liable to be harmed by the non-combatants and also say that it is permissible for him to repel their attack.

Now, we can imagine a modified version of the Tactical Bomber case in which the bomber would not be able to offer these grounds for defending himself.[18] Imagine that the reason the bomber will harm the non-combatants if he carries out his mission is that bombing the munitions factory would produce a large fire that will spread towards the village where the non-combatants live. However, the non-combatants could prevent the fire reaching their village by shooting down the bomber's plane, which would provide a shield from the fire. Can the bomber defend himself from such an attack? In this case he is not able to justify defending himself by appealing to what is impartially best. His mission is already complete and it would not be impartially better for the non-combatants to die rather than him and his crew. Furthermore, if the theory I have defended is correct, the bomber is liable to be killed by the non-combatants and they are not liable to be killed by him. So, if that theory is correct it isn't permissible for the bomber to defend himself from the non-combatants once he has carried out his mission. But I think this is just the answer that we want from a theory of self-defense. It seems to me that intuitively the bomber in this case really is not permitted to defend himself from the non-combatants.

6.8

I have been arguing that the Rights Theory provides a satisfactory account of justified threats by showing that it can explain our intuitions about Tactical Bomber, the case McMahan raised as a problem for the theory. But as I mentioned briefly in Section 6.2 the Tactical Bomber represents just one kind of justified threat because the non-combatants he attacks are not morally required to bear the cost he is going to impose on them.

I would now like to consider justified threats of the other kind, that are harming people who are required to bear certain burdens. For instance, suppose that in Machine everything is as I initially described it but the harm B has to bear for A's life to be saved is relatively minor: a mildly bruised forearm, say. In this situation it seems that B would be morally required to put his own arm in the Machine to save A since the harm he would suffer, a little bruising on his forearm, is so minor compared to a loss of life. But suppose B doesn't put his arm in the machine. As in the original case, it seems permissible for C to force B's arm into the machine for

[18] McMahan suggested a case of this kind to me in correspondence.

A's sake. However, in this case it does *not* seem permissible for B to fend off C and defend himself from her attack.

Can the Rights Theory account for this difference? Can it explain why B is not permitted to engage in self-defense in this case? What the Rights Theorist should say depends on whether we think C would wrong B by putting his arm in the Machine in this case. Some people will say that since C is only making B comply with what he is morally required to do she will not wrong him, whereas others will say that C is indeed wronging B. Either way the Rights Theory can provide a good explanation for why B may not defend himself.

First, suppose C would not wrong B. In that case, according to the Rights Theory, C retains all her rights to not be harmed by B. So, B may not defend himself from C's attack because C does not become liable to be harmed by B and would thus be wronged if B harms her in self-defense. Secondly, suppose that C really would wrong B by putting his arm in the machine. In this case the Rights Theorist must say that C lacks a right that B not attack her. However, she can still argue that B is not permitted to defend himself from C. B is, we are assuming, morally required to do what is needed to save A. So, he may not defend himself from C, since if he does so A will not be saved.

Things are a little more complicated if we imagine that B and C could share the costs of saving A or that the costs must be borne by one of either B or C, but again I think the Rights Theory can provide a good account. Suppose that B and C can share the costs of helping A by, say, both putting in their arms, so that each suffers a lesser degree of harm than they would if only their own arm was in the machine. In this case, it seems me that morality requires them to each accept a share of the harm. What if B refuses to do his part and C forces him to? Surely B is again not permitted to defend himself from this force.

There are again two ways of thinking about the rights involved and two possible, and plausible, accounts the Rights Theorist can give of why defense is not permitted in this case. First, she can say that B is not wronged when he is forced bear a fair share of the costs of helping A. Thus, C does not become liable to be harmed by B and would be wronged by any defensive action. Secondly, she can say that B is wronged even when forced to bear his fair share of the costs but still may not resist that force because he is morally required to bear those costs and will not do so if he resists C's force.

If B and C cannot divide the harm between them, then it seems they will have to use a fair procedure, such as tossing a coin, to decide who should fairly bear the harm. The Rights Theorist then has the same two options again when considering the person who refuses to bear their fair share of the harm.

Finally, some people may say, contrary to what I supposed at the beginning, that it is *only* permissible to harm/coerce X to produce a benefit for Y if X is morally required to produce this benefit for Y herself. I disagree with these people. It seems clear to me that, for instance, it is permissible for tactical bomber to drop his bomb even though, first, the bomb will kill the non-combatants for the sake of benefits to others and, secondly, the non-combatants are not required to give up their lives for the sake of those benefits. But if I am wrong about this the Rights Theory is not affected. We just saw that the Rights Theorist can give a good account of cases where someone is permissibly harmed for the sake of a benefit they are required to produce. If those turn out to be the only cases of permissible wronging then so be it: we can still say that the Rights Theory provides a good account of all cases of permissible wronging.

6.9

I have argued that a Rights Theory can be used to offer a perfectly good explanation of why people like the non-combatants in Tactical Bomber are permitted to defend themselves against justified attacks. Before concluding, I would like to briefly argue that there can be no plausible alternative to the Rights Theory's explanation for why the non-combatants are permitted to defend themselves in the Tactical Bomber case that we began with. If we assume, as McMahan does, that the bomber retains his right not to be harmed, it can only be permissible to harm him if substantial good would be produced. And the non-combatants would not produce any substantial good by harming him; in fact, by hypothesis, they would make things substantially worse since they would prevent him from carrying out his just mission.

What else is there left to appeal to? McMahan points to the fact that if the non-combatants do not defend themselves they will be wronged (McMahan 2008, p. 10). But this fact is not enough on its own to make killing the bomber permissible, as long as he retains his rights not to be killed. Compare: suppose that the mafia say to you, "We'll kill you unless you assassinate Dai." Dai is perfectly innocent and thus fully in possession of a right not be harmed/killed. If you refrain from killing Dai you will be wronged by the mafia, but all the same you are not permitted to kill him. We might not blame you for doing so, given the enormous duress the Mafia have put you under, but it would still be wrong. You cannot do whatever you like to prevent yourself being wronged; you must act within the constraints of the rights that other people have. You are not permitted to wrong them (absenting a sufficient impartial justification), even though doing so might be necessary to protect your own rights.

We could say that things are entirely different when the person you would wrong in trying to protect your rights is the very same person that would otherwise wrong you. We could say that the bomber in Tactical Bomber has a right against the non-combatants that they not harm him and yet that it is permissible for the non-combatants to kill him, given that he would otherwise wrong them. It seems to me that this would be very strange. What could be meant by saying that the bomber has a right against the non-combatants that they not kill him but one that all the same doesn't constrain them from killing him? This would not be like any other right we know and so we should be very hesitant to suppose it exists.

I thus do not see how the fact that a person is going to be wronged can make it permissible for her to harm another unless that fact alters the rights that the other person has. The Rights Theory seems to me the only plausible option for explaining how it can be permissible to harm someone who imposes a justified threat.

To conclude, we have seen that the best version of the Rights Theory of self-defense can be used to give a plausible account of self-defense against justified threats, one that fits with our pre-theoretical intuitions about such threats. This shows that the Rights Theory can avoid what McMahan and others take to be a serious problem. It also has important implications for the morality of non-combatant behaviour during wartime since it shows that non-combatants may defend themselves even from combatants who are on the side of justice, such as those in McMahan's Tactical Bomber example.

References

Hart, H. L. A. (1982) *Essays on Bentham* (Oxford: Oxford University Press).

McMahan, J. (2005) "The Moral Basis of Liability to Defensive Killing," *Philosophical Issues* 15: 386–405.

——(2008) "Justification and Liability in War," *Journal of Political Philosophy* 16/2: 227–244.

Thomson, J. J. (1971) "A Defense of Abortion," *Philosophy & Public Affairs* 1/1: 47–66.

——(1991) "Self Defense," *Philosophy and Public Affairs* 20/4: 283–310.

——(1992) *The Realm of Rights* (Cambridge: Harvard University Press).

——(2008) "Turning the Trolley," *Philosophy and Public Affairs* 36/4: 359–374.

Wenar, L. (2011) "Rights," in E. N. Zalta (ed.) *The Stanford Encyclopaedia of Philosophy* (Fall 2011 Edn), available at <http://plato.stanford.edu/archives/fall2011/entries/rights>.

7

Self-Defense Against Justified Threateners

Jeff McMahan

7.1 The Tactical Bombers

The *tactical bomber* is a well-known figure in philosophical iconography. He usually appears along with the *terror bomber* in discussions of the Doctrine of Double Effect. But I want to use him, together with his crew, to explore a different issue: the permissibility of self-defense against a person who acts with moral justification in posing a threat of harm to which the victims are not liable and that would infringe their rights.

The tactical bomber usually appears as a lone figure but I would like for him to have a crew. I will refer to him and his four crew members as the *tactical bombers* or, for brevity, the bombers. Assume that they conduct all of their military decision-making collectively and that in all the cases I will consider they reach their decisions unanimously and then act in concert.

The tactical bombers are fighting in a just war of humanitarian intervention in a distant country. Their mission, if successful, will prevent 100 innocent civilians in the state in which the intervention is occurring from being killed by soldiers of that state. These civilians are strangers to the bombers; they bear no special relation to them.

Here are some of the other features of the example, along with some assumptions I will make.

1. It is unavoidable that when the tactical bombers bomb their military target, which is located on the enemy's border with a neutral country, the explosion will hurl heavy debris onto a tiny village across the border, killing its five inhabitants as a side effect.
2. Although these five neutrals live in the same village, they are not otherwise specially related to one another. They are not, for example, members of the

same family. We might suppose that they have chosen to live in this remote village because each is reclusive. Because of the absence of special relations among them, there is no reason to suppose that the harm that any one of them is permitted to cause in defense of another exceeds what the other would be permitted to cause in her own self-defense.

3. The only two effects that are relevant to the permissibility of the bombing are the intended saving of the 100 civilians and the foreseen but unintended killing of the five villagers. Although the bombing will destroy a military target, it will not kill or incapacitate any enemy soldiers or otherwise impede their war effort. The just cause of the war in which the tactical bombers are fighting is the saving of the lives of civilians in the enemy state; thus the success of the tactical bombers' mission would constitute a partial achievement of the just cause.
4. The bombers' mission is necessary for the saving of the 100 civilians. There is no other way the civilians can all be saved, and indeed no other way that *any* can be saved.
5. I will assume that the number of civilians that would be saved sufficiently exceeds the number of villagers that would be killed to make the bombers' action proportionate in what I call the "wide" sense—that is, proportionate in the relation between its relevant good effects and its harmful effects on people who are not liable to suffer those harms, or indeed any harms.
6. Because the bombers' aim is just and their action is necessary and proportionate, their bombing of the military target is morally justified in the fact-relative sense. Assume that they know this, so that their action is justified in the evidence-relative and belief-relative senses as well. Although the villagers' right against attack has been neither waived nor forfeited, it is overridden—that is, there is a lesser-evil justification for killing them as a foreseen but unintended effect of the bombers' action.
7. The bombers might or might not be morally *required* to drop the bomb. The position I will defend would be more plausible if the bombing were morally required, but the position seems correct even if the bombing is merely justified but not required.
8. The villagers would not be morally required to act on their own to save the 100 civilians at the cost of bringing about their own deaths, either as a means or a side effect. That is, they would not be required to actively sacrifice their lives to achieve the tactical bombers' mission.
9. Those involved in the immediate conflict—the tactical bombers and the villagers in the neutral state—know all the relevant nonmoral facts, such as that dropping the bomb is necessary for saving the 100 innocent civilians but will kill the five villagers.

If the tactical bombers complete their mission, the ratio of innocent people saved to innocent people killed will be 20 to one. This seems proportionate even when the asymmetry between killing and letting die is taken into account. Compare the familiar *Trolley case* in which a runaway trolley is careering down the main track where it will kill five people unless it is diverted onto a branch track where it will kill only one. Most people believe that it would be permissible, and therefore proportionate, for a bystander to divert the trolley even though the ratio of people saved to people killed is only five to one. This supports the claim that the bombers' action is also proportionate, given its significantly higher ratio of people saved to people killed. But the comparison is not conclusive because there is another seemingly relevant difference between the cases—namely, that the killing in the trolley case is done via the redirection of an existing threat while that by the bombers is done via the creation of a new threat. If killing via the creation of a new threat is substantially more objectionable morally than killing via the redirection of a threat, then the fact that killing one to save five is proportionate in the trolley case may not show that killing one to save 20 is proportionate in the case of the tactical bombers. I suspect, however, that even if the difference between creating and redirecting a threat is significant, it is not sufficiently significant to outweigh the difference between the two cases in the ratio of people saved to people killed. (Despite this difference between the two cases, as well as another that I will discuss later, I will sometimes appeal to trolley cases to elucidate certain claims.)

The claim made earlier in point 6 is that the tactical bombers' action is justified. I mean by that more than that it is permissible. An act is *permissible* if it is not wrong, all things considered. An act is *justified* if it is permissible *and* there is a positive moral reason to do it. (That it is permissible presupposes that the positive reason or reasons to do it outweigh any and all countervailing moral reasons not to do it.) An act is *required* if one has decisive moral reason to do it, so that not to do it would be wrong, or impermissible.

The claim that the tactical bombers' action is morally justified is supported by what Parfit calls the *Consent Principle*, which says, roughly, that an act is wrong if it treats people in a way to which they would not have sufficient reason to consent (Parfit (2011), p. 184). It seems that the five innocent villagers could rationally consent to be killed as a side effect of saving the much greater number of civilians. But the 100 civilians could not rationally consent to be allowed to be killed in order that the five not be killed. The Consent Principle therefore seems to imply not only that the bombers are justified in dropping their bomb but that they are morally required to do so. I take no position on the validity of the Consent Principle, but the fact that it is not obviously implausible and has this implication provides some support for the assumption that it is at least morally justifiable for the bombers to drop their bomb.

The tactical bombers are what I call *justified threateners*—that is, people who act with moral justification but whose justified action will wrong or infringe the rights of others—in this case, the villagers' right not to be killed. (I distinguish between *violations* of rights, which are all things considered impermissible, and *infringements* of rights, which are all things considered permissible. Judith Thomson uses these terms differently. She uses "infringement" to refer to all acts that contravene rights and "violation" to refer to those instances of infringement that are all things considered impermissible.) A justified threatener differs from a *just threatener*, who threatens to inflict a harm to which the victim is *liable*, or that the victim *deserves*. Just threateners do not wrong their victims.[1] Their victims have no right not to be harmed—at least in a certain way, for a certain reason, and by certain agents—and normally have no right of self-defense against the harm to which they are liable. There are, however, cases in which a person who is liable to be defensively killed may permissibly engage in harmful defensive action against a just threatener. Suppose, for example, that an agent of a terrorist organization has just learned that the organization has hidden a large bomb where its detonation tomorrow will kill hundreds of innocent people. He has decided, on moral grounds, to go during the night to disarm and destroy the bomb. But there are limits to his moral scruples and at present he is about to commit a murder. He sees that a police sniper is about to shoot him. He can save himself only by killing the sniper. Although he is liable to be killed by the sniper, he has, and can be motivated by, a lesser-evil justification for killing the sniper in self-defense if his own survival is both necessary and sufficient for preventing the detonation of the bomb. (This is also a case in which the sniper's liability justification for killing the agent is overridden by considerations of consequences. If the police sniper knew that killing the agent would prevent the saving of hundreds of innocent people, it would be wrong for him to shoot the agent, despite the fact that the agent had forfeited his right not to be killed.)

The tactical bombers are not just threateners vis-à-vis the villagers. Unless the bombers are prevented from doing so, they will wrong the villagers, or infringe their rights. Suppose the villagers have access to an anti-aircraft weapon and can shoot down the bombers before they drop their bomb. Are the five villagers

[1] I have elsewhere suggested that we should distinguish between a *perfectly just threatener*, who would cause harms only to people who are liable to suffer them, and an *imperfectly just threatener*, who would intentionally cause harms only to those who are liable to them but would also unavoidably cause unintended but proportionate harms to some people who are not liable to them. See Jeff McMahan, "Just War," *Ethical Perspectives* 19 (2012), pp. 257–261.

permitted to kill the five bombers in self-defense, when this will thwart the latter's morally justified action?

The problem of defense against a justified threatener does not often arise in war. But it can occur both as an *in bello* problem and an *ad bellum* problem. As an example of the latter, suppose that the best or perhaps the only way that a country can effectively defend itself against an unjust aggressor is to fight from prepared defensive positions in the territory of a small neighboring country. Because this would involve destructive fighting on its territory, the small country refuses to permit the threatened country to take up positions there. And suppose that it is morally permitted to refuse. But suppose also that the country faced with aggression nevertheless has a lesser evil justification for going to war against the small country as a means of securing access to its territory for defensive operations. May the small country fight in defense? Most people think it may.

One historical example that has at least some of these features is the Winter War between the Soviet Union and Finland. The Soviet Union needed access to a section of Finnish territory to be better able to defend Leningrad against the Nazis. It offered an exchange of territory that would have given Finland an area of the Soviet Union larger than the area of Finland that the Soviets were requesting. The Finns refused and the Soviet Union then went to war to seize the relevant territory. Suppose the Finns were morally permitted to refuse but that the Soviets nevertheless had a compelling lesser evil justification for trying to secure effective defenses against a Nazi attack. The later Nazi siege of Leningrad, in which more than a million civilians died and another million Red Army soldiers were killed, shows that the Soviets' fears were justified. Yet virtually everyone outside the Soviet Union thought the Finnish defensive war against the Soviet Union was just and admirable, and even today the war is regarded among Finns almost as a holy war.

Most people with whom I have discussed the case of the tactical bombers and the villagers believe that the villagers are permitted to shoot down the bombers' plane, killing the crew and thwarting the mission. I am sympathetic to this intuition and once sought to defend it (McMahan (2005), pp. 386–405). But the more I have thought about the case, the more I have come to distrust my intuitions about it. I now think that the balance of reasons favors the conclusion that the villagers are not morally permitted to kill the bombers in self-defense. (As I will indicate later, however, there are variants in which it is more plausible to suppose that they are permitted to shift the costs of the bombers' action to them.) But I do not claim to have decisive arguments for the conclusion that the villagers may not shoot down the bombers' plane. At a minimum, however, my arguments do show more clearly what is at issue in this case.

7.2 Proportionality in Defense Against Justified Threateners

There are various possible justifications for defensive killing. Several of these clearly do not apply to defense by the villagers against the bombers. Some people, for example, believe that it can be a justification for killing that a person deserves to die, or be killed. Many and perhaps most defenders of capital punishment believe this. But the fact that the tactical bombers do not intend to kill the villagers, together with the fact that their action is justified in all three senses (fact-relative, evidence-relative, and belief-relative), rules out the possibility that they deserve to die.

Consent may also have a role in justifying certain killings. Defenders of euthanasia generally claim that, when a person is capable of giving or withholding rational consent, her consent is a necessary condition of the permissibility of euthanasia. And some just war theorists argue (mistakenly, in my view) that in general the justification for killing in war is that when people adopt the role of soldier, they thereby tacitly consent to be attacked by enemy combatants in conditions of war.[2] But even these theorists do not claim that combatants consent to be attacked by enemy civilians threatened as a side effect of their justified military action.

Another form of justification for killing is that it is, in the circumstances, the lesser evil, impartially considered. This does not mean simply that the harm inflicted through killing is less than the harm that is thereby averted. It means, rather, that there is no way other than killing some innocent people to avert a *substantially* greater harm to other, more numerous, innocent people. The bombers, for example, have a lesser-evil justification for killing the villagers as an unavoidable and unintended side effect of their action. It is, indeed, because of this that the villagers cannot have a lesser-evil justification for killing the bombers if that would prevent them from carrying out their mission. Self-defense by the villagers would intentionally kill the same number of people it would save and would also prevent an additional 100 people from being saved. (Although this is irrelevant here, most people believe that the proportionality constraint on a lesser-evil justification for intended killing is stronger than that which applies to a lesser-evil justification for killing that is foreseen but unintended.)

Although self-defense by the villagers cannot be justified on grounds of desert, consent, or lesser evil, there remain two possible grounds of justification: first, that

[2] For criticism of the claim that soldiers consent to be attacked by enemy combatants, see Jeff McMahan, *Killing in War* (Oxford: Oxford University Press, 2009), pp. 51–59; and Jeff McMahan, "Duty, Obedience, Desert, and Proportionality in War," *Ethics* 122 (2012), pp. 146–151.

the bombers are liable to be attacked and, second, that even if the bombers are not liable, the villagers have an agent-relative permission to defend themselves. I will consider both these possible justifications, but we should first consider whether defensive action by the villagers is ruled out on the independent ground that it would prevent the saving of the 100 civilians. If it is, it is then irrelevant whether the bombers are liable to attack, for thwarting the mission would be wrong even if it could be done without harming the bombers.

Suppose the villagers have a remote control device capable of jamming the bomb doors of the bombers' plane. They can use it to save themselves without harming the bombers, though at the cost of preventing the 100 innocent civilians from being saved. Is it permissible for them to use this device? In describing the example, I stipulated that they would not be required to act to save the civilians at the cost of their own lives. From this it seems a short step to the conclusion that they are also not required to allow themselves to be killed by action that would save the civilians, provided that they can prevent that action in a way that causes no additional harm.

Consider, by way of analogy, a variant of the Trolley case. A runaway trolley is careering down the main track where it will kill five people trapped on that track. A bystander has access to a switch that can turn the trolley onto a branch track on which a single person is trapped. Most people believe that the bystander has a lesser-evil justification for turning the trolley, thereby killing the trapped man rather than allowing the five to be killed. But suppose the trapped man has access to two switches, one that can turn the trolley onto the track on which he is trapped and another than can jam the action of switch controlled by the bystander. Virtually everyone accepts that it is permissible for the trapped man not to use the first switch that would turn the trolley so that it would kill him rather than the five. But if this is true, it seems that it should also be permissible for him preemptively to block the bystander's use of the other switch that would turn the trolley toward him.

In this case, as I noted earlier, the ratio of people who are prevented from being saved to those who avoid being killed (five to one) is lower than it is in the case of the tactical bombers (100 to five, or 20 to one). So one might argue that while it is permissible for the trapped man to jam the bystander's switch, the difference in numbers in the case of the bombers makes it impermissible for the villagers to jam the bomb doors. One might argue, in particular, that action that saves only five lives but ensures that 100 people will be killed rather than saved is *disproportionate*, even if it does not directly kill anyone. The alleged disproportionality of the villagers' action might be seen as a corollary of the proportionality of the bombers' initial action. If it is proportionate for the bombers to kill five as a side effect of saving 100, it may seem that it must be disproportionate to save those five at the cost of preventing the saving of the 100.

But proportionality is not merely a matter of numbers, even when all those whose lives are at stake are equally innocent, or have an equal right not to be harmed or killed. Proportionality is also sensitive to facts about agency. If effective defensive action by the five villagers would unavoidably *kill* 100 innocent bystanders as a side effect, that action would indeed be disproportionate in the wide sense. But the same conclusion does not necessarily hold when their defensive action would not kill 100 people but would instead prevent them from being saved. A pair of simple examples will illustrate this point. Suppose that I am about to be killed by a culpable threatener. If the only way I can defend myself is through defensive action (perhaps the use of a grenade) that will kill two innocent bystanders as a side effect, then I am not permitted to engage in effective defensive action. Such action would be disproportionate in the harm it would inflict on people who are not liable to be harmed in my defense. But suppose that I am about to be killed by a culpable threatener in different circumstances. I can kill him without killing anyone else. But I know that he is a celebrated surgeon who is scheduled to perform two life-saving surgeries tomorrow that no one else in the world is capable of performing. If I kill him today, I will prevent him from saving two innocent people tomorrow. But in this case it is intuitively permissible, and therefore not disproportionate, for me to kill him in self-defense.

The explanation seems to be that the deaths that my action will cause by preventing people from being saved have less weight in the assessment of proportionality than deaths that I might cause by killing.[3] This difference between killing people and preventing people from being saved may be sufficiently important to make defensive action by the villagers proportionate as well. If the bombers' action is proportionate even though it kills people, the villagers' jamming the bomb doors may also be proportionate given that it only prevents people from being saved. This may be true even though the villagers' action results in a significant net loss of lives, while the bombers' action results in an equally significant net saving of lives. The mere fact that the villagers' defensive action would bring about the greater evil is insufficient on its own to make that action disproportionate.

This is of course not to say that the numbers are irrelevant. There is *some* number of innocent people whose lives would be saved by the bombers' action that

[3] For a plausible general defense of the idea that "preventing from saving" is a conceptually and morally distinct category from killing and letting die, and that it is morally closer to letting die than to killing, see Matthew Hanser, "Killing, Letting Die, and Preventing People from Being Saved," *Utilitas* 11 (1999), pp. 277–295.

would make it impermissible for the five villagers to defend their lives by jamming the bomb doors. If, in other words, the number of innocent people who will otherwise be killed is sufficiently large, morality can require people to allow their right not to be killed to be infringed by a justified threatener. Indeed, the number of innocent people who will otherwise be killed might be so large that the five villagers could be morally required to act to save them even at the cost of sacrificing their own lives, either as a means or a side effect. Whether this number is larger than the number that would require the villagers to *allow* themselves to be killed is a question I leave open here.

7.3 Liability to Be Killed

My provisional conclusion is that it would be permissible for the villagers to defend their own lives at the cost of thwarting the tactical bombers' mission, provided they do so without causing bad effects other than preventing the saving of the 100 innocent civilians. Perhaps this is wrong; certainly if the number of innocent people whom the villagers' defensive action would prevent from being saved were significantly larger, their defensive action would be wrong. But I will assume that 100 is below the threshold at which thwarting the bombers' mission becomes impermissible.

Given this assumption, it is important to determine whether the tactical bombers, in the original case in which jamming the bomb doors is not an option, make themselves liable to be killed by justifiably threatening to infringe the right of the villagers not to be killed. If they do, the case for the permissibility of defense by the villagers may seem conclusive, for their defensive action would be discriminate (in that it would not infringe the rights of those it would intentionally kill), proportionate, and necessary. But if the tactical bombers are not liable, defensive action by the villagers seems presumptively wrong, as it would kill certain people who retain their right not to be killed as a means of saving an equal number of other people, and it would have significantly worse consequences overall, impartially considered.

Whether the tactical bombers make themselves liable to be killed in defense of the civilians is a disputed issue within the ethics of defense. Some philosophers argue that the bombers are not liable, others that they are. While most of the contending theories of self-defense imply that they are not, some imply that they are. Curiously, the theory of self-defense that has perhaps been most influential—the *rights-based account*—has no explicit implication about the case at all. This theory, originally advanced by Judith Thomson, holds that a person who will otherwise violate another person's right not to be killed has no right not to be killed if killing him is necessary to prevent him from violating the other's right (Thomson 1993, pp. 383–410). While Thomson claims that defensive action is permissible to prevent *violations* of rights, she says nothing about the permissibility of defensive action to prevent permissible *infringements* of rights. There is, therefore, a sense in which the theory is silent about whether the villagers may shoot down the bombers. Yet, because it purports to be a complete account of self-defense but provides no basis for claiming that the bombers are liable, it seems to imply that they are not liable. There would have to be an addition to the theory for it to imply that justified threateners lose their right against attack or become liable to attack.

One of the most restrictive accounts of self-defense, the *culpability account*, holds that a person can be liable to defensive killing only if he culpably poses (or is culpably responsible for) a threat of serious harm to someone who is not liable to that harm. Because the bombers are not culpable for the threat they pose to the villagers, they cannot be liable to defensive attack according to the culpability account. If the villagers attack them, therefore, they will be acting wrongly because they will be threatening to violate the bombers' right against attack. If the villagers are even minimally culpable for their attack, they are then liable to preemptive defensive killing by the bombers. Perhaps, however, the fact that they will be killed by being buried under a mound of debris if they do not attack in self-defense is sufficient to make their defensive action excusable. If their defensive action would be fully excused, they would not be culpable, in which case they too would not be liable to defensive action by the bombers. Hence the bombers, though justified in dropping their bomb, would have no justification *grounded in self-defense* for preemptively killing the villagers before the villagers could kill them. They might, of course, have a justification for preemptively and intentionally killing the villagers grounded in the importance of achieving their mission. And, like the villagers, they might be excused for killing people who will otherwise kill them without justification.

The culpability account is, in my view, excessively restrictive. It forbids self-defense in cases in which there is good reason to believe that the target of defensive action is liable. These are cases in which one person acts permissibly (at least in the evidence-relative sense) in a way that foreseeably imposes a small risk of harm on others but through bad luck ends up threatening the life of an innocent person. In such a case, when the threatened person can either allow herself to be killed or kill the person who threatens her, the fact that the initial threatener made the choice to expose other people to risk makes him liable to suffer the costs of his own choice, even though he has acted neither wrongly (in the evidence-relative sense) nor culpably.

Another account of self-defense, the *responsibility account*, holds that the criterion of liability to defensive attack is moral responsibility for a threat of wrongful harm to another. This account therefore seems to imply that the tactical bombers are liable to be killed by the villagers, for they do seem to be responsible for a threat of wrongful harm—namely, harm that would infringe the villagers' rights. And if the bombers are liable to be killed, it seems that they can have no right of defense against the defensive action of the villagers.[4]

I find these implications counterintuitive. Many people, of course, will not find it counterintuitive to suppose that the villagers are permitted to shoot down the bombers in self-defense. But what is counterintuitive is the claim that, while the five villagers are permitted to kill the five bombers in self-defense, the bombers are not permitted to kill the villagers in self-defense. For that to be true, it seems that there must be some significant moral asymmetry between the villagers and the bombers. Yet on the assumptions most favorable to the villagers, both groups act with moral justification in threatening to harm the other. The only difference is that the bombers have attacked *first*. But that is of course precisely what they were morally justified in doing.

There is a further way in which the claim that the bombers make themselves liable to attack is counterintuitive. Recall that if the bombers are liable to attack, attacking them does not wrong them or infringe their rights; for they have forfeited their right against attack. Any necessary and proportionate defensive action taken against them does not, therefore, threaten them with *wrongful* harm. According to the responsibility account, such defensive action cannot be a basis of liability. As we have seen, these claims imply both that the villagers have a liability justification for killing the bombers in self-defense and that the bombers have no liability justification for killing the villagers in self-defense. But because the reasons grounded in liability seem in this case to be agent-neutral, these judgments apply not only to action by the villagers but also to action by third parties. In that case, wholly impartial and disinterested third parties should be justified in killing the bombers in defense of the villagers. (This presupposes the earlier conclusion that the killing of the bombers is not ruled out solely because it would prevent the saving of the 100 civilians.) But because third parties would not, by hypothesis, be posing a threat of *wrongful* harm, the bombers would have no liability justification for attacking them in self-defense. This seems highly implausible. For in attempting to drop their bomb, the bombers are acting on the basis of impartial moral reasons—reasons that might even ground a moral *requirement* to drop the bomb.

[4] For a powerful defense of this view, see Adam Hosein, "Are Justified Aggressors a Threat to the Rights Theory of Self-Defense?," in this volume.

Their action would not violate anyone's rights (though it would justifiably infringe those of the villagers). Indeed, even if what they do is not morally required, it is nevertheless morally admirable, for they are exposing themselves to risk in order to do what they have most moral reason to do. Self-defense by the villagers, by contrast, would be based entirely on reasons of self-interest and would produce a significantly worse outcome, impartially considered. It is therefore implausible to suppose that morality permits neutral third parties to act in support of the villagers' self-interested aims but forbids the morally motivated bombers to act in self-defense.

The implications of the assumption that the bombers make themselves liable to be killed in defense of the villagers become even more implausible when we consider defense by third parties who are not disinterested. It is, for example, utterly implausible to suppose that the bombers' own compatriots, or their allies in their just war, could have an agent-neutral liability-based justification for killing them.[5] But perhaps—though I think this is unlikely—one could argue that, although such people would actually have a liability justification, it would be wrong for them to act on it because they share the aim that justifies the bombers' action.

A more telling objection is that, if there is an agent-neutral liability justification for killing the bombers, it seems that it must extend even to the unjust combatants against whom the bombers are fighting, who do not share the bombers' aim.[6] That, however, is deeply counterintuitive. These unjust combatants are among those who threaten the 100 civilians, among others, with death. It is their wrongful action, or the wrongful action of those with whom they are colluding, that has made the bombers' action, including the threat it poses to the villagers, both necessary and justified. They are, in other words, among those who not only are responsible for the threat to the 100 civilians but also bear primary responsibility for the threat to the five villagers. Admittedly, this latter responsibility gives them a special reason to protect the villagers. But it also gives them a special reason not to kill the bombers, as they—the unjust combatants—are also among those who bear primary responsibility for the situation that the bombers are now in. If the unjust combatants were not fighting an unjust war, the bombers would have no reason to drop the bomb that will kill the villagers. It is counterintuitive to suppose that, to save five innocent people they are responsible for putting at risk, the unjust combatants are permitted to kill another five people who are attempting to save *100*

[5] For a point that does not address the issue of liability but is nonetheless closely related, see Stephen R. Shalom "Killing in War and Moral Equality," *Journal of Moral Philosophy* 8 (2011), pp. 495–512, at p. 501.

[6] For a defense of this claim, see Uwe Steinhoff, "Jeff McMahan on the Moral Equality of Combatants," *The Journal of Political Philosophy* 16 (2008), pp. 220–226.

different innocent people whom the unjust combatants, or their collaborators, will otherwise intentionally and wrongly kill.

One might agree that the unjust combatants are not permitted to kill the bombers but also claim that this is not because the bombers are not liable to be killed. One could argue that even though the bombers are liable to be killed, the unjust combatants may not prevent the killing of only five villagers at the cost of preventing the saving of the far greater number of innocent civilians whose lives they, or their fellow soldiers, now threaten. To assess this suggestion, consider a variant of the case in which the 100 civilians are no longer threatened by the unjust combatants. Suppose that the unjust combatants who can shoot down the bombers also have the power to ensure that the 100 civilians will not be killed, either by simply not killing them, or perhaps by preventing their fellow soldiers from killing them. And suppose that they have had a change of heart and want to do what is right. Assuming that they cannot communicate with the bombers, they have two options. They can kill the bombers, thereby saving the villagers, and then spare the lives of the 100 civilians. Or they can refrain from killing the bombers, who would then save the 100 civilians, though at the cost of killing the villagers as a side effect. What ought they to do? Either way, the 100 civilians will be unharmed. So their choice is effectively between (1) intentionally killing five people who are acting in a way that is morally justified in the belief-relative, evidence-relative, and fact-relative senses (and whose justification derives from the unjust combatants' own prior wrongdoing) and (2) unintentionally allowing five innocent bystanders to be killed. It seems that those who accept that there is a general moral asymmetry between killing and letting die, and those who believe that intention is relevant to permissibility, should conclude that the unjust combatants ought not to kill the bombers. But if the bombers have made themselves *liable* to be killed, then presumably the unjust combatants ought to kill them rather than allow them to kill the villagers as a side effect. Yet this seems wrong. Given the background to this choice, it is hard to believe that the bombers have no right not to be killed *by the unjust combatants*, who are morally responsible for the threat of wrongful harm that their justified action is intended to prevent.

Those who claim that the bombers are liable to self-defensive action by the villagers might argue at this point that it is possible to forfeit one's right not to be killed vis-à-vis some but not others. Thus, the bombers might forfeit their right vis-à-vis the villagers but not vis-à-vis the unjust combatants. But it seems that this strategy will have to become implausibly complex and ad hoc if it is to yield reasonable conclusions about this case. One would have to claim that the bombers forfeit their right not to be killed vis-à-vis the villagers themselves, their friends and families and perhaps their civilian compatriots generally, as well as vis-à-vis disinterested third parties, but *not* vis-à-vis the bombers' own compatriots and allies or the unjust combatants against which they are fighting. It would be hard to explain and defend such a claim. Those who want to defend the permissibility of self-defense by the villagers would do better to pursue an alternative justification that does not claim that the bombers are liable. (I will consider the most promising such justification in the next section.)

Some people may be more troubled by the idea that the bombers lack a right of self-defense than by the claim that it is permissible for the villagers to attack them in self-defense. Such people might argue that even if the bombers are liable, their liability consists only in their forfeiture of the right not to be attacked in defense of the villagers. Their loss of this right does not entail the loss of their right of defense as well. Thus, although the villagers and third parties have a liability justification for killing the bombers, the bombers retain their right of defense against those who would attack them.

This claim is doubtfully coherent. The logic of liability is that if one is liable to be harmed in a certain way, for a certain reason, by certain people, one can have no right of defense against being harmed in that way, for that reason, by those people. (As the earlier example of the agent of the terrorist organization shows, it is possible, though rare, for a person who is liable to be harmed to have a lesser-evil justification for self-defensive action. But that is not what is generally meant by a right of self-defense. In the example, the innocent person about to be murdered by the agent would have a right of self-defense while the agent would not, though it might be wrong, all things considered, for the victim to act on that right and justifiable for the agent to act in self-defense despite lacking a right to do so.) That liability to suffer a certain harm excludes a right of defense against that harm is explained in part by the fact that the determination of liability to defensive harm is a matter of justice in the ex ante distribution of unavoidable harm. One cannot have a moral right to harm people as a means of preventing them from acting justifiably to produce a more rather than less just distribution. One cannot have a right to harm people to prevent them from justifiably doing to one what one has no right that they not do to one. So if the tactical bombers are morally liable to be harmed in defense of the villagers, they cannot have a right to inflict defensive harm on those who have a liability justification for harming them.

If I am right that liability is determined by considerations of justice in the distribution of unavoidable harm, it may well be true, in addition, that those who are liable to a certain harm are not permitted to prevent that harm even in a way that would not require them to cause harm to anyone. This seems true at least in most cases that are likely to occur. But, as we saw in the case of the terrorist agent, a person who is liable to be harmed may have a lesser-evil justification for engaging in self-defense. And there is at least one other type of exception—namely, when a person who is liable to be harmed has a better distributive option than any available to those who would otherwise harm him in accordance with his liability. If the liable person could, through preventive or defensive action, achieve a more just distribution of the unavoidable harm than others are capable of achieving, then he or she can be justified in engaging in preventive or defensive action to achieve that distribution.

7.4 Justification Excludes Liability

Thus far it may seem that the responsibility account has the implausible implications I have described: that the tactical bombers are liable to be killed in defense of the villagers, that neutral third parties therefore have a liability justification for killing them, and that the bombers have no right of self-defense either against the villagers or against third parties (though they might have a different justification for defensive action derived from the importance of achieving their mission). Some proponents of the responsibility account, myself included, have sought to qualify the account to avoid being committed to these implausible implications. In earlier work, I have suggested that if one is objectively morally justified, or morally justified in the fact-relative sense, in acting in a way that will cause wrongful harm to others, the justification exempts one from liability to defensive action (McMahan 2009, pp. 38–51). If that is right, the responsibility account does not imply that the bombers are liable to defensive attack either by the villagers or by third parties.

But the claim that justification excludes liability is controversial and has been vigorously challenged.[7] Perhaps the strongest objection comes from the domain of corrective justice, in the form of putative counterexamples from the law of torts that are held to reflect the requirements of morality. Suppose, for example, that a passerby finds a person in a diabetic coma. If the diabetic does not receive a shot of insulin within minutes, he will die. The passerby knows that the house immediately across the street from where the diabetic lies belongs to someone who has a bountiful supply of insulin. That person not being home, the passerby breaks in, takes some insulin, and saves the life of the diabetic. He has acted with moral justification but is nonetheless legally liable to compensate the owner of the insulin for any damage done to the house and for the taking of the insulin without the owner's consent. As I indicated, many people think that tort law here expresses the demands of morality—that is, that the passerby's liability to compensate the owner is not merely legal but moral as well.

[7] See, e.g., Uwe Steinhoff, "Jeff McMahan on the Moral Inequality of Combatants," *Journal of Political Philosophy* 16 (2008), pp. 220–226; Uwe Steinhoff, "The Moral Equality of Modern Combatants and the Myth of Justified War," *Theoretical and Applied Ethics* 1 (2012), pp. 35–44, esp. p. 37; and Hosein, "Are Justified Aggressors a Threat to the Rights Theory of Self-Defense?" (in this volume).

One possible response to this challenge is that there is a fundamental difference between liability to pay compensation and liability to suffer defensive harm, so that while justification does not exclude liability to compensate those one has harmed, it does exclude liability to defensive harm. One reason why this might be true is that to hold a justified threatener liable to compensate his victim is not to permit anyone to prevent his justified action, whereas to hold him liable to defensive action is to permit others to prevent the justified action. In the case of the diabetic, for example, even if one thinks that the passerby owes compensation to the owner of the insulin, one should accept that the owner, had he been home and reluctant to part with any of his insulin, would not have been permitted to engage in harmful defensive action against the passerby to prevent her from taking the insulin. The passerby's moral justification does seem to exempt her from liability to defensive harm. So even if the general claim that justification excludes all forms of liability is false, it may still be true that justification excludes liability to defensive harm, and that is all that is necessary to rule out the claim that the bombers are liable to defensive action either by the villagers or by third parties.

Another possibility is that the original, stronger claim that moral justification excludes all forms of moral liability is true and that the law of torts departs from corrective justice when it holds an agent who has acted with moral justification liable to compensate those whom his justified action has wronged. In the case of the diabetic, for example, it is not unreasonable to suppose that no one is liable to pay compensation to the owner of the insulin. If he had been at home and had seen the diabetic in need of insulin outside his door, the owner would have been morally required to give up some of his supply to save the diabetic's life, in which case he may not have been able to demand compensation from anyone. The sacrifice of the insulin may simply have been what morality required of him. But given that he was not at home at the time the insulin was needed, the passerby acted in his absence to fulfill the duty he would have had if he had been at home.[8] Thus no one is liable to compensate the owner for the loss of what he was morally required to sacrifice.

It may, however, seem unfair to the owner to force him to bear the full cost of saving the diabetic. Perhaps the ideally fair way to deal with problems such as the rescue of the diabetic is to have a fair scheme of social cooperation that requires everyone in a society to make a contribution, proportional to their income or wealth, to a fund for the compensation for people who suffer a loss through brute bad luck. Since it is brute bad luck for the owner of the insulin that the diabetic

[8] On the permissibility of a third party's fulfilling another person's enforceable duty, see Victor Tadros, *The Ends of Harm: The Moral Foundations of Criminal Law* (Oxford: Oxford University Press, 2011).

collapsed where he did, the burden of the rescue ought not to be imposed on the owner alone. It should also not be imposed on the passerby alone, who acquired the moral duty to take the insulin by the entirely fortuitous circumstance of being present where the diabetic collapsed. Rather, the burden of the rescue should ideally be shared by everyone in the society (or indeed by everyone in the world). When the cost of the rescue is dispersed in this way, the loss to any one person is negligible. Though anathema to libertarians and members of the American Republican Party, such a scheme could work to the expected benefit of the great majority of citizens in a society. The more antecedently egalitarian the society, the more likely it would be that the scheme would work to the expected benefit of all.

But what if there is no such scheme in place? No existing society has such an arrangement and none is likely to have one anytime soon. One might therefore argue that although the passerby would be exempted from liability if there were such a scheme, she is liable to compensate the owner in conditions in which no such scheme exists. There is nothing puzzling in the idea that liability can be conditional in this way. Yet even in the absence of an ideal redistributive scheme, there are other ways of allocating losses caused by the action of morally justified agents that are more just than holding such agents liable to compensate the victims of their justified action. One such option is to require the beneficiaries of the justified action to compensate the victims. For example, rather than allowing the cost of saving the diabetic to be imposed on either the owner or the passerby, the diabetic ought to pay that cost himself by compensating the owner. This is not ideally fair, assuming that the diabetic's misfortune was itself the result of brute bad luck, but it is fairer than having the benefit go to the diabetic while the burden goes to someone else. When a burden is borne by someone who on balance benefits from it, it is compensated for in a way that it is not when it is borne by someone who derives no benefit.

To claim that those who have suffered a loss to prevent others from suffering an even greater loss ought to be compensated by the beneficiaries of their sacrifice is not necessarily to claim that the beneficiaries are *liable* to provide such compensation. In the case as I have presented it, the diabetic is unconscious; he has not done anything that could make him liable to any sort of harm, whether compensatory, retributive, or defensive. That he has a duty to compensate the owner therefore cannot be a matter of liability. But it is a matter of justice nonetheless. Not all considerations of justice in the distribution of harm are a matter of liability. The diabetic has been greatly benefited at the cost of someone else. Even if he fully compensates that person, the resulting situation will be vastly better for him than it would have been if the person had not been harmed for his benefit. The diabetic can therefore have no reasonable objection to being required to restore the owner to the position he would have been in had he not made (or been forced to make) the sacrifice, when the outcome of this would still be much better for the diabetic than what would have happened to him in the absence of the sacrifice.

One might reasonably draw a different conclusion in a variant of the case in which the diabetic's predicament is not a matter of brute bad luck. If the diabetic acquired the disease from overeating, in the knowledge that obesity is a significant risk factor, or if he had left his own supply of insulin at home through recklessness or negligence, his duty to compensate the owner might well be a matter of liability rather than a matter of simply paying the cost of benefits he has done nothing to deserve. It is even more obvious in this version than it is in the original that the duty to compensate the owner lies with the diabetic rather than with the passerby.

Suppose the diabetic had been able to save himself by breaking into the owner's house and taking the insulin he needed. In that case it seems reasonable to suppose that he would thereby have made himself liable to compensate the owner—though, significantly, not liable to defensive action. If that is right, this may seem to be a counterexample to the claim that justification excludes liability. But that claim is that *moral* justification excludes liability. And it may not be that in taking the insulin the diabetic would be acting for a moral reason. Even though the outcome in which he takes the insulin is impartially better, his justification seems prudential rather than moral. He would be acting irrationally, but not immorally, if he refrained from breaking in. If that is right, then this is not a counterexample to the claim that moral justification excludes liability. That is, the diabetic would be liable to compensate the owner but the passerby would not be. In contrast to the diabetic, the passerby would be acting immorally if he failed to break in and take the insulin for the diabetic.

What if the diabetic, having been saved by the passerby, is incapable of compensating the owner? Assuming there is also no social scheme for spreading the costs of brute bad luck, one might think that the passerby would then be liable to compensate the owner. But it seems no more just to transfer the costs of the rescue to the passerby, who has already devoted her time to the rescue, than to allow them to lie with the owner. While the best outcome in these restricted circumstances might be for the owner and the passerby the divide the costs evenly between them, it does not follow that that the passerby is liable to compensate the owner for half of his losses. Indeed, it seems implausible to me, regardless of what the law says, to suppose that third parties would be morally permitted to coerce the passerby to provide that compensation, given that she has acted with full moral justification. If third parties have any reason to intervene, it is to make some voluntary contribution of their own to the compensation of the owner.

The main point of the discussion in this section has been to suggest that action that is morally justified does not, on its own, make the agent liable to compensate those who are harmed by the action in ways to which they are not liable. (I say "on its own" because there may be background conditions that, together with the justified action, make the agent liable. One such condition might be that the agent's prior wrongdoing has created the conditions that now justify his infliction of harm on someone who is not liable to that harm. Another might be that he has a professional or other special duty to pay or take on himself the costs of his own justified action. I will return to this second consideration in Section 7.6.) I have sought to defend this claim by arguing that in the case of the diabetic and other cases of the same sort, the justified agent is not liable to compensate the victim. This, in turn, supports the more general claim that justification excludes liability (in the absence of special background conditions of the sorts just noted).

It is worth mentioning, however, that the case of the diabetic differs in one important respect from the case of the tactical bombers. Whereas the owner would have a duty to provide the needed insulin were he at home, I have stipulated that the villagers (who are the cost-bearers in this case, as the owner is in the diabetic case) would not be required to act in a way that would sacrifice their own lives to save the 100 civilians. But the owner's duty in the case of the diabetic does not substantially affect the morality of the redistribution of costs. Suppose that the cost to the owner of saving the diabetic's life were substantially greater, so that if he were at home he would have no duty to provide the life-saving resource. It would instead be a matter of supererogation. The passerby could nevertheless still be justified in taking the resource necessary to save the diabetic. That the owner would have had no duty to surrender that resource does seem to make it more imperative that he be compensated for the loss. But it does not affect my earlier conclusion that, in the absence of a social arrangement for spreading the costs of brute bad luck, the duty of compensation would lie with the diabetic, who is the beneficiary of the owner's loss, rather than with the passerby. It also seems plausible to suppose that, even if the owner had no duty to provide the life-saving resource, the passerby's justification in taking it would shield her from liability to harmful defensive action by the owner. The owner would, it seems, be permitted to thwart the passerby's efforts by other means, but not by means that would involve the infliction of serious or substantial harm on the passerby.

There may, of course, be contingent reasons why it would be undesirable for the law to require involuntary beneficiaries of the sacrifices of others to compensate their benefactors. I will not consider those reasons here, as they are largely irrelevant to the question whether justified threateners are liable to defensive harm or liable to compensate the nonliable victims of their action. It is worth noting, however, that there is also a contingent reason not to hold justified threateners such as the passerby liable to compensate those on whom they impose proportionate losses. This is that the anticipation of a duty to pay compensation might deter potential rescuers from saving people whom they should be encouraged to save. And of course holding justified rescuers liable to defensive action would do even more to deter rescues that should instead be encouraged.

In concluding this discussion of the possible liability of justified threateners, it is perhaps worth observing that some writers have assumed that it is intuitively obvious that justified threateners are liable to compensate their nonliable victims, while if the potential victims manage to defend themselves preemptively, they owe no compensation to the justified threateners they have harmed. One such writer, Uwe Steinhoff, thinks that this reveals a moral asymmetry between the tactical bombers and the neutral villagers. He writes that "the fact—if it is a fact, and I think it is—that the innocent victims of the bombers can demand compensation for the mutilations and losses they have suffered from the bombers while the bombers cannot demand compensation for the losses and harms they have suffered due to the defensive action of the innocents, shows that a moral asymmetry is at play here. The bombers have wronged the innocents, and not vice versa" (Steinhoff 2012, p. 360). But the case of the insulin shows that the intuitions about compensation to which Steinhoff appeals are not so robust as he supposes.

7.5 Self-Defense as an Agent-Relative Permission

I have argued that the tactical bombers' justification for dropping the bomb exempts them from liability to defensive killing by the villagers. But it does not follow from this that it is impermissible for the villagers to kill them in self-defense. Even though the bombers have neither waived nor forfeited their right not to be killed, and even though that right has not been overridden (that is, even though the villagers cannot justify killing them by appeal to a consent-based justification, a liability justification, or a lesser-evil justification), there remains one way in which it might be argued that defensive killing by the villagers would be justified. This alternative form of justification once seemed plausible to me and I defended it in earlier work (McMahan 2005, pp. 386–405).[9] What I suggested is that the villagers have an *agent-relative* permission to defend their right not to be attacked even against justified infringement,

[9] For an ingenious defense of a general account of self-defense based on the assumption that there are agent-relative permissions, see Jonathan Quong, "Killing in Self-Defense," *Ethics* 119 (2009), pp. 507–537.

provided that they would not be required to sacrifice their own lives for the sake of the tactical bombers' goal. To say that their permission is "agent-relative" is to say that it does not extend to third parties. Only the villagers themselves are permitted to kill the bombers.

I noted at the beginning of this section that the rights-based account of self-defense advanced by Thomson does not address the question whether those who threaten another's right with justified infringement thereby lose their own right against necessary and proportionate defensive action. If Thomson's rights-based account were extended to justify not only defense against rights violations but also defense against justified infringements, it would be too permissive. In the case of the tactical bombers, it would permit neutral third parties to intentionally kill five morally justified agents, thereby also preventing the saving of 100 innocent people, as a means of preventing the justified killing of only five other innocent people—that is, the same implausible conclusion that is implied by the supposition that the bombers are liable to be killed. It is more plausible to suppose that if there is a permission to defend a right against justified infringement, it applies only to the possessor of the right—in this case, that it applies only to the villagers themselves.

It is tempting, however, to suppose that if a person has an agent-relative permission to defend her right against justified infringement, that permission must extend as well to those who are specially related to her, such as her parent or spouse. The permission, in other words should extend to the agent and to certain third parties to whom the agent is specially related, though not to unrelated third parties. But this suggestion creates various problems. One is a slippery slope problem—namely, where is the line to be drawn between special relations that are sufficiently important to justify the extension of the permission and those that are not? But a more important objection is that a permission to defend *oneself*, when that permission is not agent-neutral, has a different source from a permission to defend someone else to whom one is specially related, when that permission is also not agent-neutral. One's relation to oneself seems morally quite different from one's relation to others to whom one is specially related.

Most of us accept that we have special duties to at least some people to whom we are specially related, duties that we do not have to others to whom we are not specially related in the relevant way. Such duties are often referred to as "associative duties." If there are associative duties, there must also be associative permissions—permissions to give some degree of priority to the interests or well-being of certain people to whom one is specially related.

Most people also believe that there are agent-relative permissions—permissions to give a certain priority to the objects of one's own special concern, including oneself. It is, however, more problematic to suppose that there are duties to oneself in addition to a permission to give some priority to oneself. It seems, for example, that self-sacrifice is always permissible, provided that it is not worse for others. It may be prudentially irrational, but it is not immoral. But that is difficult to reconcile with the idea that one has duties to oneself. It might be claimed that, as the object of these duties as well as their subject, one could always waive one's right to the performance of the duty by oneself. But that would mean that such duties could never be binding. The notion of a duty to oneself would, at least in practice, be empty.

If a person has an agent-relative permission to defend himself, someone specially related to him might have an associative permission or duty to defend him as well. But the sources of the two permissions are different. They derive from different relations: self-identity in the one case and some other relation, such as the parent-child relation, in the other. If a potential victim who has only an agent-relative permission to engage in self-defense may be defended by someone specially related to her, that is because the other person has an associative permission, not because the potential victim's agent-relative permission extends to the specially related person as well.

It is possible that there are no agent-relative permissions but that there are associative permissions. If that is true, there can be cases in which a person has neither an agent-neutral nor an agent-relative permission to defend herself and yet someone specially related to her does have an associative permission, or perhaps even an associative duty, to defend her—for example, a case in which, while a person has no right of self-defense against a justified threatener, her parent is nevertheless permitted to defend her.

My principal concern here is to determine whether victims of justified threateners who are not liable to the harms they would suffer are permitted to act in *self*-defense. So I will continue to concentrate on what it is permissible for potential victims to do rather than on what it might be permissible for third parties to do, whether they are specially related to the potential victims or not.

When, in earlier work, I sketched the argument that the villagers have an agent-relative permission to defend themselves from the bombers, I assumed that their permission was also an agent-relative *justification*. Then on the further assumption that justification exempts an agent from liability to defensive action, I argued that the villagers' defensive action against the bombers would not make them liable to counter-defensive action by the bombers. Yet because the bombers are also not liable to attack, they retain their right not to be attacked. Since the villagers threaten to infringe their right against attack, they too have an agent-relative permission to attack the villagers as a means of self-defense.

Since each party to the conflict has an agent-relative permission to attack the other in self-defense, I suggested that the situation might be referred to as a "symmetrical defense case." This term was meant to indicate a rough moral parity between the parties. Most accounts of the morality of self-defense imply that there cannot be such cases. They assume that if one person has a right to attack another, the other must lack a right not to be attacked and therefore cannot have a right of defense against what he has no right not to have done to him. I think, however, that there are symmetrical defense cases.

It is comparatively easy to imagine cases in which it is permissible in the evidence-relative sense for each of two people to attack or kill the other. All that has to be true in such cases is that each person is epistemically justified in believing that the other threatens to harm her in a way that is unjustified in the fact-relative sense. It is more difficult, however, to find cases in which each of two people is justified in the fact-relative sense in attacking or killing the other. But there do seem to be cases of this sort. Suppose that two captured Roman prisoners of war are credibly threatened by the guards at the Colosseum that unless they fight to the death as gladiators, they will both be killed.[10] Suppose that there is no difference between them that would give one of them a duty to sacrifice himself for the sake of the other. And it cannot be the case that each of them is morally required to sacrifice himself to the other, for in that case if both tried to do their duty, neither would kill the other and both would be killed by the guards. Perhaps the ideal solution would be for them to agree to a random procedure, such as a coin toss, to determine which would have to allow himself to be killed by the other. But we can imagine that they cannot communicate, or that the Emperor has threatened to have them both killed if there is the slightest evidence of a thrown match. In these circumstances it seems wrong to insist that neither may kill the other, so that they will both be killed. It is better that one should live than that both should die. It seems, therefore, that each has a lesser-evil justification for trying to kill the other, at least if that makes it more likely that one will survive than it would be if they were both to refuse to fight. If this is right, this is a symmetrical defense case in which each is justified in the fact-relative sense. So in principle such cases are possible. But while I once thought that the conflict between the bombers and the villagers is such a case, I no longer think so.

To explain why the conflict between the tactical bombers and the villagers is not a symmetrical defense case, and in particular why self-defense by the villagers cannot be justified by an appeal to an agent-relative permission, it will be helpful to

[10] I borrow this example from *Killing in War*, p. 58. The same point might be illustrated by a case in which two people simultaneously climb into a lifeboat that will sink with more than one occupant.

review a particular line of argument in the history of the debate about self-defense and agent-relative permissions. In earlier work, I defended the culpability account of self-defense but was disturbed by its apparent inability to justify the self-defensive killing of someone who wrongly but nonculpably threatens one's life. I suggested that one might appeal to the claim that, in cases in which both the threatener and the potential victim are entirely innocent, so that considerations of justice favor neither, the victim may be permitted to give priority to her own life—that is, that she may have an agent-relative permission to engage in self-defense. But I then rejected this suggestion on the ground that it also implies, implausibly, that it is permissible for an innocent person to kill an innocent bystander as a means of self-preservation (McMahan 1994a, pp. 268–271).[11] If this is right, the same objection applies to the idea that one can appeal to an agent-relative permission to justify the killing a justified threatener in self-defense. That appeal would justify too much. But more recently I noted that a promising response to this objection is that the relevant difference between intentionally killing an innocent (or, as I would now say, nonresponsible) threatener in self-defense and intentionally killing an innocent bystander in self-preservation is that whereas the first form of killing does not use the victim as a means, the second does (McMahan 2009, pp. 170–173). Borrowing a distinction first introduced by Warren Quinn, I noted that the first form of killing is merely "eliminative," while the second is "opportunistic," and that it is plausible to suppose that the constraint against opportunistic harming is stronger than that against eliminative harming (Quinn 1989, p. 344). This could also explain why the appeal to an agent-relative permission might justify the self-defensive killing of a justified threatener without also justifying the self-preservative killing of an innocent bystander when other relevant considerations are equal. This is because the constraint against the intentional killing of an innocent bystander is stronger because that killing is opportunistic.

I went on to argue, however, that there are instances in which the agency involved in the intentional killing of an innocent bystander in self-preservation is eliminative rather than opportunistic. Suppose, for example, that to avoid being killed by a culpable threatener, one must quickly cross a narrow, wobbly public bridge.[12] Yet there is an innocent bystander sitting in the middle of it enjoying the view. In one version of this example, if one runs onto the bridge, this will jostle the bridge, foreseeably causing the bystander to plunge to her death. In another

[11] The same point was made independently at roughly the same time by Michael Otsuka, who also rightly defended the responsibility account when I mistakenly defended the culpability account. See his "Killing the Innocent in Self-Defense," *Philosophy and Public Affairs* 23 (1994), pp. 74–94.

[12] I take this example from Thomson, "Self-Defense," p. 290. It is also discussed in Noam J. Zohar, "Collective War and Individualistic Ethics: Against the Conscription of 'Self-Defense,'" *Political Theory* 21 (1993), pp. 606–622, at pp. 612–613.

version, one must deliberately shake the bridge to dislodge her. Few believe that it would be permissible to do either. In the first case one's harmful agency seems neither opportunistic nor eliminative, for these are forms of *intended* harming. In the first case the harm one causes is not intended at all but is merely foreseen. In the second case, one does intend to affect the bystander in a way one knows will be harmful but one's agency seems eliminative rather than opportunistic, for one does not need to *use* the bystander in any way; indeed, one would survive if she were not there at all. In either case, therefore, if one has the kind of agent-relative permission that would justify the eliminative killing of a nonliable justified threatener in self-defense, one must be permitted to kill the bystander either as a side effect or even as a means of self-preservation. Hence the appeal to an agent-relative permission to justify self-defense against a nonliable threatener, such as a nonresponsible threatener or a justified threatener, cannot escape the original objection after all. For if there were an agent-relative permission, it *would* justify killing innocent bystanders as a means of self-preservation in certain cases, such as the second bridge case, in which it is counterintuitive to suppose that killing is justified.

Jonathan Quong has argued, however, that the notion of opportunistic using must be extended to include the harmful using not only of a person but also of that to which the person has a right, or claim (Quong (2009), pp. 525–532).[13] On the general point about the concept of harmful opportunistic agency, Quong seems right. But his application of this broader notion to the bridge cases seems strained. He discusses only the first version of the bridge case. What he says is that "because the bridge... is so wobbly that it cannot sustain two people at the same time, it seems best to treat the bridge as an amount of physical space that can only feasibly contain one person. To get on one part of the bridge is effectively to seize the whole bridge." For one to run onto the bridge in an effort to flee from the threatener is thus to use a space to which the bystander "has a prior claim," grounded presumably in prior occupancy. Merely to run onto the bridge as a means of escape, and certainly to shake it to dislodge the bystander, are, Quong claims, instances of the intentional and harmful using of something to which the bystander has an exclusive right, at least at that time. They are therefore instances of harmful opportunistic agency in Quong's extended sense. They are not, after all, counterexamples to the claim that the intentional killing of an innocent bystander in self-preservation must violate the constraint against opportunistic using, as I intended them to be.

[13] Quong does not articulate his view in quite this way but for consistency of exposition I have paraphrased his view by reference to Quinn's distinction.

As I noted, Quong seems right to claim that opportunistic using can include using not just a person but also her property. Suppose, for example, that two people need a certain medicine to survive and one of them owns it. If the other seizes it and administers it to himself, it may be plausible to suppose that he violates the constraint against harmful opportunistic using. But it seems implausible to suppose that the bystander has anything like a comparable right or claim to the space occupied by the public bridge, so that stepping into that space constitutes the use of something to which she has an exclusive right at the time. Merely running onto the bridge does not seem morally tantamount to harmfully *using* the bystander as a means of saving one's life. Even shaking her off seems clearly the elimination of an obstacle rather than the strategic use of her resource for one's own benefit. Indeed, even if one were the legal owner of the bridge, it seems that it would be impermissible to run onto it knowing that that would kill the bystander (unless, perhaps, she had been explicitly warned against trespassing) and certainly impermissible to shake her off of it. If that is right, the second bridge case remains a counterexample to the claim that the killing of an innocent bystander in self-preservation must be an instance of opportunistic agency.

So, again, the original claim stands: if the appeal to an agent-relative permission can justify the villagers in killing an equal number of nonliable people (the bombers) in self-defense, it can also justify people in killing an equal number of innocent bystanders in self-preservation, provided that the form of agency involved is not opportunistic—that is, provided that the innocent bystanders are killed either as a side effect or eliminatively, as in the two bridge cases.

When advocates of the agent-relative permission claim that it can justify the killing of a justified threatener in self-defense, they are claiming that it can override two distinct constraints: the constraint against harming and the constraint against intending harm (because eliminative killing in self-defense is intended killing in the sense relevant to the constraint).[14] For convenience we can say that these two constraints combine to form the constraint against intended harming, which is stronger than the constraint against foreseen but unintended harming. Because of the comparative strengths of the two constraints, the advocates' view has further implausible implications concerning numbers. They claim that even on the assumption that the five bombers are not liable to be killed, the five villagers may intentionally (that is, eliminatively) kill them in self-defense. Assuming that the constraint against intended harming of nonliable people is significantly rather

[14] For what I, following Quinn, take to be the relevant sense, see Quinn, "Actions, Intentions, and Consequences;" and Jeff McMahan, "Revising the Doctrine of Double Effect," *Journal of Applied Philosophy* 11 (1994), pp. 201–212.

than only marginally stronger than the constraint against the foreseen but unintended harming of nonliable people to an equal degree, it seems to follow that if the villagers could jam the bomb doors (leaving the bombers unharmed) only in a way that would kill six or more innocent bystanders as a side effect, they would be permitted to do so. For while the number of victims would be greater, the constraint that would be overridden is much weaker. If the villagers' only defensive option were to kill the bombers eliminatively, the claim that there is an agent-relative permission implies that that option would be permissible. If their only option were to jam the bomb doors, killing six innocent bystanders, or perhaps even more, as a side effect, they must have an agent-relative permission to do that as well. It is unclear which option would be permitted if both were possible.

Because they accept that there is a general moral asymmetry between doing and allowing, many deontologists believe that it is impermissible for people threatened with death to kill an equal number of innocent bystanders as a side effect of self-preservative action. Many others accept a stronger restriction, claiming that the killing of innocent bystanders as a side effect of self-preservation can be permissible only when the number saved is greater than the number killed. Some think the number saved must be significantly greater than the number killed. But few believe that it is permissible for people threatened with death to kill a greater number of innocent bystanders as a side effect of self-preservation. Yet if the claim that there is an agent-relative permission is to imply that it can be permissible to kill a nonliable justified threatener defensively in self-defense, it must also imply that acts of self-preservation can be permissible when they kill, as a side effect, more nonliable people than they save (and even when the killings occur through the creation of a threat rather than through the redirection of an existing threat). Those who find this counterintuitive should reject the claim that the villagers have an agent-relative permission to kill the tactical bombers in self-defense.

7.6 Killing in Self-Preservation Without Thwarting the Justified Action

Although I have argued that the villagers' killing of the bombers in self-defense cannot be justified by appeal to an agent-relative permission, it does not follow that there are no agent-relative permissions. I suggested that it is plausible to suppose that the villagers are permitted to jam the bomb doors if they could do that without harming the bombers. But it would not be permissible for a disinterested bystander to do that—that is, it would not be permissible for a neutral third party to do what would save five nonliable people, in a way that would prevent the saving of

100 nonliable people. Indeed, it might even be permissible for a third party to prevent the villagers from jamming the doors (though not, I think, by killing them). If the villagers are permitted to jam the bomb doors, therefore, their permission must be agent-relative. They are not required to allow themselves to be sacrificed for the sake of the greater number. They may have an agent-relative permission to prevent the saving of a greater number, but not by killing an equal number.

In the case as I initially presented it, the villagers have two distinct moral reasons not to shoot down the bombers. They have a reason not to thwart the mission and a reason not to kill people who are not liable to be killed. By appealing to a variant in which the mission could be thwarted without killing the bombers, I suggested that the first of these reasons may not be decisive on its own. We can now examine the second reason on its own by considering variants in which the villagers can defend their lives by killing the bombers but without thwarting the bombers' mission.

One can imagine a number of such variants involving different modes of agency. Here are four.

(1) Although the bombers cannot do this themselves, the villagers can cause the bombers' plane to crash onto the military target, thereby killing the bombers but also saving both the 100 civilians and the five villagers. This would be an instance of opportunistic killing.

In the remaining three variants, the military target has been destroyed and the debris from the explosion is heading toward the villagers.

(2) The villagers can shield themselves from the debris by using a remote control device to fly the bombers' plane into it. This too would be an instance of opportunistic killing.
(3) The villagers can create an explosion that would deflect the debris away from them but also destroy the bombers' plane. This would be an instance of foreseeable but unintended killing via the creation of a threat.
(4) The villagers can somehow deflect the debris away from themselves but only in a way that will cause it to collide with and destroy the bombers' plane. This would be an instance of foreseeable but unintended killing via the redirection of an existing threat.

Given the assumption that the bombers are not liable to be killed in defense of the villagers, it seems that neither instance of opportunistic killing can be justified. Even those who believe that the killing of the bombers in the original case can be justified by appeal to an agent-relative permission may agree with this if they also accept that self-preservative killing of a nonliable person via opportunistic agency can be justified, if at all, only as the lesser evil.

In the third variant, the killing of the bombers would be neither opportunistic nor eliminative but merely a side effect, albeit one caused by the creation of a new threat. One might think it relevant in this case that the bombers are responsible for the threat the villagers can avert via the creation of a threat to the bombers. But if my earlier argument that the bombers' responsibility for the threat does not make them liable to defensive harm because their action was justified (in both the evidence-relative and fact-relative senses), then the fact that they created the debris seems irrelevant.

It may help in thinking about the third variant to consider a parallel trolley case. Suppose a runaway trolley is heading for five people trapped on the track. The only way they can prevent it from killing them is to detonate a bomb that will both derail the trolley and kill five innocent bystanders standing near the track. Defenders of the agent-relative permission in the original version of the tactical bombers case accept that it is permissible for them to detonate the bomb. But if my argument in the preceding section is correct, that is in fact impermissible. A neutral third party would certainly not be permitted to detonate the bomb, saving five but also killing five. If this trolley case is relevantly analogous to the third variant, then it is not permissible for the villagers to deflect the debris by a means that will kill the bombers.

It may also help in evaluating the fourth variant to consider an analogous trolley case. If the five people who are trapped on the main track have access to a switch that will direct the trolley onto a branch track on which five other equally nonliable people are trapped, may they pull it? Again, it seems that a neutral third party may not. Yet it may seem intuitively plausible to suppose that the five potential victims may. If they may, that must be because they have an agent-relative permission to kill when the numbers are equal and the killing is unintended and brought about via the redirection of an existing threat. Perhaps the redirection of a threat away from oneself but toward another is morally intermediate between failing to save a person at great cost to oneself and other ways of killing a person to avoid a great cost to oneself. I am uncertain what to think about either the fourth variant or the analogous trolley case.

One might argue that the villagers are permitted to kill the bombers in the fourth variant, and perhaps even in the third, on the ground that the bombers ought to bear the cost of their own voluntary action. Suppose, for example, that the bombers can attack the military target, thereby saving the 100 civilians, in either of two ways. If they attack it in one way, the debris will land on the villagers, but if they attack it the other way, the debris will collide with and destroy their plane (and they have no parachutes). Call this the *Two-Option Bombing* case. Some would say the bombers have a duty not to impose the costs of saving the civilians on innocent bystanders rather than on themselves and thus must attack the target in the second way. And it is this same duty that justifies the villagers in refusing to bear the costs of the mission and imposing them on the bombers instead.

Yet again, it may be illuminating to consider a sequence of simple trolley cases. The first is the standard trolley case in which a bystander, B1, can pull a switch to divert the trolley away from the five and onto a track that branches off to the right where it will kill another innocent bystander, B2. Assume, as most people believe, that it is permissible for B1 to turn the trolley toward B2. In the second case, B1 is himself trapped on a track that branches off to the left. There is no branch to the right. B1 has the switch and can divert the trolley away from the five but only onto the track on which it will kill him. Assume, as most people believe, that it is permissible for him not to pull the switch. Finally, in the third case, B1 has the switch and is trapped on the left branch track while B2 is trapped on the right branch track. B1 can do nothing, allowing the trolley to kill the five, divert the trolley toward himself, or divert it toward B2. Call this third case the *Three-Option Trolley* case.

It is tempting to argue that because the first case shows that B1 is permitted to divert the trolley toward B2 while the second case shows that he is permitted not to divert it toward himself, it follows that he is permitted in the third case not to divert it toward himself but to divert it toward B2 instead. If this is correct, it may seem that a parallel conclusion follows in the Two-Option Bombing case—namely, that it is permissible for the bombers to conduct the attack in the way that will direct the debris toward the villagers rather than toward themselves.

Although I believe this is the correct conclusion about the Three-Option case, it does not follow from the claims about the first two cases. What it is permissible to do can depend on what alternatives there are. It might, therefore, be permissible for B1 to divert the trolley toward B2 when there is no alternative other than allowing it to kill the five, but not permissible when B1 can also save the five by diverting it toward himself. When there is this additional option, there may be what Frances Kamm calls "contextual interaction." For example, an issue of fairness may arise that is not present when the only alternative to allowing the five to be killed is to divert the trolley toward B2.

It seems to me that B1 is nevertheless permitted to divert the trolley toward B2 in the Three-Option Trolley case. We may sometimes do unto others what we are permitted not to do unto ourselves.[15] But it also seems to me that if B1 has diverted the trolley toward B2 and B2 can divert it away from herself, though only in such a way that it will end up on the left branch track and kill B1, it is permissible for B2 to save herself by diverting it in this way. (This seems true even though B1, unlike the bombers, has merely redirected a threat toward B2 rather than creating a new threat to her.)

[15] Judith Jarvis Thomson disagrees. See her "Turning the Trolley," *Philosophy and Public Affairs* 36 (2008), pp. 359–374.

To the extent that this is plausible, it supports the claim that the villagers may deflect the debris toward the bombers in the fourth variant noted earlier.

These remarks about the fourth variant of the bombers case, the Two-Option Bombing case, and the Three-Option Trolley case presuppose that the bombers have no special duty to bear the costs of their action that B1 does not have. But the tactical bombers are professional combatants fighting in a just war. Such people are almost universally recognized to have a special duty to take certain risks and even accept certain harms during their military operations to avoid causing harm to innocent bystanders. Indeed, the special duty is generally acknowledged even by combatants themselves. Thus, the *U.S. Army/Marine Corps Counterinsurgency Field Manual* asserts that "combat, including counterinsurgency and other forms of unconventional warfare, often obligates Soldiers and Marines to accept some risk to minimize harm to noncombatants" (*U.S. Army / Marine Corps Counterinsurgency Field Manual* 2007, p. 244). This may be a reason for thinking that in the Two-Option Bombing case, they must attack their target in the way that will cause the debris to strike them rather than the villagers.

Suppose the bombers have a special duty to bear the costs themselves but that they instead attack the target in the way that sends the debris toward the villagers. In that case, they are responsible for unjustifiably creating a lethal threat to the villagers and that makes them potentially liable to be killed in any one of the three ways by which the villagers might protect themselves from the debris, including opportunistically killing the bombers by flying their plane by remote control into the debris.

Suppose, however, that although the bombers *would* have a duty to attack the target in the way that would send the debris toward their plane, they do not have that option. Their only option is to attack the target in the way that will hurl the debris onto the villagers. In that case, when they justifiably drop their bomb in the only way that is possible in the circumstances, they do nothing to make themselves liable to be killed. But the claim that they *would* have a professional duty to impose the cost of their action on themselves rather than on innocent bystanders may still be relevant to whether it is permissible for the villagers to deflect the debris away from themselves when this would unavoidably redirect it toward the bombers. One might argue that if the duty that the bombers would have to impose the cost on themselves if they could would be an enforceable duty, the villagers can be understood to be permissibly enforcing that duty when they deflect the debris, even when the bombers have been unable to fulfill that duty themselves. Indeed, one might think that the bombers ought even to consent, if they could, to the redirection of the debris.[16] For

[16] The view that rights of defense can be grounded in the enforcement of duties that people have not to cause harm is developed with great ingenuity by Victor Tadros in *The Ends of Harm: The Moral Foundations of Criminal Law* (Oxford: Oxford University Press, 2011).

their situation is analogous, not to that of B1 in the Three-Option Trolley case, but to that of the owner of the insulin in the example discussed in Section 7.4. It is in part because the owner would have a duty to provide the insulin if he were home that it is permissible for the passerby to take it in his absence.

It is important to note that this argument, if successful, would have limited application in the debate about the permissibility of defense against justified threateners. The scope of the argument is limited to cases involving justified threateners who have a special professional duty to bear risks and harms rather than impose them on innocent bystanders. If the tactical bombers were not professional combatants but civilian pilots who had decided to undertake this justified mission on their own initiative, perhaps because no professional combatants were available to do it, the villagers would not be justified in deflecting the debris on the ground that the pilots had a professional duty to bear the costs of their action. This is because these civilian pilots would not have had a professional duty to conduct the attack, if they could have, in a way that would have sent the debris toward themselves.

There are two reasons for doubting whether this argument for the permissibility of deflection by the villagers is successful. One is that it is doubtful whether the special duties of professional combatants include a duty to sacrifice their lives to avoid killing innocent bystanders. Even professional duties have limits. Thus, the *Counterinsurgency Field Manual* that recognizes a duty of combatants to take risks also explicitly says that "combatants are not required to take so much risk that they fail in their mission or forfeit their lives" (*Counterinsurgency Field Manual* 2007, p. 245). And even if B1 were the Safety Officer for the trolley company, it is not obvious that in the Three-Option Trolley case he would have a special duty to divert the trolley toward himself rather than toward B2.

But suppose that in the Two-Option Bombing case the tactical bombers do have a professional duty to attack the target in the way that will direct the debris toward themselves rather than toward the villagers. It still does not follow that, if their only option were to attack in a way that would direct the debris toward the villagers, the villagers would then be permitted to deflect the debris on the ground that they were simply enforcing the bombers' duty to bear the costs of their own action. For not all moral duties are enforceable. This is recognized in the idea that there can be a "right to do wrong"—that is, the idea that a person can have a claim-right against others not to prevent him from acting wrongly.

The duty that the insulin owner would have if he were at home to provide insulin to the diabetic does seem enforceable even when he is not at home. But suppose that I have a moral duty to contribute a large sum of money to a charity organization but cannot fulfill that duty because I am away on an extended mountain-climbing expedition. It does not seem that it would be permissible for the organization to take the money from my bank account, supposing it were able to do so. I am not sure what makes this duty different, if it is, from that of the insulin owner. If we had a criterion for distinguishing between enforceable and unenforceable duties, it might explain why this case seems different from the insulin case. And it would tell us whether the alleged special duty of the tactical bombers to bear the costs of their mission to save the civilians was enforceable by the villagers (or a third party) even when the bombers do not have the option of attacking in a way that would send the debris in their direction rather than toward the villagers. This is an issue about which I am uncertain.

But suppose, for the sake of argument, both that the bombers have a professional duty to bear the costs of their mission when they can and that this duty is enforceable by potential victims and third parties in circumstances in which the bombers are unable to fulfill the duty on their own. There must still, it seems, be restrictions on the means by which they might be made to bear those costs. Granting these assumptions, it seems permissible for the villagers to deflect the debris from themselves, even if it will then unavoidably kill the bombers. It is less clear, however, that it would be permissible for them to deflect the debris by detonating a bomb that would also kill the bombers as a side effect. And it is doubtful whether it would be permissible for them to use the bombers as a shield by taking remote control of their plane and flying it into the debris.

7.7 Conclusion

It is difficult to say whether the villagers may kill the bombers in self-preservation even when their doing so would not thwart the bombers' justified mission. Whether that would be permissible depends on, among other things, the villagers' mode of agency, whether the bombers have a professional duty to bear the costs of their justified action rather impose them on innocent bystanders, and, if so, whether that duty is enforceable. Insofar as the justification for self-preservative killing depends on the bombers' professional duty, it does not apply to other cases in which justified threateners do not have such a duty. That the justification for the killing of the bombers is precarious even when killing them would not thwart their mission reinforces the earlier conclusion that the self-defensive killing of the bombers in the original case is impermissible.[17]

[17] I am grateful for helpful discussion of the issues discussed in this article to Crystal Allen, Gustaf Arrhenius, Yitzhak Benbaji, Tim Campbell, Michael Da Silva, Kim Ferzan, Major Ian Fishback, Helen Frowe, Adam Hosein, Graham Long, David Mapel, Michael Otsuka, Jonathan Parry, Jonathan Quong, Stephen Shalom, Uwe Steinhoff, Victor Tadros, Alex Voorhoeve, Alec Walen, Noam Zohar, and, especially, Shelly Kagan, Frances Kamm, and Larry Temkin.

References

Hanser, M. (1999) "Killing, Letting Die, and Preventing People from Being Saved," in *Utilitas* 11: 277–295.
Hosein, A. (2014) "Are Justified Aggressors a Threat to the Rights Theory of Self-Defense?," in this volume.
McMahan, J. (1994a) "Self-Defense and the Problem of the Innocent Attacker," in *Ethics* 104: 252–290.
—— (1994b) "Revising the Doctrine of Double Effect," in *Journal of Applied Philosophy* 11: 201–212.
—— (2005) "The Basis of Moral Liability to Defensive Killing," in *Philosophical Issues* 15: 386–405.
—— (2009) *Killing in War* (Oxford: Oxford University Press): 51–59.
—— (2012) "Just War," in *Ethical Perspectives* 19: 257–261.
—— (2012) "Duty, Obedience, Desert, and Proportionality in War," in *Ethics* 122: 146–151.
Otsuka, M. (1994) "Killing the Innocent in Self-Defense," in *Philosophy and Public Affairs* 23: 74–94.
Parfit, D. (2011) *On What Matters*, Volume One (Oxford: Oxford University Press).
Quinn, W. S. (1989) "Actions, Intentions, and Consequences," in *Philosophy and Public Affairs* 18: 334–351.
Quong, J. (2009) "Killing in Self-Defense," in *Ethics* 119: 507–537.
Shalom, S. R. (2011) "Killing in War and Moral Equality," in *Journal of Moral Philosophy* 8: 495–512.
Steinhoff, U. (2008) "Jeff McMahan on the Moral Equality of Combatants," in *The Journal of Political Philosophy* 16: 220–226.
—— (2012) "The Moral Equality of Modern Combatants and the Myth of Justified War," in *Theoretical and Applied Ethics* 1: 35–44.
—— (2012) "Rights, Liability, and the Moral Equality of Combatants," in *Journal of Ethics* 13: 339–366.
Tadros, V. (2011) *The Ends of Harm: The Moral Foundations of Criminal Law* (Oxford: Oxford University Press).
Thomson, J. J. (1991) "Self-Defense," in *Philosophy and Public Affairs* 20: 283–310.
—— (2008) "Turning the Trolley," in *Philosophy and Public Affairs* 36: 359–374.
U.S. Army/Marine Corps Counterinsurgency Field Manual (Chicago: University of Chicago Press, 2007).

8

Just War Theory, Intentions, and the Deliberative Perspective Objection

Kasper Lippert-Rasmussen

8.1 Intentions and the Ethics of War

Intentions play a significant role in just war theory. Standard theories of what make it permissible to initiate wars, i.e. theories of *jus ad bellum*, insist that the intention underlying resorting to war must be admissible (Caney 2005: 191, McMahan 2005: 4, Norman 1995: 118). Hence, a state may wage war with the intention of protecting itself against aggression, but it may not wage war with the intention of killing enemy non-combatants, even if it does so in the course of protecting itself against aggression. Similarly, traditional theories of which action in war are permissible, i.e. theories of *jus in bello*, embody the doctrine of double effect (henceforth: DDE) (Walzer 2006: 152–159). On Warren Quinn's non-absolutist formulation, DDE holds that "the pursuit of a good tends to be less acceptable where a resulting harm is intended as a means than where it is merely foreseen" (Quinn 1994: 176).[1] A corresponding, absolutist version of DDE holds that "the pursuit of a good is morally unacceptable where a resulting harm is intended as a means unlike where it is merely foreseen." Most defenders of DDE endorse a non-absolutist version to accommodate intuitions about the moral permissibility of intending harm when necessary to avoid disastrous consequences, and for that reason, I focus on non-absolutist versions in what follows.[2]

[1] By "unacceptable," Quinn means morally unacceptable. Presumably, "tends to" indicates that Quinn thinks that differences in intentions do not render actions harder to justify in all contexts. Finally, Quinn would also say that intending harm as an end is less acceptable than merely foreseeing harm, all other things being equal.

[2] The distinction between absolutist and non-absolutist versions is largely irrelevant to the arguments in this paper.

DDE is widely thought to explain and be supported by the potentially differential permissibility of the following pair of cases often discussed in relation to *jus in bello*:

(*Tactical Bomber*) A pilot bombs a munitions factory. Destroying it is her means of depriving enemy combatants of ammunition and, thereby, of ultimately ending the war. She knows that her raid will inevitably kill a significant number of non-combatants as a side-effect.

(*Terror Bomber*) A pilot bombs a city. This is a means of killing enemy non-combatants and terrorizing the surviving ones and, thereby, undermining the enemy's will to continue fighting and, thus, ultimately ending the war. The number of non-combatants that she intentionally kills through her raid is identical to the number the tactical bomber knowingly kills in her raid.

Intuitively, the tactical bomber's raid is morally more acceptable than the terror bomber's despite the fact that they kill and save the same number of people.[3] The fact that many people find terrorism much less acceptable than conventional warfare, even when the latter involves a greater number of casualties and more suffering, reflects this differential assessment (McMahan 2009: 346–347).[4] DDE explains and is supported by these facts in terms of differences in intentions.

In the following three sections, I critically explore Scanlon's ingenious attempt to account for the differential permissibility of acts of war involving the intentional killing of non-combatants and acts of war involving the non-intentional killings of non-combatants independently of DDE. In Section 8.5, I describe an argument canvassed by Thomson and Scanlon. This argument—the deliberative perspective objection—derives the conclusion that intentions are irrelevant to the permissibility of action from the fact that it seems peculiar to suggest to an agent that the permissibility of an action that she considers performing depends on the intention with which she will perform it, if she does. I critically respond to this argument in Sections 8.6 to 8.8. My overall conclusion is that neither Scanlon's

[3] By "more acceptable," I do not mean "morally permissible all things considered." Whether the raid is the latter depends on whether further conditions are satisfied, e.g. whether there is proportionality between the harms involved in the raid and the good consequences it produces. Many incorporate the proportionality requirement into DDE (e.g., Walzer 2006: 153), but in the present context, we can simply set the proportionality condition—and any other non-intention-related condition bearing on moral permissibility all things considered—aside.

[4] It is not essential to the terror bomber case that it involves *terrorizing* the non-combatants or intending to terrorize the non-combatants (cp. Kamm 2008: 159–161): We can imagine the tactical bomber case to have this former effect as well. What is essential is that the death of the non-combatants is intended as a means of achieving the end. Nor is it clear if it is essential to the terror bomber case that it involves the killing of *non-combatants*. Presumably, some friends of DDE may think that killing combatants intentionally is less acceptable than killing them unintentionally. However, other friends of DDE might think that since combatants are liable to be killed, or perhaps even in some cases deserve to be killed, harm to them is irrelevant for the purpose of applying DDE. To avoid this issue about the exact specification of DDE, I focus on cases involving harm to non-combatants.

non-intention-based account of the differential permissibility of the tactical and the terror bomber's actions, nor the deliberative perspective objection, suffices to reject DDE or, more generally, to refute the relevance of intentions to permissibility.

8.2 Scanlon on DDE

Some critics of DDE do not share the intuitions underlying DDE. Others share the intuitions but contend that these are not best explained by intentions. Scanlon is a critic of the latter kind. He agrees that even though the tactical bomber acts permissibly, the terror bomber may not. However, this differential permissibility has nothing to do with intentions. Rather, the explanation lies in the existence of "a class of exceptions to the general prohibition against the use of deadly force":

> In war, one is sometimes permitted to use destructive and potentially deadly force of a kind that would normally be prohibited. But such force is permitted only when its use can be expected to bring some military advantage, such as destroying enemy combatants or war-making materials, and it is permitted only if expected harm to non-combatants is as small as possible, compatible with gaining the relevant military advantage, and only if this harm is "proportional" to the importance of this advantage. (Scanlon 2008: 28)

Since the terror bomber's raid does not bring about any "military advantage, such as destroying enemy combatants or war-making materials," but only the non-military advantage of "undermining morale" (Scanlon 2008: 29), her action is not a member of the class of exceptions to the use of deadly force. This is unlike the tactical bomber's action that does bring a military advantage, i.e. the destruction of "war-making materials" in the form of munitions.

Scanlon finds that, in general, intentions are irrelevant to the moral permissibility of actions.[5] However, in his view, they are highly relevant to the assessment of the reasoning process behind the agent's act. Accordingly, he distinguishes between two different uses of moral principles:

> As guides to deliberation, moral principles answer a question of permissibility: "May one do X?" They also explain the answer by identifying the considerations that make it permissible or impermissible to do X under the circumstances in question...In what I will call

[5] I say "in general" because Scanlon wants to allow for certain exceptions, e.g. cases where the agent has promised to act with a certain intention or cases where the meaning of action changes when done with a particular intention. So, for instance, he thinks that firing an employee with the intention of getting rid of a minority member has a different meaning from firing an employee, who happens to be a minority member, with the intention of making a necessary economic cut in the number of staff and that, because of this difference in the meaning of the two actions, the former may be impermissible and the latter permissible (Scanlon 2008: 69–74) (see Lippert-Rasmussen 2012). It is not clear how Scanlon can allow that intentions may bear on permissibility of action in these indirect ways and, at the same time, canvass the deliberative perspective objection (see Lippert-Rasmussen 2010).

their critical employment, however, a principle is used as the basis for assessing the way in which an agent went about deciding what to do on some real or imagined occasion. Used in this way, it provides the basis for answering a question of the form, "In deciding to do X under those circumstances, did Jones take the proper considerations into account and give them the right weight?" (Scanlon 2008: 22)

Employing this distinction, Scanlon submits that the terror bomber made up her mind about what to do in a flawed way when she regarded the fact that, by killing a large number of non-combatants, she would demoralize the enemy, thereby ending the war as a fact counting in favour of the raid. Yet, the impermissibility of her action is not due to her flawed reasoning. Rather, it is due to the fact, as explained earlier, her action does not fall under the scope of Scanlon's exception to the general principle forbidding the killing of innocents.

Turning to the tactical bomber, her reasoning was not flawed in the same way as the terror bomber's reasoning. That her raid destroys the munitions factory and, thus, shortens the war *does* count in favor of the raid. Also, since her raid falls under the stated exception, it is permissible. But what makes the raid morally permissible is not the flawless reasoning behind the tactical bomber's decision to carry out the raid.

To recapitulate, Scanlon agrees that the terror bomber case is morally problematic in two ways that the tactical bomber case is not. First, using moral principles as guides to permissibility, we find that only the action of the latter may be morally permissible. Second, employing moral principles critically, we see that only the terror bomber's reasoning is flawed. The variation in intention is crucial to the second difference, and this gives some support to Scanlon's error theory regarding DDE, i.e. that many confuse the two uses of moral principles and misidentify the source of their differential moral assessment of the two bombers as differential permissibility rather than the differentially assessed reasoning behind their actions. Hence, Scanlon's criticism of DDE has two components: 1) a non-intention based account of why what the terror bomber does is impermissible, while what the tactical bomber is not and 2) an error theory, i.e. an account of why defenders of DDE are under the false impression that intentions make a difference to permissibility. In the next two sections, I explain why neither is fully satisfactory.

8.3 Scanlon's Non-Intention Based Account

To see why Scanlon's account of the differential permissibility of the terror and the tactical bomber case in terms of "a class of exceptions to the general prohibition against the use of deadly force" fails to offer a sufficiently general explanation, consider the following case:

(*Terror Bomber**) A pilot bombs a city to kill enemy non-combatants, because she foresees that this will demoralise them, and as a result thereof, they will destroy a vital munitions depot. If they do, the enemy will run out of munitions, and this will cause the achievement of the terror bomber's ultimate aim of ending the war. The number of non-combatants that the bomber intentionally kills through her raid is identical to the number the tactical bomber knowingly kills in her raid.

This terror bombing case involves the "destructive and potentially deadly force of a kind that would normally be prohibited" (Scanlon 2008: 28). But it "can be expected to bring some military advantage, such as destroying enemy combatants or war-making materials"—indeed, the very same military advantage as Tactical Bomber—and, accordingly, Terror Bomber* falls under the scope of Scanlon's exception, if Tactical Bomber does. Yet, unlike Tactical Bomber, Terror Bomber* is the sort of case DDE discriminates against. Hence, Scanlon's exception does not account for the kind of differential assessment of pairs of cases that DDE accounts for. This casts doubt on the first component in Scanlon's critique of DDE.

Could Scanlon's exception be reformulated to meet this challenge? To accommodate Terror Bomber*, one might suggest that it is reformulated along the following lines—call the resulting principle "Scanlon's Exception*": The use of "destructive and potentially deadly force of a kind that would normally be prohibited" is permitted only when its use can be expected to *directly* bring some military advantage, such as destroying enemy combatants or war-making materials. "Directness" should then be understood as a matter of the length of the relevant causal chains. Scanlon's exception so reformulated is immune to Terror Bomber*, because the military advantage is not immediately causally downstream from the raid, i.e. it is not an immediate causal effect of the raid.

However, Scanlon's Exception* is indefensible in my view. First, which causal chains are direct depends on how we individuate the different causal links in the chain. This can be done in many ways—notably, we can have a more or less fine-grained individuation of causal links depending on whether we locate these events at a macro- or at a microscopic level—and it is not clear why one rather than another way of individuating causal links would be the correct way to do so. Moreover, however we resolve the issue of individuation it is hard to see that the length of causal chains has a moral relevance in itself. The length of causal chains may well correlate with other factors, for example, the probability of the relevant good or bad outcomes, that are morally significant, but this has no tendency to show that the length of causal chains has a moral relevance *per se*.

Second, even if Scanlon's Exception* successfully accounted for the impermissibility of actions, the explanation of which one would otherwise ascribe to DDE, it introduces a new problem, which is that it is unable to explain the permissibility of *tactical* bombing raids where the causal chain from the dropping of the bombs to the achievement of a military advantage is very long, i.e. indirect. Yet, it is implausible that a tactical bomber has any moral reason to select a bomb that brings about the relevant military advantage directly over one that does so indirectly, when all other things are equal. Indeed, could she reduce the number of non-combatants killed by using the one that brings about the military advantage indirectly, she would have a decisive reason to do so.

A similar line of argument rebels against Scanlon's Exception**: The use of "destructive and potentially deadly force of a kind that would normally be prohibited" is permitted only when its use can be expected to bring some military advantage, such as destroying enemy combatants or war-making materials *and this advantage is not causally downstream from the death of non-combatants.* Scanlon's Exception** does not imply permissibility of the action of the Terror Bomber*, since the military advantage involved is causally downstream from the death of non-combatants. Yet, Scanlon's Exception** is implausible in the light of a scenario where a bomber is told that she can carry out her raid either by selecting a bomb that has a 99 per cent chance of bringing about the military advantage and, thus, end the war causally downstream from the death of non-combatants and a 1 per cent chance of doing so causally upstream from the death of non-combatants, or by selecting a bomb that is guaranteed to bring about the military advantage causally upstream from the death of non-combatants, but will involve slightly more non-combatant casualties than the first bomb. If intentions are irrelevant to the case—say the bomber simply intends to drop the bombs—she should choose the former bomb (cp. McMahan 2009: 369). But on anything more substantial than a tie-break version—and such a weak version will not do when the purpose is to explain the differential permissibility of the pairs of action that DDE explains—of Scanlon's Exception**, she would act impermissibly, whereas she would act permissibly if she selected the latter bomb, thereby killing more non-combatants. I tentatively conclude that Scanlon's Exception (and its reformulated versions) fails to explain the differential permissibility of the pairs of cases that DDE explains.[6]

[6] I say "tentatively," because Frances Kamm has explored a complex "downstreamish," non-state-of-mind account of the essence of non-consequentialist constraints on harming (Kamm 2007: 130–189) that accommodates many of the intuitions normally adduced in defence of DDE. However, this is not the place for a discussion of her intricate examples and principles, e.g. the doctrine of the triple effect.

8.4 Scanlon's Error Theory

Crucial to the second element in Scanlon's critique of DDE is his claim that DDE derives illicit support from our confusing the critical employment of moral principles with the use of moral principles as guides to deliberation. To test this claim, compare the following two cases:

(*The Altruistic Terror Bomber*) This case is like the original terror bomber case except that the bomber will achieve a huge personal economic benefit if she carries out the raid and that she considers this irrelevant to what she should do and decides to go ahead with the raid simply to end the war and thereby minimize the overall number of non-combatant deaths.

(*The Amoral Bomber*) This case is like the original tactical bomber case except that the pilot is indifferent to the non-combatant casualties. Also, she does not carry out the raid with the intention of ending the war by destroying the factory, although she will in fact do both. Rather, she is motivated to carry out the raid solely by a tiny personal economic gain and by her belief that carrying out the raid is a means of obtaining this. This bomber is a principled amoralist and gives weight to the interests of others in her deliberations only when she believes that doing so will maximise her own self-interest.

In Scanlon's elaboration of the critical employment of moral principles, he indicates that a positive assessment of the agent's reasoning depends on factors such as whether the agent takes "the proper considerations into account" in her deliberations and gives "them the right weight" (Scanlon 2008: 22). Clearly, the amoral bomber does neither. In fact, the amoral bomber's reasoning is even more flawed than the reasoning of the altruistic terror bomber as it involves giving no weight to moral concerns, or to those facts on which moral concerns supervene, at all. The only factor to which the selfish bomber ascribes weight is the fact that her action will promote her self-interest. Suppose—quite implausibly to my mind—that nearly everyone thinks that an amoralist's reasoning is more flawed than that of an altruistic moralist with, let us suppose for the sake of argument, mistaken moral views—on Scanlon's view, it is a mistake to think that the fact that the raid will kill a large number of non-combatants and, thus, put an end to the war counts in favour of carrying it out. Suppose also that Scanlon's error theory is correct, i.e. that the reason many find DDE plausible is that they confuse the employment of moral principles as guides to deliberation and the critical employment. In that case, we should expect that many proponents of DDE would deem the amoral bomber's action to be impermissible and the altruistic terror bomber's action permissible provided that they think that the two cases differ in terms of moral permissibility. My conjecture is that they will do the reverse. They will agree that the amoral bomber's reasoning is appalling, but say that, by sheer coincidence, she nevertheless acted permissibly. Also, they will agree that while the altruistic terror bomber's deliberations are much better—perhaps even praiseworthy in certain ways—what she does is nevertheless impermissible. If this conjecture is correct, Scanlon's error theory is false. Proponents of DDE *are* sensitive to the fact that a certain feature may affect the assessment of deliberation and permissibility of actions differentially, and yet, they do think that intentions matter to the permissibility of actions.[7]

Summing up the discussion in this and the previous sections, I conclude that Scanlon fails to offer an account of the judgements of differential permissibility of pairs of action that DDE purportedly explains and that his error theory fails to support the hypothesis that opponents and supporters of DDE are not simply engaged in different kinds of assessment—assessment of deliberation and assessment of permissibility of actions. We need another argument to reject DDE.[8]

8.5 The Deliberative Perspective Objection

Recently, Judith Jarvis Thomson (1991, 1999) and Thomas Scanlon (2000, 2008) have offered a general argument intended to demonstrate the irrelevance of intentions to permissibility (see also Jonathan Bennett 1981: 96–98), whether in the way DDE implies or, with the exceptions mentioned in footnote 5, in any other way. I shall dub it the deliberative perspective objection against DDE. The objection invites us to imagine an agent who asks herself: "Is it permissible for me to do X?" As a help in her deliberations, she is then offered the following two-component conditional advice: "If, were you to do X, you would do X with the intention to Y (for example, kill the non-combatants), then it is impermissible for you to do X. But if, were you to do X, you would do X with the intention to Z (for example, destroy the munitions factory), then it is permissible for you to do X". Proponents of the deliberative perspective objection contend that such an advice is "a queer performance" (Thomson 1991: 293), an "absurd" idea (Thomson 1999: 515), or something "you would not say" (Scanlon 2000: 305; 2008: 20) and "should not say" (Scanlon 2008: 30). Thomson puts it this way (with Scanlon's (2008: 20) endorsement): "Can anyone really think that the [agent] should decide whether he may drop the bombs by looking inward for the intention with which he would be dropping them if he dropped them?'" (Thomson 1991: 293). They infer the irrelevance of intentions to permissibility from these observations of queerness and peculiarity.

[7] Thomson suggests a slightly different error theory according to which intentions are relevant to the assessment of character and that friends of DDE confuse this relevance with relevance to permissibility of actions (Thomson 1999: 517). This hypothesis is vulnerable to a line of argument similar to the one suggested here.

[8] The option of rejecting intuition of differential permissibility in the terror and the tactical bomber remains, of course.

Thomson's way of putting the deliberative perspective objection is problematic in the light of Scanlon's distinction between two uses of moral principles provided that a property may make an action morally impermissible even if it is not the case that an agent should decide whether she may perform the act by asking herself if the action would have this property, were she to perform it. I think this is possible and that Scanlon's distinction allows this to be the case. For instance, an act may be impermissible, because it fails to manifest spontaneous generosity, and yet, agents should not decide whether to perform this act by asking themselves if it would manifest spontaneous generosity, were they to perform it. Similarly, from a third-person perspective, one might hold that acting in an offensive way is morally permissible for someone, because she does not know the relevant local conventions. Yet, she herself cannot base her view about the permissibility of her conduct on this fact.

Note also that the phrasing of Thomson's challenge is unfortunate, because friends of DDE are not committed to the extreme view that the most important, let alone the only, factor that determines permissibility is the agent's intention, and surely, it would be an extreme view that agents should determine the permissibility of an action that they consider performing *only* on the basis of what intention will lie behind it. To the extent that Thomson's question has force, a significant part of it might derive from its not being clear whether the thought that Thomson doubts that anyone really has is the thought that the intention of the bomber is *all* that matters to the permissibility of her raid.

Setting aside these reservations about the way in which Thomson puts the objection, we can present the deliberative perspective objection as follows:

(1) If the intention with which an agent performs an action makes a difference to its permissibility, then it would not be odd for an agent mulling the permissibility of her performing a certain action to consider with which intention she would perform the action, were she to perform it, in order to determine the action's permissibility.

(2) But it *is* odd for an agent mulling the permissibility of her performing a certain action to consider with which intention she would perform the action, were she to perform it, in order to determine its permissibility.

(3) Hence, the intention with which an agent performs an action makes no difference to its permissibility.

In my view, the deliberative perspective objection to DDE is inconclusive. I concede that, in many contexts, an advice of the relevant sort is odd, so to that extent, I accept (2). However, I reject (1), because the oddness in question does not derive, even indirectly, from the putative fact that intentions are irrelevant to moral permissibility in general, and can be explained independently of any such claim (see Sections 8.7 and 8.8).

8.6 The Dialectical Context of the Deliberative Perspective Objection

Before proceeding to explain why I reject (1), I must say something about the argumentative context of the deliberative perspective objection. Neither Thomson nor Scanlon is very articulate about the nature, as opposed to the source (i.e., on their view, the irrelevance of intentions to permissibility), of the infelicity of the advice offered in the scenario that the deliberative perspective objection sketches. Specifically, they do little to link this infelicity to the irrelevance of intentions to moral permissibility, which presumably, it must be for it to count as a reason to reject DDE.

If (we think) intentions are irrelevant to moral permissibility, there is an obvious sense in which we will think the relevant advice is queer etc., i.e. it points to a factor that is irrelevant to the question at hand. But, presumably, moral irrelevance-queerness is not the issue at stake here initially, because the deliberative perspective objection is supposed to be one that can be offered even to those inclined to think that intentions bear on the moral permissibility of actions. Hence, the relevant queerness is one that such addressees must be able to concede initially even if, by way of further inference, they will be compelled to reject DDE.[9] If it were not, the deliberative perspective objection would beg the question against proponents of DDE. That is, if all (2) amounts to is the claim that it is odd for an agent mulling the permissibility of her performing a certain action to consider facts that are irrelevant to permissibility, of which facts about the agent's intentions are one kind, then the argument begs the question against supporters of DDE. They *do* think that intentions are relevant to permissibility, and obviously, *they* should not be impressed with an argument involving a premise, i.e. (2) under the present interpretation that amounts to sheer counter-assertion in the relevant dialogical setting.

Ever since Anscombe's DDE-based denunciation of Truman's DDE-informed decision to bomb Hiroshima and Nagasaki (and long before that, for that matter), some moral philosophers have defended and others have rejected DDE. Each

[9] One such further inference might appeal to an ancillary premise that no fact can bear on the permissibility of an action if, from a first-person perspective, this fact cannot coherently form the basis of the agent's assessment of permissibility. However, my examples of spontaneity and lack of knowledge of local customs defeat this premise.

side has offered various arguments to try to persuade the other party, neither party managing to offer conclusive arguments. The reason that the deliberative perspective objection holds the promise of breaking this stalemate is that it poses the question of the relevance of intentions to permissibility from the perspective of the deliberating agent—a perspective previously not normally taken in the debate when assessing the relevance of intentions to permissibility of action—and does not pose the question from an ex post or a third-person perspective. It specifically appeals to the putative fact that it seems absurd for an agent deliberating about what to do that she should think that facts about the intention with which she will perform the available action settles the issue of which actions are permissible.[10]

To see this, consider first the *retrospective analogue* of the agent-perspective puzzle. That is, suppose someone contemplates the intention with which she performed one of her past actions in order to establish if what she did was impermissible. In this case, it is not absurd for the agent to try to establish with which intentions the action was performed to determine whether her past action was morally permissible. Indeed, this was exactly what Anscombe did in her classic piece on war: She determined the permissibility of a past action—the bombing of Hiroshima—on the basis of the intention with which it was carried out. However, if the infelicity of the advice imagined in the deliberative perspective puzzle is constituted by the general irrelevance of intentions to moral impermissibility, the retrospective version of the deliberative perspective objection should fare no less well. But, in its retrospective version, the infelicity evaporates, or at least it is invisible to proponents of DDE. If some critics of DDE think that it exists even in the retrospective case, I suspect the infelicity that they sense is simply the infelicity of letting a factor, which in their view is irrelevant, determine their assessment of the permissibility. In that case, friends of DDE simply do not sense *this* infelicity, and appeals to it beg the question against them.

Consider next the *third-person perspective analogue* of the agent-perspective puzzle. That is, suppose an agent deliberates how to act and a bystander aware of the agent's deliberations asks herself which of her available actions are permissible without offering any advice to the agent. To assert that it would be queer from the third-person perspective to think that the intention of the agent is relevant to the permissibility of her action would, I take it, simply amounts to asserting something that friends of DDE are committed to denying. In general, from a third-person perspective, one must take the agent's future intentions as given, and if, as defenders

[10] I am not saying that this appeal does not beg the question against no defender of DDE. For instance, Nagel's account of DDE in terms of the magnification of evil intended from the point of view of the agent suggests that he rejects (1) (see Nagel 1986: 184).

of DDE do, one thinks that intentions influence permissibility, nothing seems odd about the bystander believing that the intentions of the agent matter to the permissibility of whatever she does.

Fortunately, neither Thomson nor Scanlon offers the deliberative perspective objection in its unconvincing retrospective or third-person form. [11] Hence, we should take a closer look at the scenario to which the deliberative perspective objection appeals, to see if the relevant infelicity can be explained in different ways. I offer two such explanations.

8.7 The Queerness of Treating One's Future Intentions as Given

The first alternative explanation hinges on the fact that the advice might easily be taken as an invitation to the agent to treat her future intentions not as an object of deliberation, but as a constraint in her deliberations, and that, in general, it is odd to invite agents to take their future intentions as fixed in a way that determines which of their options are morally permissible rather than to expect them to shape their intentions in the light of their deliberations, including their deliberations about what they are morally required to do. Moreover, the very fact that the agent asks for advice may be thought to pragmatically imply that she is seeking to and believes herself capable of making her intentions conform with the outcome of her moral deliberations, and the advice that she should ponder with which intention she will perform the action, if she does, contradicts this pragmatic implication.[12] By way of illustration of the claim put forward in the first sentence in this section, suppose a prospective bomber ponders whether to carry out the war-winning raid, decides not to do so in spite of the promising prospects, and then justifies her inaction by saying: "I knew the best thing for me to have done was to have carried out the raid with the intention to destroy the factory. But I also knew that if I were to

[11] Cp. how Kamm (2008: 168) summarises the deliberative perspective objection: "This is because, as Thomas Scanlon has argued, in most cases an agent can decide whether an act is permissible by considering properties and effects the act would have independently of considering with what intentions she would do the act." Admittedly, Thomson does appeal to one such case, i.e. she asks if the intention of the doctor really can make a difference to whether killing a terminal patient suffering tremendously is permissible. But there are other problems with her use of this case. First, defenders of DDE may agree that it is impermissible to kill the terminal patient. In their view, killing the patient with the intention of relieving her suffering is permissible, but killing her intending her death is impermissible. Second, defenders might say that DDE discriminates against intending harm, and in the case at hand, intending the patient's death is not intending harm considering the alternative. Hence, DDE does not apply to the case at hand.

[12] I owe this point to Gerald Lang.

carry out the raid, I would do so with the intention to demoralise the enemy by killing non-combatants. Hence, I did the best I could." What strikes one as odd here, even if one thinks the agent made the right decision, is that the agent deliberated as if her future intentions were not something to be left up to her, but something that was externally given to her and settled, morally speaking, what she should do rather than something she could and should shape in accordance with her beliefs about moral permissibility. This is why it would neither be odd for some third party to complain that she did not carry out the raid with the intention of destroying the factory, nor for some agent to ponder the intention with which she performed some past act with an eye to determining whether she acted impermissibly.

Admittedly, as the case of predictable weakness of the will reminds us, it is not always odd for an agent to treat her future subjunctive intentions as fixed in her deliberation. Sometimes agents are literally incapable of exercising control over their future intentions or know from past experience that even if they are capable of exercising such control, they will not do so. But not only are such cases abnormal. Cases that appear in the literature on DDE are, in this respect, quite normal, and it is not as if the prospective bomber must, as a result of weakness of her will etc., predict her future intentions with respect to the raid.

Note, finally, that the present account explains why neither Thomson nor Scanlon offers the third-person perspective or the retrospective version of the deliberative perspective objection, since, clearly, one does not now control the intentions of others or with which intentions one acted in the past.

The following point might be pressed into service against this observation: According to Scanlon, we do not even control our future intention "since it is not open to us to choose which ultimate reasons to act on" (Scanlon 2008: 88). Hence, Scanlon might acknowledge no relevant difference between the deliberative perspective and the third-person/retrospective versions, and in the light of that, it could be conjectured that he might as well have offered the third-person/retrospective version even if he does not. The claim preceding the former sentence, however, seems implausible. If, by "intention," we mean the plan that guided the agent's action (Scanlon 2008: 10), as is the meaning that seems generally employed in discussions of DDE (for example, Nagel 1986: 179–180), agents normally control which plans they adopt (Walen 2004: 343). Surely, the prospective bomber controls which plan she will adopt to end the war, and more generally, very many of our deliberations are premised on the assumption that we are faced with different possible plans for future courses of action, and we need to decide which one we will commit ourselves to.

If, by "intention," we mean the features that the agent took to count in favour of her action (Scanlon 2008: 10), and I think this is the sense of "intentions" that

Scanlon has in mind when he claims that we do not control our "ultimate" intentions, then his no-control claim seems plausible. Just like we do not directly control what we believe in general, we do not directly control which features we think speak in favour of some action. Yet, two problems arise. First, which features of an action that, ultimately, an agent takes to speak in favour of, as opposed to which of these features she acts on, is not what defenders of DDE normally have in mind. A terror bomber who defers to authority and adopts a plan to kill non-combatants violates DDE even if she takes it that, ultimately, it never speaks in favour of killing non-combatants that doing so will bring an end to a war.

Second, we exercise sufficient control over our intentions for DDE to apply even when "intention" is understood as a matter of which subset of features we act upon of those we take to favour an option. Specifically, in our deliberations and, thus, in our resulting actions, we may decide not to let ourselves be influenced by what we take to be a feature favouring the performing of a certain action. For instance one might believe that a person deserves to be blamed for an action, but not think that one has sufficient evidence to warrant blaming her, given the institutional rules regulating the blame one can dispense in one's official role. A university lecturer may believe that a student has downloaded an essay from the internet and yet disregard this believed fact in her deliberations about how the essay should be marked, because she does not possess the officially required evidence.

8.8 The Queerness of Answering a Different Question: Actualism vs. Possibilism

The second alternative explanation contends that the oddness of the advice consists in the fact that it fails to address the question with which the agent struggles and, accordingly, is infelicitous in the way that any response to a question purporting to be an answer, but really is not, is. To show this, I need to introduce the distinction between actualism and possibilism.

Actualism is the view "that the values that should figure in determining which option is the best and so ought to be done out of a set of options are the values of what would be the case were the agent to adopt or carry out the option, where what would be the case includes of course what the agent would simultaneously or subsequently in fact do" (Jackson and Pargetter 1986: 233). Possibilism is the view that "it is only necessary to attend to what is possible for the agent" (Jackson and Pargetter 1986: 233).

Jackson and Pargetter (1986: 236–240) believe actualism is the correct view. However, for present purposes, I remain neutral on this issue. The distinction is relevant to the deliberative perspective objection, because actualism implies that the advice given in the scenario appealed to in the deliberative perspective objection—"If, were you to do X, you would do X with the intention to Y (for example, kill the non-combatants), then it is impermissible for you to do X. But if, were you to do X, you would do X with the intention to Z (for example, destroy the munitions factory), then it is permissible for you to do X"—is not an answer to the question nagging the deliberating agent, i.e. "Is it permissible for me to do X?"

Let me explain. An actualist proponent of DDE who believes the bomber will carry out the raid, if she does so, with the intention to kill the non-combatants, might advise her that carrying out the raid is impermissible for her. Nevertheless, this actualist might consistently think that the right answer to the question of whether it is permissible for the prospective bomber to carry out the raid with the intention to destroy the munitions factory is "Yes". After all, it might be possible for her to carry out the raid without intending to kill the non-combatants even if, as a matter of fact, she will intend to kill the non-combatants, if she carries out the raid. Hence, actualists, or someone torn between actualism and possibilism, as in fact I think most of us are, might say that the oddness that Thomson and Scanlon point to reflects that the answer offered—even if it has the form "If you do X with the intention to Y, it is impermissible for you to do X. If you do X, but not with the intention to Y, then it is permissible for you to do X" and, thus, covers all possible ways of doing X with some intention or other—is not really an answer to the question posed—"Is it permissible for me to do X?" The right answer does not involve the relevant sort of conditional clause, but is a "yes" or "no"—full stop—answer premised on the intention that the agent will in fact have if she carries out the raid.

No such divergence arises for a comparable proponent of DDE who is a possibilist. For her, if the agent could carry out the raid with a morally acceptable intention, she should carry it out even if, in fact, she will not carry it out with such an intention if she proceeds with the raid. Yet, the issue of actualism vs. possibilism is one on which few hold firmly settled pre-reflective views, and to the extent that we have actualist leanings, we should (and I suppose, will) find the proposed advice odd in part, because it does not address the agent's question, but a different one.

It might be replied that my explanans implies that the comparable disjunctive answer to the retrospective question "Was it permissible for me to do X?" should be odd in the same way as the answer to the agent's prospective question "Is it permissible for me to do X?", and yet, I claim it is not. A similar point applies to the third-person perspective analogue of the deliberative perspective objection.

In response, I note that the reason the disjunctive answer is not infelicitous in the retrospective case is that while, strictly speaking, it fails to answer the question, it does so indirectly, because it clearly sets out what the agent needs to do to answer the question, i.e. to settle what her past intention was. Hence, the disjunctive answer to the retrospective question is not infelicitous for the same reason that the answer—"Look at the shopping list!"—to the question—"Were we supposed to buy apples?"—is not, despite the fact that, strictly speaking, it too fails to answer the question posed. It provides an indirect answer by informing the agent that she will find out what the answer is by glimpsing at the shopping list, i.e. it informs her of a procedure that she can follow to answer the question.

On the assumption that our future intentions are, to some extent, up to us, the conditional advice provides no comparable indirect answer to the prospective question, because on the stated assumption, the agent cannot predict what her own future intentions will be, given that she acts in a certain way and then, on that basis, determines the permissibility of an action that she ponders. This procedure presupposes that no moral question pertaining to what the agent's future intentions ought to be arises. Hence, on my view, Thomson's inward gaze quest for future intentions passage does indeed describe an absurdity.[13]

8.9 Conclusion

Scanlon's account of the differential permissibility of acts of war involving the intentional killing of non-combatants and similar acts involving non-intentional killings independently of DDE is unconvincing. Moreover, while there is something peculiar about advising a deliberating agent that the permissibility of an action that she considers carrying out depends on the intention with which she will perform it, if she does, this infelicity does not derive, even indirectly so, from the general irrelevance of intentions to moral permissibility. Rather, it is explained by the oddness of inviting the agent to treat her future intentions as fixed in her deliberations and by the fact that, from an actualist perspective, the advice does not address the question posed by the agent. Hence, the deliberative perspective objection neither rebuts the relevance of intentions to permissibility, nor demonstrates that the focus of just war theory on intention is mistaken. Whether intentions are relevant to permissibility in relation to war or elsewhere is another and broader question, which this paper bears on, but in no way settles.[14]

[13] The third-person analogue of the deliberative objection can be dealt with in the same way.

[14] A previous version of this paper was presented at a conference at University of Sheffield, "War and Innocence," 25–27 August 2010. I thank the participants—especially, Daniel Halliday, Frances Kamm, Gerald Lang, Graham Long, David Mapel, Jeff McMahan, Iddo Porat, Daniel Statman, Daniel Schwartz, and Victor Tadros—for helpful comments.

References

Bennett, J. (1981) "Morality and Consequences," *The Tanner Lecture on Human Values*, vol. 2 (University of Utah Press) 45–116.

Caney, S. (2005) *Justice Beyond Borders: A Global Political Theory* (Oxford: Oxford University Press).

Jackson, F. and Pargetter, R. (1986) "Ought, Options, and Actualism," *The Philosophical Review* 95.2: 233–255.

Kamm, F. M. (2007) *Intricate Ethics* (New York: Oxford University Press).

——(2008) "Terrorism and Intending Evil," *Philosophy & Public Affairs* 36: 157–186.

Lippert-Rasmussen, K. (2012) "Intentions and Discrimination," *Journal of Moral Theory* 9.1: 55–74.

——(2010) "Scanlon of the Doctrine of the Double Effect," *Social Theory and Practice* 36.4: 541–564.

McMahan, J. (2005) "Just Cause for War," *Ethics & International Affairs* 19.3: 1–21.

——(2009) "Intention, Permissibility, Terrorism, and War," *Philosophical Perspectives* 23: 345–372.

Nagel, T. (1986) *The View from Nowhere* (New York: Oxford University Press).

Norman, R. (1995) *Ethics, Killing, and War* (Cambridge: Cambridge University Press).

Quinn, W. (1994) *Morality and Action* (Cambridge: Cambridge University Press).

Scanlon. T. S. (2000) "Intention and Permissibility," *Aristotelian Society Suppl. Volume* 74.1: 301–317.

——(2008) *Moral Dimensions: Permissibility, Meaning, Blame* (Cambridge, MA: Belknap Press of Harvard University Press).

Thomson, J. J. (1991) "Self-Defense," *Philosophy & Public Affairs* 20: 283–310.

——(1999) "Physician-Assisted Suicide: Two Moral Arguments," *Ethics* 109: 497–518.

Walen, A. (2004) "Permissibly Encouraging the Impermissible," *The Journal of Value Inquiry* 38: 341–358.

Walzer, M. (2006) *Just and Unjust Wars* (New York: Basic Books).

9

Risking and Protecting Lives

Soldiers and Opposing Civilians

Noam Zohar

Introduction: Double Effect, Double Intention, and Preventing Harm

A fairly large segment of recent debates about the morality of conduct in warfare has focused on the question of civilian casualties. Much hangs on the way the question is formulated, and I will argue later that one prevalent formulation is highly misleading; but we must begin somewhere, so I shall at first set forth the question in that very form, which speaks of "preventing" such casualties. The twofold question is thus: "(1) Do soldiers have a duty to prevent deaths of non-combatants; and if they do, (2) to what extent must they incur risk for the sake of such prevention?"

My main purpose—after clearing up some of the confusion arising from this misleading formulation—is to work toward a better definition of norms and guidelines for particular, characteristic scenarios. In order to do that, I shall first have to briefly cover some well-known ground, recapitulating the discourse that provides the context for the question itself and for its common formulation in terms of prevention. I will then focus on some of the arguments surrounding "preventing harm to opposing non-combatants." I hope to show that, although there is some merit in the claim that soldiers are not obligated to risk their lives in order to protect civilians other than those under the domain of their own state, this is irrelevant for most combat situations. For actual warfare ethics, the question is not one of prevention but rather of a nefarious permission for soldiers to harm civilians or put them at significant risk, for the sake of the soldiers' enhanced safety.

The widespread moral indignation that rightly motivates the war against terrorism depends crucially on the moral assessment of foreseen (though unintended) killing of non-combatants. Since some extent of such killing seems unavoidable in many contemporary settings, those seeking—and claiming—to fight in a morally justified way must account for how their actions are significantly different from those of intentional terrorists and indeed permissible. Unless such an account can be provided, states and armies will have to yield the moral high ground that they aspire to hold in their campaigns against insurgents and terrorists; the battle will then be reduced, at best, to one between two sorts of terrorists—intentional and unintentional. Even if it is granted that intentional terrorism is still worse than the unintentional kind, all parties will have on their hands the blood of the innocent.[1]

Permission for such unintended killing is commonly asserted by citing the classical doctrine of double effect (DDE). But this venerable doctrine merely defines conditions under which a bad (side) effect, if unintended, shall not preclude an action undertaken for the sake of a legitimate purpose (= the main or intended effect). The doctrine does not offer a justification for the distinction between intending a bad effect—to be specific, in the present context, killing people—and knowingly bringing it about. Rather, this distinction serves as the doctrine's point of departure.

It seems that most (if not all) contemporary combat activities cannot be permitted without this crucial distinction. But in order to sustain the distinction, it is necessary to counter the accusation that both kinds of killing involve callous disregard for human life. For the intentional terrorist, there is only one defense against that accusation, namely, asserting tragic necessity. He would rather not have to kill innocent people, but it is unfortunately required in order to free his nation from (say) repressive tyranny. The obvious retort is that rejecting that kind of justification is the very core of the just war tradition: however justified the goals of a war may be, they cannot translate into a permission to kill non-combatants. People's lives have inherent value; they carry a weight that cannot be swept aside by the force of military necessity. But then mere lack of intention also does not amount to respecting the value of the victims' lives. If the DDE were to allow an agent to pursue a worthy goal while having no regard for people killed incidentally, it would indeed amount to an endorsement of unintended terrorism.

The DDE, as restated in Mangan's oft-cited modern formulation, seems to avert this pitfall through the condition of proportionality, requiring "that there be a proportionately grave reason for permitting the evil effect."[2] But in the context of warfare, this condition will mostly not pose a significant hurdle. In effect, it allows the value of human lives to be outweighed by any military-political objective deemed to

[1] For an extended discussion, see Rodin (2004).

[2] Mangan (1949: 43), whose discussion summarizes the 19th century detailed formulation by Joannes Gory (see Mangan 1949: 60–61).

be important. Sufficient importance is routinely taken to exist, except when the number of non-combatant casualties is extremely large (and note that the restrictions of proportionality could in principle be accepted by terrorists).[3]

We should therefore not be surprised that the following guideline regarding unintended harm to non-combatants has been presented as an expression of the traditional law of warfare (specifically, the 1907 Hague conventions): "the attacker may, given the presence of innocents in a combat zone, do anything that it would be permissible to do if there were no innocents there—subject to the restrictions entailed by the principle of proportionality... This... allows the indiscriminate shelling or bombing of defended areas containing innocents" (Cohen 1989: 33).[4] This formulation has been recently quoted sympathetically by Pavlischek (2010: 29), claiming that it represents "the more traditional understanding of double effect."

This version of the DDE implies the following perverse permission. Suppose a military unit is assigned an important military objective, and by consulting standard operating procedures a plan is devised—let us call it "Plan A"—that will lead to the objective while causing some non-combatant deaths. If these are assessed (rightly, let us stipulate) as not disproportionate in light of the important objective, it seems that the unit and its planners have no obligation to consider or to seek non-standard Plan B, whereby they can attain the same objective with fewer non-combatant casualties, or the more imaginative Plan C, which can (almost surely) spare the non-combatants altogether. This cannot be right, yet it is precisely what is prescribed by the above guideline, which mandates ignoring the presence of the non-combatant victims (provided that the proportionality threshold has been met).

Instead, moral guidance for combat must give serious weight to human lives. A crucial improvement is thus found in the New Catholic Encyclopedia[5] (NCE) formulation of the DDE, which explicitly adds a requirement of necessity: the unintended bad effect must be necessary, not in the sense that it serves as a means toward the good objective but in the sense that it is unavoidable—the good objective cannot be attained except through the act that also produces the bad effect.[6]

[3] Admittedly, the challenge for terrorists would be greater, since harming many civilians is inherent to their strategy, and thus they might more often run afoul of the proportionality condition.

[4] Cohen's discourse on "Bombardment and Civilian Casualties" (1989: 25–35) explicitly takes issue with Walzer's view (presented later) regarding the soldiers' obligation to accept certain risks; but see further in my discussion of the "Proximity" scenario later in this paper.

[5] Volume 2 (1967), 1020–1022.

[6] This seems to be stated explicitly in the classical source of the DDE, namely, the discussion of self-defense in Aquinas's *Summa Theologica* (Part 2 of Part 2, Question 64 Article 7). Aquinas states that "if a man, in self-defense, uses more than necessary violence, it will be unlawful."

This version of the DDE excludes, in principle, both Plan A and Plan B: neither is necessary, since Plan C is available. As we shall see later, things are by no means so simple, as it is naïve to assume that there is no difference between the plans in terms of their various costs. But even without attending to costs, it is crucial to note that the lack of necessity will often not be obvious. Within the framework of Plan A, each of its component-acts is necessary. Consider an officer engaged in working out its details, looking at maps and intelligence reports, and noticing with alarm that one of these acts is likely to bring about non-combatant deaths. Having stopped to assess proportionality (and being satisfied in that regard), he might well move ahead, deeming the act necessary. It is only by thinking outside the box of standard procedures that Plan B will be noticed; and only by a further exercise of the imagination that Plan C might be devised—rendering some or all of the non-combatant deaths unnecessary and thus impermissible.

It follows that if the necessity condition is to have practical value, it is morally imperative that a tension be retained between the importance of military objectives and the value of civilian lives. This must be expressed through a constant balancing, with proactive attention regularly directed to seeking alternative plans, reducing or eliminating harm to non-combatants. Otherwise, the near-absolute priority that is routinely assigned to military objectives will effectively allow soldiers to kill non-combatants as long as that is not what they intend—amounting to unintended terrorism.

Walzer (1977: 155) thus insists that the DDE must be explicitly amended to require a "double intention," the second intention being "that the foreseeable evil be reduced as far as possible." Specifically, recognizing the presence of the non-combatants who are being put at risk requires an effort to reduce both the magnitude of that risk and the extent of the expected harm.

Walzer also demands that such an effort involve a willingness, on the part of the soldiers, to themselves incur some risk for the sake of preventing non-combatant casualties. As I have argued elsewhere (Zohar 2007), this cannot be accepted as a necessary condition for validating the "second intention" (in the following discussion, I shall focus on the issue of risk and safety for the soldiers). The underlying consideration is that true respect for human life requires a genuine effort to spare the lives of non-combatants in the course of military operations. Accordingly, the IDF code of ethics (revised version, 2000) speaks of such an effort without explicitly referring to undertaking risk:

"Purity of Arms" (Morality in Warfare)

The soldier shall make use of his weaponry and power only for the fulfillment of the mission and solely to the extent required; he will maintain his humanity even in combat. The soldier shall not employ his weaponry and power in order to harm non-combatants or prisoners of war, and *shall do all he can to prevent harm to their lives*, bodies, honor and property. (Emphasis added.)[7]

From here it is easy to see how the language of "prevention" (or also: "protection") has gained prevalence in discourse about war ethics. Those who, like Walzer, reject the crude application of DDE that would in effect allow disregard for opposing non-combatants, demand that military campaigns be accompanied by a consistent effort to prevent harm to non-combatants.

Yet there is something curious about talk of "preventing" here, as though someone else is about to harm these civilians and the virtuous soldier is being asked to protect them. Actually, the question is not about *preventing* harm but rather about *refraining* from inflicting it. Yet it is easy to see how this way of putting things arises naturally in the context of verifying necessity. Permission for the planned military operation is assumed, since the proportionality condition is met. Thus it is taken as given that the operation will go ahead, causing non-combatant casualties. The necessity condition requires an effort to find alternative plans, averting (or at least reducing) these casualties; this is plausibly described as "preventing" them, or even as "protecting" the putative victims. Yet as I shall proceed to argue, framing the issue in these terms can entail a morally corrosive confusion—especially in light of the difference in costs between alternative ways of obtaining the military objective

Sparing Lives: Costs, Risks, and Necessity

The preceding discussion about plans A, B and C omitted the crucial dimension of costs. Costs are, however, inherent to the question of necessity. If we are to deny that Plan A (with its concomitant civilian deaths) is necessary on the grounds that Plan B is available, we must face the question of constraints. Suppose that Plan B requires a great concentration of forces, drawing on most of our strategic reserves, and therefore no responsible commander would consider adopting it. Risking our side's entire strategic prospects is an unacceptable cost of Plan B. The comparison needed to determine necessity must therefore be subject to a constraint of the

[7] This is my own translation, with an effort toward literal fidelity. The official IDF English version takes somewhat greater freedoms, such as adopting gender inclusive language and shifting to the plural: "The IDF servicemen and women will use their weapons," etc. Significantly for the discussion here, it substitutes "avoid causing harm" for "prevent harm." See <http://dover.idf.il/IDF/English/about/doctrine/ethics.htm>, reproduced also at <http://zionism-israel.com/hdoc/IDF_Ethical_Code.htm>.

form: "Is there an alternate Plan B that can achieve the same objective as Plan A, without incurring cost X?"

There are many kinds of costs. Plan B may be literally more expensive, for example, in that it utilizes costly precision ordnance. Or it might take more time, either in execution (the objective will be attained, but a few hours later) or in preparation (to work out its details, the unit's operation officer and her team will have to spend several extra hours). Or, finally, plan B might involve a slightly higher risk to the soldiers. Should any or all of these costs be translated into constraints on the comparison between the prospective plans?

Note that virtually every kind of cost can be seen as entailing a military disadvantage. Using up expensive materiel, delaying the achievement of an important objective, taking up the limited time of key personnel, exposing one's soldiers to extra risk—each of these might entail some sub-optimal outcome down the road. In one sense, risk to one's soldiers is, of course, uniquely unpalatable. Yet any military disadvantage can also imply a greater risk of casualties.

Realizing this, one way of response can be to insist on a strict constraint, disallowing any cost whatever. Plan B shall count as a viable alternative to Plan A only if (besides reducing non-combatant deaths) all other things are equal. If Plan B involves expending an extra round, dollar, or minute—and needless to say, if it involves even a minuscule extra risk to our soldiers—then it is ruled out, and Plan A is deemed as meeting the necessity condition: under the given constraint, there is no other way of achieving the military objective.

Clearly, such an approach renders the necessity condition effectively vacuous. The lives of these people—the prospective non-combatant victims—have value, in theory; and to this lip service is paid: we would spare them if it would cost us nothing. But in reality this value will be routinely outweighed by the importance of our military objectives. On rare occasions, perhaps, an alternative plan will present itself, whereby the victims' lives can be spared at no cost (of any kind), and then we shall indeed steer clear of gratuitous bloodshed. But in practice, when the standard operating procedures yield a single plan A, even the effort needed to look beyond that will be construed as an undue burden. Rather than seeking a more complicated way to achieve the same objective, the officers' time will surely be better spent in thinking a step or two ahead, planning for the day after tomorrow.

This helps explain why Walzer insists on a willingness to incur some cost, which he defines poignantly in terms of risk undertaken by the soldiers themselves. Without such willingness, there is no balancing of values: the lives of the opposing civilians are simply swept aside, and those who bring about their deaths exhibit a disregard for human life similar (though not identical) to that which characterizes terrorism.

Nevertheless, as we have seen, there are those who expressly reject Walzer's position. I shall dub their position "Soldiers' Safety First" (SSF), since it places the safety of soldiers above that of the local civilians.[8] Some SSF proponents have offered a seemingly compelling argument against what they call a "duty to protect" local civilians in the course of military action. They argue that no such duty should be recognized—particularly if that would impinge upon the military operations, and most emphatically if it would involve any risk to the soldiers themselves. Thus J. Fleury asserts that "soldiers do not have the same positive duty to protect innocents among the enemy population, as they have to protect their own population."[9] This claim has been endorsed and defended extensively by Asa Kasher and Amos Yadlin, who take special care to steer clear of any form of nationalist or ethnocentric stance. The soldiers owe less to the local civilians not because of their alien ethnicity, nor even because they are not co-citizens. It is simply that the soldiers are agents of their state, and a state owes special duties of protection only to people residing under its control.[10]

This is true as far as it goes, but as I shall proceed to show, is virtually irrelevant to moral guidance in the setting of military action. As I suggested earlier, the false impression of its relevance reflects a confusion that is due, at least in part, to the ambiguity in the talk of "protection" (or "prevention") in this context. In order to dispel the ambiguity and reduce the confusion, I will begin with two scenarios in which what is required of soldiers seems rather clear-cut. These will furnish the sharpest contrast as a backdrop for analyzing more perplexing situations, and also spell out the notion that—*pace* adherents of SSF—respect for human life is inseparable from consideration of risk. I will then move on to several more complex scenarios that lie in between, in one sense or another.

Risk and Protection: Two Initial Scenarios

1. *Humanitarian aid*

Kasher and Yadlin derive what is perhaps the most compelling support for their position from an analogy to duties of rescue and protection owed by the state

[8] See Kasher and Yadlin (2005: 14–15). Clearly, the prioritization enumerated there is meant to trump the earlier-stated condition of "minimizing collateral damage" (p. 11).

[9] As cited in Pavlischeck (2009: 30); I have been unable to locate Fleury's 1998 military research paper cited there.

[10] Kasher and Yadlin (2005, 2006); and more recently their exchange (2009) which also includes a response by Walzer and Margalit, whose earlier essay (2009) had occasioned the response by Kasher and Yadlin.

and its agents in cases of natural disasters. Part of the very purpose of the political association constituting a state is providing protection and help, particularly in life-threatening situations. In the face of plague or fire, for example, health-care workers or firefighters are the agents of the government (whether national or local), fulfilling its special obligations toward those residing in its domain. As such, they may also be expected to incur some risk in the course of their urgent work. Neither these agents nor the state itself have any similar obligations toward people in other countries, far or near.

Likewise, argue Kasher and Yadlin, for soldiers, whose mission is to protect their compatriots from certain man-made disasters: they have no duty of protection toward other people, including the civilians of the territory where the soldiers operate in the national defense. As I indicated earlier, this is perfectly correct as far as it goes; let me now introduce a scenario that will help to see just how far that may be.

Think of a humanitarian aid operation, delivering crucial food to a population; the operation comes under attack by armed groups (who seek to disrupt and/or seize the supplies, in either case preventing them from reaching the starving people). Foreign soldiers are present, as they are conducting a military operation in the same territory. Are these soldiers required to undertake risk (or to incur other costs, for example, to divert their efforts from their military mission) in order to protect the flow of aid, and thereby the lives of the population who needs it for survival? Here Kasher and Yadlin's argument seems convincing: whatever these soldiers would owe their own people if something similar should take place back home, they have no similar obligations to these other people.

Indeed, it would be foolhardy and illicit for a commanding officer to order his or her soldiers into such action. Even if the problems in delivering food were aggravated by the soldiers' military campaign, their duty in that regard is fully discharged by removing whatever obstacles they have introduced. They must ensure that their own operations pose no hindrance to the food's delivery, and conduct any co-ordination with the aid operation required for its safe passage. They are not obligated further to counteract the threat to the food supply introduced independently by local evil forces.[11]

This scenario truly involves protection, and is well served by the comparison to relief in the face of natural disasters. Let us now examine to what extent this might

[11] The qualifier "independently" is meant to suggest that if the threat to the food supply was somehow caused by the army's military operations, that army may have a special obligation to contribute to a remedy.

be relevant to combat situations, and whether it offers any support for a broad SSF position.

2. *Free-fire zone*

In the course of anti insurgency/anti-terrorist military operations, soldiers are located in an urban environment, and face possible attack. A "free-fire zone" is declared, that is, an instruction is issued that anyone approaching within a certain distance of their outpost be deemed a threat and shot. Let us suppose that efforts are undertaken to inform the local residents of this instruction, but it is known that some are unaware of it or are unable to entirely avoid the area that has been declared off-bounds. During the night, figures are seen approaching. Is it permissible to shoot them?

This can be construed in terms of incurring risk to the soldiers for the sake of protecting civilians. Imagine a debate between two soldiers. One says: "How can I shoot at these people, who may well be civilians?"—and the other answers: "Well, by not shooting you are risking your own life (as well as mine). We are not obligated to protect these civilians, certainly not where—as in our current situation—we thereby endanger ourselves."

This version of SSF is, however, clearly misguided. The question here is not about preventing harm or protecting lives—it is about directly harming and killing. Suppose that if an enemy combatant gets too close and a shootout takes place, the odds are even, i.e., there is a 50 per cent chance that one of the soldiers will be killed. But suppose also that a person crossing the forbidden line is—with a probability of 98 per cent—a non-combatant. If our soldiers' safety is deemed paramount (as argued by Kasher and Yadlin—subject only to protecting the lives of our civilians and to fulfilling the military mission), then eliminating the 1 per cent risk to one of them justifies the near-certain killing of a noncombatnt. This is of course an unacceptable conclusion, although it would presumably be endorsed also by Cohen, who would allow soldiers to behave as if no non-combatants are present. So such a free-fire zone is an impermissible tactic. The soldiers must wait for the person to come nearer, or shine a light to better determine who is approaching, even if they thereby incur some risk—not because they must "protect" non-combatants, but because they have no permission to slay them.

One could start asking about proportionality or necessity; as we shall see later, delineating those conditions can in some cases present no small challenge. But doing so here would be misguided, since such shooting cannot in any event be justified by the DDE. In fact, what we have here is an act with just a single effect. To try a DDE justification, one would have to resort to sophistry, for example, "I am shooting at this suspected terrorist, not intending the effect of killing a non-combatant." Or maybe one would employ tools of act-individuation: "I intend this qua shooting a suspect, but do not intend it qua slaying a teenager hurrying to get medication for her ailing father." It is this type of "mental gymnastics" that has given DDE a bad name.[12]

I do not mean to deny that some acts can be ambiguous, and that their proper description can depend on mental states. It is just that given the probabilities as stipulated, the agent cannot in good faith declare (or think) "I do not intend this as slaying a non-combatant." A serious concern with probabilities is required in attending to what it means to foresee (or to intend) a particular effect or result. If a doctrine of "minimizing risk to our soldiers" implies acting to enhance their safety even when the acts consist (almost certainly) in gratuitous killings, then neither the doctrine nor the ensuing acts are consistent with valuing human lives.

In our first scenario—Humanitarian Aid—what is at stake for the soldiers is indeed preventing harm to alien civilians, and the SSF argument was seen to have merit. By contrast, in the second scenario—Free-fire Zone—an argument in terms of SSF would be spurious. Here, putting the question in the terms cited at the outset ("should soldiers risk their lives to prevent harm to opposing civilians?") represents a breath-taking distortion. What places the soldiers at risk is not any attempt to serve local civilians, but entering the enemy area. There is no question of incurring risk in order to protect anyone. Rather, the question is: "May soldiers kill non-combatants in order to enhance their own safety?"—to which the answer is emphatically: "No." These two diametrically opposed scenarios can now serve as a backdrop for considering more complex ones.

Complex Scenarios

3. *Proximity (with a note on human shields)*

In this ubiquitous scenario, the soldiers' fire is directed against an appropriate military target, but there are non-combatants nearby. This kind of case has furnished the classic examples of double effect in warfare: the act of shooting has two clearly distinct effects, one legitimate and important, the other bad and undesired.

[12] Another try is to change the unit of analysis from the acts of individual soldiers to the unit's policy. On this view, the deed in question is the organization's act of declaring a free-fire zone. Its legitimate and desired effect is safeguarding the unit's soldiers; the unfortunate side-effect is shooting the civilians. Even if one were to buy in to this, the declaration would still not be permitted by DDE, since the shooting is the means by which the safety is achieved. And at any rate, even though it is appropriate to think also in terms of collective agency, that cannot be a substitute for moral evaluation of the actions of individual persons.

This is also the original context of the discussion of double intention. Suppose again that—after excluding options with disproportionate civilian casualties—there are several ways of destroying the target. How should the planners assess the competing risks? Is it appropriate to frame the question here in the contested terms introduced earlier (as done by the adherents of SSF), asking about soldiers incurring costs—and risking their lives—to prevent harm to non-combatants?

This time, let us suppose that standard operating procedures indicate Plan B, which involves a high probability of some civilian deaths. But one of the planners thinks up Plan C, much safer for the non-combatants but somewhat riskier for the soldiers. Walzer seems to require that they should adopt this alternate plan; does that mean that he is asking them to risk their lives *in order to protect* these (alien) non-combatants? Are the proponents of SSF right in claiming that this case is akin to scenario 1 (Humanitarian Aid)?

Before answering, let us consider an additional possibility. Another planner proposes Plan A, which—again, compared to Plan B—is even safer for the soldiers, but is expected to kill even more non-combatants (though still within the bounds of proportionality, since the target is quite important). Following the same linguistic form, it seems that a shift to Plan A would amount to allowing the soldiers *to cause extra civilian deaths* in order to enhance their own safety—plainly an impermissible option, akin to scenario 2 (Free-fire Zone).

If substituting Plan C for Plan B counts as "protecting non-combatant lives," then substituting Plan A for Plan B should count as "causing non-combatant deaths." But both these accounts are equally unwarranted, because they characterize the act not in terms of its actual effect(s), that is, the difference in outcome as compared to what would have happened were the act not performed, but rather as compared to some other act. In particular, when this alternate act is simply what is suggested by standard operating procedures (or perhaps, just whatever the planners happened to think of first) it is a morally arbitrary baseline.

The same is true with regard to choosing how to describe the soldiers' action in terms of its effect on their own fate. Are they "risking their own lives" or "enhancing their own safety?" As long as the selection of description depends on comparison to something else they could have done instead, it is subject to arbitrariness or bias.

In fact, in the various "Proximity" cases the soldiers cannot be said in good faith to be "protecting" the non-combatants at all. They are in any event *killing* the non-combatants, or at least endangering them, except perhaps in the limiting case of Plan D that entirely avoids the bad side-effect. Even that does not really constitute *preventing* harm to non-combatants; rather it is a matter of refraining from harming them.

Along similar lines, the soldiers are risking their lives not by the selection they make among the available plans but rather by the very enterprise of engaging the enemy or of moving into enemy territory, and then specifically by setting out to achieve the military objective in question. The choice among the several ways to do that is, in this regard, a choice about how to *minimize* this risk (= maximize their safety).

Thus the terms employed in the initial formulation are by no means the most natural manner of reflecting the quandary posed by Proximity scenarios. If the only objectives were "protecting" opposing non-combatants and avoiding risk to our soldiers, they could both be achieved wonderfully by withdrawing our forces altogether, or better still, by not undertaking military action in the first place. The soldiers, however, reject this option—rightly, let us grant, in light of the great importance of the campaign's goals in general, and of the current objective in particular. By committing to this objective, they are also unfortunately committed both to risking their own lives and to endangering non-combatants. The quandary is how to balance these negative outcomes. Putting the issue instead in terms of "risking soldiers' lives to prevent harm to non-combatants" is quite artificial; rather than illuminating the problem, it merely facilitates a bogus analogy to the Humanitarian Aid scenario. The analogy is bogus because the issue here is not whether the soldiers have any special obligation to "protect" these non-combatants, but whether they are permitted to kill them. A demand to refrain from killing people need not invoke any special obligation.

Returning to the DDE perspective, the question is—as discussed earlier—what constraints should define the "necessity" condition. For example, Plan B is only necessary if Plan C (with fewer non-combatant casualties) is ruled out on account of excessive risk to our soldiers.

Cohen (1989: 3) insists that "The law of war implies that soldiers are not obligated to raise their already high risks to even higher levels in order to lower further the risk to innocents in combat zones ... even where [departure by the innocents is] not possible[13] ... the rights of innocents are defeasible when honoring those rights would push the soldiers' risks beyond what it is reasonable to expect any group to endure." This sounds reasonable, not only in terms of law but also in terms of morality; and Cohen rightly notes that the risks to soldiers are repeated and hence cumulative. Here are the kinds of odds he has in mind:

[13] Kasher and Yadlin (2009) do seem to endorse efforts to avert Proximity situations, by issuing advance warnings and calling upon civilians to leave the prospective combat areas. But where such efforts have been ineffective or ignored, they join forces with Cohen and other members of the SSF camp.

In the Normandy campaign a rifleman in the Ninetieth Division could expect to last fourteen days before becoming a casualty. By contrast, in heavily bombed Germany, a civilian had only a one in seventy chance of being killed or seriously wounded by a bomb during the six years of the war.

I suspect the odds against the civilian would look rather worse were the focus narrowed from Germany in its entirety to certain particular locations. But the point regarding soldiers is well taken: if the odds in a particular battle or campaign are already as high as those against riflemen on D day and its sequel, it is hard to justify adding any significant risk, especially if the risk to non-combatants is quite low already. In other Proximity cases, the comparison will yield an opposite conclusion, and it will be clear that attaining somewhat greater safety for soldiers who are already relatively safe cannot justify imposing significant risks on non-combatants. Thus Cohen's approach—looking closely at the comparative magnitude of risks—actually undermines his sweeping rule, quoted earlier, that calls for virtually ignoring the presence of non-combatants near military targets.

At any rate, the bogus analogy to Humanitarian Aid scenarios should be avoided, along with any arbitrary formulation in the terms employed at the outset of our enquiry. The lives of non-combatants must be respected, hence necessity may not be defined so as to exclude any risk to soldiers, however small it may be. Alternate plans that reduce risk to non-combatants must be sought and adopted even if they involve additional risk to the soldiers—up to some hard-to-define limit, lower than the intolerable level rejected by Cohen, but definitely higher than zero.

A note on human shields

Up to now, I have been discussing Proximity scenarios as simply given: as it happens, there are non-combatants near the target, so that attacking the target has the side effect of harming them. But the literature on ethics of warfare—and the reality that it (partly) reflects—includes also the special case of a "human shield," where the proximity is intentionally set up by the enemy combatants in order to "shield" themselves from our fire. The shield is moral rather than physical; it is designed to work through deterrence, in that moral considerations (such as those enumerated earlier) will bar us from shooting at the military target (see Nozick 1974: 35).

Often it will be the case that applying the revised DDE—exercising the requisite double intention, and according sufficient weight to the lives of the civilian "shields"—will still allow the soldiers to attack despite the knowledge that the human shield will be killed. This can be due to the importance of the target and to the likelihood that there will be few options of executing the attack while sparing the "shields," or at least of achieving this without unacceptable losses to the soldiers. But it may well be that even apart from that, there are special reasons to disregard the moral bar formed by the presence of the shield.

The reasons are rather straightforward. Respecting the said moral bar has two unacceptable results. First, it rewards brutal immorality by granting its perpetrators immunity from military action. Second, it encourages further employment of human shields, in the long run placing in jeopardy an ever-greater number of non-combatants. The enemy operatives who employ human shields are breaking the rules, and the only hope of getting them to stop is to refuse to go along with them—that is, to disregard the moral bar they have thrust in our path.

Policy considerations of this kind are akin to those adopted by some governments facing hostage situations. In both cases, these considerations act to override the rights of the innocent victims, since respecting those rights would unacceptably deliver coercive power into the hands of the most ruthless evildoers, as well as produce harm to more victims down the road.

Yet my main concern here is not to defend the permission to shoot without regard for the lives of shields or hostages. Rather, it is to emphasize that even if such a permission exists, it is based on the said policy considerations, which apply narrowly (if they apply at all) to these perverse settings, where the moral bar has been intentionally manipulated by the enemy. Since it is only this intentional manipulation that warrants such considerations, extra care must be taken to avoid conflation of Proximity scenarios in general with those involving "human shields." Every fighting organization (regular or irregular) will have many of its bases, installations, and staging areas in proximity to civilian habitations. And despite urgent calls and demands to leave their homes which have (or are about to) become a combat zone, many non-combatants have no realistic option of safe evacuation. Thus a position that sweepingly reduces Proximity scenarios to the terms of "human shields" is entirely unjustifiable.

4. *Force protection*

Up till now, I have been examining scenarios where soldiers' safety figures as a factor in—or constraint upon—the selection of the means for pursuing a military objective. Sometimes, however, a unit's mission may consist directly in "force protection," that is, in defending another unit from enemy fire. Here the soldiers' safety itself constitutes the military objective. If there are non-combatants near the source of this enemy fire, the defending unit faces a special kind of Proximity scenario.

In classic Proximity scenarios, risks to soldiers and to opposing non-combatants operate as competing constraints upon the pursuit of a military objective whose importance derives from its function in the overall battle plan and from the goals of the war itself. These objectives and goals furnish the crucial "grave reason" that outweighs, in the assessment of proportionality, the very lives of innocent people. Indeed, the same objective and goals are what justifies the sacrifice of the soldiers' lives as well. In other words, whatever balance is struck between risks to non-combatants and to soldiers, the combined harm to both is justified by the military objective, because of its role in attaining the goals that (we assume) justify the military campaign.

For the sake of clarity, let us consider a Force Protection scenario in which the unit requesting protection (say, from mortar fire) is not currently engaged in action, and thus defending it does not directly serve any (other) military objective. Of course, avoiding casualties (and demoralization) is important for the success of the overall campaign. Moreover, soldiers are people and it is important to save their lives—which are here under direct attack. But the absence of current engagement can often mean that the soldiers of the threatened unit are able to provide for their own safety by taking temporary protective measures such as getting under cover (or remaining therein), selecting a roundabout route, and the like.

Now suppose that the defending unit consists of an artillery battery, this being the most effective weapon by which to quickly target the enemy mortars. But it becomes evident that a group of vans carrying non-combatants[14] are passing near the source of enemy fire, so that the artillery shelling (by its very nature, which hits an area rather than a precise point) will hit the vans along with the mortar-shooters. The crucial issue is thus timing: How urgent is it to take out those mortars? Suppose it is known that in twenty minutes the civilian vehicles will have moved on (such things are nowadays often knowable with drones providing real-time intelligence). Should not the defending unit hold its fire, advising the threatened unit to hunker down for the time being? Indeed, even if the threatened unit is on its way to strike some military objective, waiting might be possible.[15] If, however, its soldiers are inescapably exposed or are unable to take cover since they are in the midst of battle, there might not be time to wait or to seek alternatives, and DDE may mandate destroying the mortars despite the loss of civilian lives.

But who is to judge the urgency—and hence the moral permissibility—of Force Protection actions? The inherent difficulty of these scenarios lies in the split agency. The commander who must decide about endangering non-combatants is not the same commander who is considering how best to ensure the safety of his soldiers. They are in separate locations and do not have timely access to the same

[14] We might imagine that they are a convoy of evacuees who have heeded the army's calls to depart from combat zones.

[15] It is worth noting that even in the midst of a low-intensity engagement there might be options of temporary evasive action.

information. Therein lies the particular moral feature of such situations, namely, the salience of moral interdependence.

The commander of the threatened unit is likely to be unaware of the presence of non-combatants near the source of the mortar fire directed at his unit. Hence in calling for an artillery barrage to suppress the mortars he is unable to weigh the risk to non-combatants against the risk to his soldiers—something he can (and ought to) do in many classic Proximity scenarios. Likewise, the artillery commander—who is in a position to assess risk to non-combatants—will likely not know the degree and the urgency of the danger to the soldiers of the threatened unit, and thus is also unable to balance the competing moral factors.

However, it is precisely such a balancing that is morally required (and prescribed by the DDE, properly rendered). To reiterate, *pace* the SSF approach, failure to accord significant weight to non-combatant lives amounts to unintended terrorism.[16]

This implies, first of all, an imperative of communication. Those requesting protection should give consideration to the possible moral costs of artillery fire in populated areas, and thus ought to indicate how urgent their need is. More important, those about to shoot must inform the requesting unit of the presence of non-combatants. Ideally, they should together address the problem and try to agree on an overall assessment. In practice, the requisite, nuanced give-and-take will often be extremely difficult to achieve via rushed and restricted voice communication. But the basic, crucial information should be conveyed and then weighed.

The inherent moral interdependence means that the commanders must rely on each other and be able to trust each other's commitment to the moral conduct of warfare. Having received the request for Force Protection, the artillery commander must be able to respond, for example, "Heavy civilian traffic near target during next 20 minutes," to which the other commander might respond, "OK, can stay under cover that long," or conversely "Sorry, but we are entirely exposed and taking casualties, your support is urgently needed right now!"

The underlying moral understandings (cf. Walker 2008) must be shared by the several agents and be part of the organizational culture. Moral responsibility begins with individual agents—both ordinary soldiers and officers—but is also crucially a matter for the army as a whole.[17]

[16] It is worth considering that the artillery commander might be misled by the formulation in terms of prevention or protection. If he believes that his duty toward the prospective civilian victims is a duty of "protection," he may well conclude that he owes a greater duty of protection toward his comrades, wrongly assigning absolute priority to Force Protection.

[17] I have sought here to illustrate the collective aspect of morality in warfare through this example of Force Protection, where the interdependence is immediate and the individual agents can readily identify each other. In fact, moral interdependence within an army is far more complex, involving agents who cannot identify each other, acting at disparate points in time etc. For a brief discussion of this regarding so-called "target banks" and the collection of intelligence, see Zohar (2007: 35–40).

Conclusion: You shall not kill

In employing the language of the Ten Commandments, I do not mean to posit an absolute prohibition upon causing deaths of innocent people in warfare. I do mean, however, to emphasize that in most combat situations involving possible harm to non-combatants, it is misleading to speak of the soldiers' relevant obligation in terms of "preventing" such harm. As illustrated through the various scenarios we have examined, what is at stake is not whether the soldiers shall (or should) "protect" the lives of non-combatants, but rather whether they will (or may) knowingly kill them, albeit as a side-effect of pursuing their military objectives.

Gaining clarity in this matter removes the appearance of legitimacy from the doctrine I have dubbed SSF—"Soldiers' Safety First." The detailed examination of combat scenarios involving risk to both soldiers and non-combatants served not only to decry the misleading language of "protection" and its morally dangerous effects, but also—I hope—to show what is required when the lives of opposing non-combatants are accorded proper value. Individual soldiers as well as the army as an organization are required to continually balance the lives of our soldiers and the lives of non-combatants whom we are at risk of killing.

References

Cohen, S. (1989) *Arms and Judgment: Law, Morality, and the Conduct of War in the Twentieth Century* (Boulder: Westview).

Kasher, A. and Yadlin, A. (2005) "Military Ethics of Fighting Terror: An Israeli Perspective," *Journal of Military Ethics* 4/1: 3–32.

—— (2006) "Military Ethics of Fighting Terror: Principles," *Philosophia* 34: 75–84.

—— (2009) "Israel and the Rules of War: an Exchange," *New York Review of Books* 11 June.

Mangan, J. T. (1949) "An Historical Analysis of the Principle of Double Effect," *Theological Studies* 10: 41–61.

Nozick, R. (1974) *Anarchy, State and Utopia* (New York: Basic Books).

Pavlischek, K. (2010) "Proportionality in Warfare," *The New Atlantis* Spring Issue: 21–34.

Rodin, D. (2004) "Terrorism without Intention," *Ethics* 114: 752–771.

The New Catholic Encyclopedia (1967) (New York: McGraw-Hill).

Walker, M. (2008) *Moral Understandings* (New York: Routledge).

Walzer, M. (1977) *Just and Unjust Wars: A Moral Argument with Historical Illustrations* (New York: Basic Books).

—— and Margalit, A. (2009) "Israel: Civilians and Combatants," *New York Review of Books* 56/8: 21–22, 14 May.

Zohar N. (2007) "Double Effect and Double Intention: A Collectivist Perspective," *Israel Law Review* 40/3: 730–742.

10

Non-Combatant Liability in War*

Helen Frowe

10.1 Introduction

The principle of non-combatant immunity holds that it is impermissible to target non-combatants in war. The principle is thought to hold universally: it covers all non-combatants in all conflicts. Most just war theorists argue that this is because non-combatants are not *liable to defensive killing*, by which they mean that non-combatants have done nothing to lose their rights against intentional attack. Intentionally killing them will therefore wrong them. But of course, just war theorists usually allow that it *is* permissible to target combatants during war. The traditional explanation of why combatants have lost their rights against intentional attack is that, unlike non-combatants, combatants threaten.

But these days, not many people think it plausible to claim that non-combatants don't pose threats in war. Non-combatants make substantial causal contributions to their country's war effort. I suggest that when they are morally responsible for making these contributions, they can be liable to defensive killing if their war is unjust. In Section 10.2, I explain what I mean by an indirect threat, and argue that posing an indirect threat can render a person liable to be killed. In Section 10.3, I draw attention to the various ways in which non-combatants pose indirect threats in war.

Sections 10.4, 10.5, and 10.6 deal with various attempts to show that non-combatants are not liable to be killed even if they indirectly contribute to their country's war. I begin with David Rodin's argument that the contributions that

* Versions of this paper were presented at: Nordic Network on Political Ethics Conference on the Ethics of War, Copenhagen; Frances Kamm's seminar on killing in war, Harvard University; Departmental Reading Group, Boston University; 13th Annual International Law and Ethics Conference Series, Belgrade; Departmental Seminar, MANCEPT; Nuffield College Political Theory Reading Group, Oxford University; Research Seminar, Glasgow University; Symposium on The Ethics of War and Self-Defence, University of Hull. Many thanks to the audiences for their helpful comments.

non-combatants make lie too far down the causal chain to render their authors liable (Rodin, 2008: 44–68). I then tackle Jeff McMahan's and Cécile Fabre's arguments that non-combatant contributions are causally insufficient to ground liability to defensive killing (McMahan, 2009: 225; Fabre, 2009: 36–63). I also consider Fabre's argument that non-combatants are not morally responsible for their contributions because they are ignorant with respect to whether they pose an unjust threat or a just threat.

I find that none of these arguments successfully undermine the idea that non-combatants are liable to defensive killing. The generally accepted ground of the principle of non-combatant immunity—that non-combatants have done nothing to render themselves liable to intentionally killing—is false. I suggest that if we want to offer grounds for protecting non-combatants in war, we would do better to turn our attention to alternative strategies. In Section 10.7, I argue that to show that a person is liable to a harm is not to show that it is permissible to inflict that harm upon her. Permissibility and liability are not two sides of the same coin. So, it is possible to concede non-combatant liability, as is consistent with many people's broader accounts of defensive killing, without granting a permission to intentionally kill non-combatants. I suggest that one argument against such a permission is that killing non-combatants serves no military purpose. However, this is simply a contingent fact about the nature of war, and ought not to be mistaken for a deep principle about the moral status of non-combatants.

10.2 Preliminaries

My view of defensive killing in war endorses four main claims. The first is that the rules of self-defence underpin the rules of killing in war. The second is that people who pose what I call *indirect threats* can be liable to defensive killing. The third is that non-combatants often pose indirect threats in war. The fourth is that non-combatants are often liable to defensive killing in war. In this paper, I will assume the first claim, and say something about the others.

A person poses a *direct threat* to you if she is going to inflict harm upon you, for example by falling on you, poisoning you, shooting you, and so on. A person poses an *indirect threat* to you if she isn't going to inflict harm upon you, but rather endangers you in some other way. For example, a person who blocks an escape route of which you need to avail yourself counts as an indirect threat. A threat of harm is *unjust* if it is aimed at someone who is not liable to bear harm. When I say that an agent is *liable to bear harm*, I mean that harming her does not wrong her. (Some people like to describe this as the claim that she has no right not to be harmed, but I generally eschew rights-talk.) In my view, a person who is liable to a harm is not permitted to defend herself against that harm.

10.3 War

We can think of many ways in which non-combatants contribute to their country's war effort. They contribute politically, perhaps by voting for the war, or writing pro-war newspaper articles. They contribute materially, by producing weapons, clothing and food for the armed forces. They also make technological contributions to war, by designing and testing weapons and machinery. And, of course, the war is financed by taxes paid by combatants and non-combatants alike.

In the light of these contributions, it is hard to credit the idea that non-combatants are not part of the threat that their country poses: that they are 'not harming'. But current international law prohibits the intentional targeting of, for example, a person working in a factory making the guns and bombs that will kill enemy combatants. The *Manual of the Law of Armed Conflict* by the UK Ministry of Defence stipulates that such people are civilians, and do not count as playing a 'direct part' in the war.

> Only combatants are permitted to take a direct part in hostilities. It follows that they may be attacked. Civilians may not take a direct part in hostilities and, for so long as they refrain from doing so, are protected from attack. Taking a direct part in hostilities is more narrowly construed than simply making a contribution to the war effort. Thus working in a munitions factory or otherwise supplying or supporting the war effort does not justify the targeting of civilians so doing. However, munitions factories are legitimate military targets and civilians working there, though not themselves legitimate targets, are at risk if those targets are attacked. Such incidental damage is controlled by the principle of proportionality. (UK Ministry of Defence, 2004: 2.5.2)

Setting aside for a moment the pragmatic reasons for why we might want to endorse this view as a matter of policy, I think it clearly mistaken as a picture of liability to defensive harm. The use of the phrase 'hostilities' to try to distinguish parts of the war, such that one might contribute to a 'war effort' without playing a part in the 'hostilities' seems wholly artificial. If being directly involved in the hostilities means firing weapons on the front line, then most combatants will not be involved in the hostilities either. And if we broaden the meaning of 'hostilities' to include the military activities behind the front line that provide intelligence, training and supplies, so that we cover all combatants, it seems arbitrary to exclude the non-combatants playing comparable roles.

Of course, this is not a new observation. Many just war theorists have pointed out that there doesn't seem to be any principled—or *morally significant*—difference between the contributions of combatants compared to those of non-combatants (Mavrodes, 1975: 117–131; Alexander, 1976: 408–415). And yet the distinction between combatants and non-combatants is supposed to give rise to an important moral difference in how members of these two groups may be treated. If the distinction between combatants and non-combatants is not underpinned by a distinction between harming and not harming, what are our grounds for insisting upon this different treatment?

Several contemporary writers have tried to answer this question. Faced with the difficulties noted earlier with the traditional ground of the principle of non-combatant immunity, these writers have focused their efforts on showing not that non-combatants don't contribute to wars, but that they are not liable to be killed *even if* they contribute. I want to show why we should not adopt the solutions that these writers have offered.

For the sake of simplicity, I will assume in what follows that we are talking about a war that is an unjust war of aggression on one side and a just war of defence on the other. My claim about liability to defensive killing applies only to the non-combatants who contribute to the unjust side of the war.

10.4 Intervening Agency

David Rodin's suggested ground for non-combatant immunity relies upon the idea that causally proximity is relevant to liability. Whilst non-combatants do threaten, the threats they pose are not causally proximate to deaths of enemy soldiers.[1] Rodin suggests that it is a necessary condition of liability to defensive force that one be currently engaged in an unjust attack. Of course, it isn't clear how we ought to cash out this idea of being 'currently engaged' in an attack. Rodin cites and dismisses various attempts at specifying a temporal measure of this condition. In their place, he argues for a *principle of intervening agency* to identify agents who are liable to defensive force.

This principle holds that if two or more agents create an unjust threat between them, and both meet a threshold of minimal moral responsibility, only the agent

[1] Rodin's view has echoes of Robert Fullinwider's claim that killing non-combatants is ruled out because such killings cannot be justified by the Principle of Self-Defence ('War and Innocence', *Philosophy and Public Affairs*, Vol. 5, No. 1 (Autumn, 1975), pp. 90–97). Fullinwider does not develop the intervening agency line, but rather stipulates that self-defence permits the killing only of direct threats. I argue against this view in Frowe (2008), Frowe (2011), Frowe (forthcoming). Larry Alexander offers a rebuttal of Fullinwider's view (Alexander, 1976) in which he suggests that, 'Although causal remoteness is relevant to the questions of whether a threat exists and whether a person is a necessary or sufficient cause of it, it is irrelevant to the right of self-defence once the threat, the necessary or sufficient causal relation, and the lack of superior alternatives to remove the threat are posited' (p. 413).

whose action came last in the causal chain counts as engaged in an unjust attack. Rodin further argues that only this agent—the proximate cause—is a permissible target of defence (Rodin, 2008: 52). Rodin offers two examples to illustrate this principle.[2]

Naughty Minister: Criminal has been released from prison as a result of financial cuts in the prison system. The cuts are a direct result of fraudulent mismanagement of the finances by Minister, who acted in the full knowledge that his actions would endanger the public. Criminal is trying to kill Victim, who can save his life either by killing Criminal, or by lethally trampling over Minister.

Provocation: Villain culpably provokes Attacker into attacking Victim. Victim can save his life either by killing Attacker, or by lethally trampling over Villain.

Rodin argues that it would be impermissible for Victim to save himself by killing either Minister or Villain in these cases. Rodin acknowledges that Minister and Villain bear perhaps greater moral responsibility for the unjust threat to Victim's life than do the intervening agents in each case. But neither Minister nor Villain is currently engaged in an unjust attack, their engagement having been 'superseded' by that of the intervening agent. This intervening action transfers liability from the causally remote agents, Minister and Villain, to the causally proximate agents, Attacker and Criminal.

Rodin thinks that it is these sorts of cases that should inform our understanding of the combatant/non-combatant relationship. Non-combatants are causally remote threats, and combatants are causally proximate threats. Since both combatants and non-combatants meet the threshold of minimal responsibility, it follows that that non-combatants are not liable to attack in war, even if we grant that non-combatants can bear greater moral responsibility for a war than do combatants. Non-combatants are not currently engaged in attacks, as required for liability, because the combatants intervene further down the causal line. Intervening agency thus gives us a principled way of sustaining non-combatant immunity in war, even if we grant the role of non-combatants in initiating and sustaining war.

Alexander considers the possibility that Fullinwider might think intervening agency relevant, and rejects this argument on the grounds that 'only the likelihood of harm, not the number of choices required to bring it about, is directly relevant' (p. 414). Alexander's alternative view of permissible defence, however, seems alarmingly permissive (even to me).

[2] The cases are Rodin's. The names of the cases are mine.

I think that many people would endorse arguments along these lines, thinking that by enlisting in the armed forces combatants 'take on' liability to harm in a way that protects their country's civilians. But I think that Rodin's argument is nonetheless mistaken. For a start, it isn't clear that this view will capture all combatants in the liability net. A combatant who loads the bullets into a gun whilst his comrade does the firing will not be liable to be killed on Rodin's account. Both combatants seem like legitimate targets (and certainly, if Rodin is defending the distinction between combatants and non-combatants, he will want to have (at the very least) frontline combatants on the liable side of the distinction).

Rodin acknowledges that his principle would require 'some finessing' to deal with these cases, along with the high-ranking military commanders who certainly seem liable to attack, but who might never go near a battlefield (Rodin, 2008: 52, fn. 14). He suggests that a plausible form of this finessing would be to 'claim that those persons who play a defined role within the command structure of an organization engaged in the infliction of harm are deemed to participate in equal measure in the proximate agency of delivery unjust harm' (Rodin, 2008: 52, fn. 14) This rather ad hoc response seems to amount to nothing more than a stipulation that the principle doesn't apply to non-combatants. Why would we define the 'organization engaged in the infliction of harm' as the military, rather than the government? Indeed, given that the government head the command structure of the military, it doesn't look like we *can* so define it. But once we include those acting at the behest of the government, it's not clear how we can exclude munitions workers employed at government-owned factories. These workers have a defined role. They operate within what can be plausibly described as a command structure (there is a hierarchy within which orders are issued). And the end they pursue is clearly that of furthering the unjust war. Unless we arbitrarily and implausibly hold that the 'organisation involved inflicting harm' is identical with 'the military', Rodin's suggestion implies that non-combatants making weapons are participating in equal measure to combatants in the delivering of unjust harms.

More generally, I don't think Rodin's principle can be sustained as an account of liability to defensive force; indeed, I think that it is undermined by Rodin's own earlier work. In *War and Self-Defense*, Rodin offers a critique of Alan Gewirth's view of moral responsibility. Gewirth argues that moral responsibility attaches to the proximate cause of a threat, because intervening agency rids those further back in the causal chain of responsibility for the threat. In effect, he says about responsibility what Rodin says about liability. But Rodin argues that we can see that Gewirth's principle is false by thinking about cases like Cheyney Ryan's *Coercion* (Ryan, 1983: 515).

Coercion: The German army capture a town. Nazi forces Mayor to shoot Citizen, on pain of Nazi shooting a much greater number of citizens.

Rodin points out that Gewirth's principle generates the result that Mayor's intervening agency supplants Nazi's responsibility for the killing. This is clearly wrong: as Rodin says, moral responsibility is not exclusive, but can be shared by a number of people (Rodin, 2002: 63). Mayor may take on some responsibility for the killing, but his doing so does not free Nazi of *his* responsibility. Both are morally responsible for the killing of Citizen.

But what also seems clear, and what Rodin overlooks, is that the same is true of these characters' liability to defensive harm. If Citizen has a gun with which he can lethally defend himself, both Nazi and Mayor seem like legitimate targets. Indeed, it would be preferable that Citizen shoot Nazi, even though Mayor clearly meets Rodin's threshold of minimal agency, and it is his action that is most proximate to the threat. If so, Rodin's principle is defeated by the very objection that he levels at Gewirth: why think of liability as an exclusive attribute, rather than a plastic, shareable attribute?

I think Rodin is mistaken, then, to think that liability is based upon this idea of being 'currently engaged in an unjust attack', such that liability can be erased by the intervention of other agents. Rather, what matters for liability is whether the threatening situation *to which one contributes* is current. What makes Nazi a legitimate target is his prior contribution to the threat currently facing the unlucky citizen. Thus, the claim that causal proximity is key to liability is false.

Again, Rodin himself commits himself to this idea in his discussion of the following case:

Goading: Villain hates Victim. He thus deliberately goads Victim into attacking him in order that he may then kill Victim on grounds of self-defence.

Rodin argues that Villain cannot invoke a right of self-defence against Victim (Rodin, 2002: 79). Why not? Well, Rodin says, because Villain is 'at fault for the creation of the threatening situation to which he now responds' (Rodin, 2002: 79). If, as Rodin claims, Villain is not permitted to defend himself against Victim, this suggests that Villain is liable to the harm that Victim will inflict. But then, what matters is not whether Villain is currently provoking Victim—whether he's 'currently engaged in an unjust attack'—but whether the threatening situation that Villain has helped create is current. With respect to non-combatants, then, our focus in determining liability should not be their causal proximity to a current threat, but their responsibility for having helped create that threat.

We might try to rescue a version of Rodin's idea by arguing that an intervening agent can voluntarily take on liability to defensive killing. This is another pretty popular idea with respect to the relationship between combatants and non-combatants. We talk of combatants 'assuming risks' on behalf of their non-combatants: by donning a uniform, a person invites enemy combatants to target them instead of the non-combatants. But I doubt that this will do the trick. It would be very odd if those posing an unjust threat got to decide amongst themselves who was liable to be killed to avert that threat, making it impermissible for their victim to aim defensive force at some group members rather than others. Liability to defensive harm doesn't seem like something we get to allocate by agreement.

This is not to deny that it is sometimes possible for a person to take on another's liability. One can insure against tort law risks, for example. But one cannot insure against liability to defensive killing, because there are some forms of liability that cannot be transferred. Even if a person volunteers to bear a defensive harm in your stead, this does not rid you of liability nor make it impermissible for your victim to kill you. Defensive liability is like criminal liability. A person cannot stand trial for murder in your place or undertake your prison sentence on your behalf. This is no less true in cases where two or more people conspire to bring about a murder. They are all liable to prosecution, irrespective of whose action came where in the causal chain.

Of course, whilst it might not be philosophically defensible, we might nonetheless think that there are pragmatic reasons for combatants to agree amongst themselves not to target non-combatants. Just combatants probably do not want their own non-combatants killed, and might thus agree not to kill non-combatants on the unjust side. But such an agreement, even if it were binding on the just combatants, would not eradicate non-combatant liability on the unjust side of the war. Such an agreement would be nothing more than an agreement not to inflict the harms *to which those non-combatants are liable*. As I say, we don't get to choose by agreement who is liable to defensive harm.

So, intervening agency, even combined with consent on the part of the intervening agent, doesn't give us a plausible way to sustain non-combatant immunity. That non-combatant contributions are causally remote does not show that they cannot be rendered liable to defensive killing by them. Indeed, parts of Rodin's own work seem to suggest that causally remote agents are liable to defensive killings if they are morally responsible for contributing to a current unjust threat.

10.5 Causal Thresholds and Proportionality

One common objection to the idea that non-combatants might be liable to defensive killing is that killing them is nearly always disproportionate to the threat they pose.

So, for example, even though McMahan and I agree that being morally responsible for an indirect threat can render a person liable to be killed, McMahan argues that when it comes to non-combatants, intentional attack would be a disproportionate response to the threat they pose. This is because McMahan's model of proportionality pays attention to the moral responsibility of the person posing the threat and, according to McMahan, non-combatants are typically only weakly morally responsible for the threats posed by their country in war (McMahan, 2009: 197).[3]

I find the idea that proportionality is sensitive to moral responsibility quite puzzling, especially in light of what McMahan says about the permissibility of killing even fully excused threats self-defence. For example, McMahan thinks it permissible to kill Homeowner in the following case.

Mistake: Homeowner sees on the news that a notorious murderer has escaped from the local prison. The murderer's innocent, identical twin brother breaks down near Homeowner's farm, and knocks on Homeowner's door to use the phone. Homeowner mistakes Twin for the murderer, and, in terror, lunges at him with a knife.

McMahan thinks that Twin may permissibly inflict defensive harm upon Homeowner even though Homeowner is fully excused, and thus has only a low degree of moral responsibility for the threat that she poses. Given the apparent permissibility of killing weakly morally responsible people in cases like this, it's hard to see why non-combatants who are weakly morally responsible for an unjust threat are off limits.

Moreover, McMahan argues that variations in moral responsibility amongst combatants are largely irrelevant when the harm to be averted is sufficiently great. If it is proportionate to kill weakly responsible combatants because of the magnitude of the harm to be averted, it is surely proportionate to kill weakly responsible non-combatants to avert that very same harm.

It seems to me that this aspect of McMahan's proportionality calculation—the degree of responsibility—is being used in two distinct ways in his work. With respect to unjust combatants, the condition is interpreted as *the extent to which the combatant is morally responsible* for posing a threat—that is, whether he is culpable, negligent, or excusably ignorant, and so on. And we are told that, given sufficient gravity of the harm, it doesn't matter very much which category of responsibility the combatant falls into. But with respect to non-combatants, the responsibility

[3] McMahan goes on to say that variations in responsibility 'are likely to have comparatively little significance, provided that the Threat is morally responsible, and particularly if he is culpable to some extent'.

aspect of the proportionality condition seems to refer to the non-combatant makes *enough of a causal contribution* to render killing her proportionate (irrespective of whether she makes it culpably, ignorantly, and so on). Hence, when McMahan says that non-combatants are only weakly responsible for threats they pose, he supports this claim not by invoking ignorance on the part of the non-combatants, but by emphasising the causal triviality of the contributions they make.

> In some unjust wars, many civilians do bear some responsibility but the degree to which most of them are responsible is very slight... They may pay their taxes, vote or even campaign for particular political candidates (sometimes on the basis of general sympathy with their overall positions on matters of policy but seldom because of the advocacy of war), participate in the culture from which the country's political leaders have emerged, fail to protest their country's unjust war, perhaps because they correctly believe that to do so would be ineffective, or perhaps because they approve of the war, and so on; but none of these things, nor even all of them together, is ordinarily sufficient for the forfeiture of a person's right not to be attacked and killed. Military attack exceeds what a person may ordinarily be liable to on the basis of these comparatively trivial sources of responsibility. (McMahan, 2009: 225)

What makes killing non-combatants disproportionate, then, is not that they are only weakly morally responsible for their contributions, but that they don't contribute *enough*.

Of course, we might think that facts about causal contribution are indeed relevant to determining proportionality (and thus liability). This could explain why McMahan thinks it permissible to kill weakly responsible Homeowner in cases like *Mistake*. Homeowner's causal contribution is very significant. In contrast, as McMahan emphasises, non-combatants typically make only small contributions to their country's unjust war. Even if McMahan's presentation of this argument conflates causal contributions with moral responsibility, he might nonetheless be right that these contributions are just too insignificant to render their authors liable to be killed.

Cécile Fabre advances a similar view in her recent work. Fabre argues that any kind of liability-based account of defensive killing must look at what non-combatants do as individuals, not merely invoke the results of group endeavours (Fabre, 2009: 61). And, in order to render their authors liable, these individual contributions must pass a threshold of causal significance. Fabre argues that most non-combatant contributions will fall below this threshold: she suggests that even if the overall output of a munitions factory constitutes a significant contribution to the war, making pieces of guns is not enough to render an individual liable to be killed.

But it seems to me a mistake to understand liability as subject to this sort of causal threshold. Such a view tells us that merely spreading the causal load for an unjust threat dissolves liability for that threat. This is pretty unattractive as a moral principle. Consider a case like *Hit*.

> *Hit*: Mafia Boss wants to take Victim out, but he cannot afford to hire Assassin, who is extremely skilled and thus extremely expensive. Mafia Boss has a whip-round amongst all the members of his mob, none of whom really like Victim. Everyone coughs up a few pounds for the assassination fund.

Each member of the mob plays only a small role in hiring Assassin. Their contribution is slight—a few pounds out of Assassin's hefty price. But if killing a member of the mob is necessary to save Victim's life, I do not think that such a killing would be ruled out on grounds of being disproportionate. Rather, I think that each member of the mob is liable to defensive killing. Victim would be permitted to kill any member of the mob (or even more than one) to save his own life. That each mobster makes only a small contribution to the threat cannot protect them from liability to defensive harm. This suggests to me that proportionality concerns the gravity of the threatened harm, and the gravity of the force used to avert it. It does not pay attention to the amount that a person contributes to a threat. And, I think that cases like *Hit* suggest that what matters for liability is whether one contributes, and not how much one contributes. Since the members of the mob responsibly contribute to a lethal threat, they are liable to lethal defence.

I think the same is true of those making weapons in munitions factories. Stipulating the existence of a causal threshold that protects non-combatants from liability just doesn't seem plausible as a general account of liability. The idea of a threshold also commits us to differences in liability in cases that should strike us as morally similar. For example, imagine that a munitions factory owner can run his factory in one of two ways. He can have a standard assembly line, in which each worker fits a particular component of every gun. Or, he can have a tandem system, where each worker independently produces an entire gun. Either way, he ends up with two hundred guns at the end of each day. Let's assume that Fabre's threshold lies somewhere between making pieces of guns and making complete guns. The workers on the assembly line model don't pass the causal threshold with respect to any particular weapon, whereas those working in tandem to produce complete weapons do.[4] Fabre's account therefore suggests that whilst the assembly line workers are not liable to be killed, the workers in the second are so liable.

[4] We can vary what the workers produce depending on where we think the threshold lies (maybe they make a tank a week, or a plane a year).

But this difference in liability hardly seems plausible. What matters, surely, is that they are contributing weapons for the unjust side of the war. It is this fact that grounds the liability of those making entire guns from scratch. If they were not sending their weapons to the war effort, or if they were not on the unjust side of the war, their contributions would not render them liable. And since those making pieces of guns are also contributing weapons for the unjust side of the war, those workers must be similarly liable. Those who conspire or collude in the creation of unjust threats cannot rid each other of liability simply by working as part of a team. And if it is not disproportionate for Victim to use force against individual members of the mob in *Hit*, I do not think it disproportionate for just combatants to use lethal force against individual workers who contribute to the unjust lethal threats that they face.

10.6 Ignorance

A third strategy for defending the claim that non-combatants aren't liable to be killed is familiar from debates about the moral equality of combatants. People frequently invoke the *ignorance* of combatants to argue that unjust combatants are not morally responsible for posing unjust threats. Fabre claims that this also applies to non-combatants, arguing that 'even if civilians who provide unjust combatants with the material resources which they need are unjustifiably contributing to wrongful killing, they are not, on the whole liable to attack' (Fabre, 2009: 56). Fabre and I agree that one can be liable to be killed only if one is morally responsible for an unjust threat. But Fabre argues that if one is unavoidably ignorant of either the fact that one poses a threat, or the fact that the threat is unjust, this negates moral responsibility (Fabre, 2009: 58).[5] So, if non-combatants are unavoidably ignorant of the fact that they pose an unjust threat, they are not morally responsible for posing that threat, and are not liable to be killed.

Fabre argues that we can see that non-combatants are unavoidably ignorant by noticing the mixed character of war. Wars often have both just and unjust phases. For example, what began as a war of aggression might become a partial war of defence if the opposing army is breaching the rules of *jus in bello*. Non-combatants who contribute to the just threats posed by combatants during these just phases of a war do not act wrongly, on Fabre's view, and are not liable to be killed.[6] Because of

[5] It isn't obvious that equal ignorance about these two facts is equally corrosive of liability. Ignorance that one poses a threat at all seems to preclude liability, but ignorance that the threat that one knowingly poses is unjust does not. However, let us grant for the sake of argument that unavoidable ignorance about a threat's justness might preclude liability as well.

[7] It isn't obvious to me that this is true. Providing support for one part of a war can facilitate the fighting of another part of that war. If, as I argue later, the onus is on agents to not contribute to unjust

this mixed character of the war, a non-combatant on even the *ad bellum* unjust side of a war cannot know whether the equipment she makes will be used for the just or the unjust ends of the war. She therefore cannot know whether she is contributing to an unjust threat, and her unavoidable ignorance protects her from liability to defensive killing.

Fabre acknowledges an obvious objection to this line of argument that finds its roots in the distinction between doing and allowing. The doing/allowing distinction gives rise to a presumption of erring on the side of *not causing* unjust harm, even if one will *allow* unjust harm as a result. So, non-combatants should not contribute to what might be an unjust threat, even at the risk of failing to rescue others from unjust harm. But Fabre argues that this objection 'has bite' only at the beginning of a war (Fabre, 2009: 60). As the war goes on, the more likely it is to acquire additional, just ends like thwarting retaliatory killings. As the chances of contributing to a just threat improve, the presumption against contributing becomes correspondingly weak. And, Fabre argues, even if non-combatants do unjustifiably contribute to unjust threats, going against this presumption, they are still not liable to defensive killing.

> [I]f *individuals'* rational and moral agency is decisive for their liability, then there should be some fit between the costs which agents, as individuals, are liable to incur for acting wrongfully, and their degree of moral responsibility for their actions. To deem them liable to be killed merely in virtue of knowingly taking the risk of wrongfully contributing to unjust lethal threats, given (a) that there is a strong chance that they will in fact either contribute to just threats or not contribute to any threat... and (b) that they cannot know either way how their contribution will be used, does not pass the fittingness test. (Fabre, 2009: 61)

Fabre is not denying that that there is a duty to avoid wrongfully harming people that outweighs the duty to help people. Indeed, she explicitly endorses this duty (Fabre, 2009: 55). But she says that choosing wrongly under the epistemic constraints described cannot render a person liable to be killed. The degree of moral responsibility that attaches to non-combatants who choose to contribute is too low to render them liable to lethal harm.

But this reply fails to hit its target. Fabre is meant to be tackling the objection that non-combatants ought to err on the side of not contributing to a war when they lack information about the justness of the war. This objection suggests that those who do not so err render themselves liable to be killed. Fabre's response is that even those who choose to contribute will lack moral responsibility for contributing and

harm even at the risk of failing to prevent unjust harm, Fabre's argument will not undermine the liability of non-combatants contributing to the just parts of an unjust war if they thereby facilitate other, unjust parts of the war.

so will not be liable. But her explanation of *why* they lack moral responsibility as laid out in (a) and (b) of the material just quoted seems to amount to little more than the claim that the non-combatants cannot know whether they will be contributing to an unjust threat. And surely the presumption that if a non-combatant doesn't know how her contribution will be used then she ought not to contribute cannot be undermined by pointing to the fact that she doesn't know how her contribution will be used. This presumption is designed to guide agents in the face of precisely the sorts of epistemic constraints to which Fabre draws attention. It thus cannot be defeated by invoking those same constraints. When an enterprise is morally mixed and one cannot know whether one will be contributing to the right parts, one must prioritise not harming the innocent over aiding the innocent. Non-combatants who opt to contribute to wars without knowing whether they will be posing just or unjust threats cannot plead ignorance in order to escape liability.

10.7 Liability and Military (In)Effectiveness

A possible source of protection for non-combatants is the *jus in bello* rule of military necessity. The rule of military necessity stipulates that harm done in wartime must produce a military advantage. Since killing non-combatants isn't usually very helpful, such killings will often fail this requirement, and will thus be impermissible. McMahan makes use of this rule in his attempt to limit a permission to kill non-combatants. However, McMahan's argument is intended to show, again, not just that it's impermissible to kill non-combatants, but that the requirement of necessity shows that non-combatants aren't liable to be killed (McMahan, 2009: 225). McMahan thinks that liability itself has a kind of internal necessity condition, such that a person can be liable to a harm only if that harm is instrumental in averting an unjust threat for which she is morally responsible (McMahan, 2009: 9). So, a non-combatant might be morally responsible for an unjust threat, for example by having voted for a war-mongering politician. But if that is her only contribution, and it lies in the past, killing her now will not be instrumental in averting the threat. Targeting non-combatants on the basis of these past contributions will serve no military purpose. McMahan argues that therefore non-combatants cannot be liable to such killings.

I think we ought to reject McMahan's claim that liability is subject to this sort of internal necessity condition. It seems to me that whether a person is liable to defensive harm rests upon facts about them, not on external facts about necessity. Consider *Lucky Escape*:

Lucky Escape: Murderer is chasing Victim and trying to kill him. Victim happens to have a parachute. He can simply jump to safety without needing to kill Murderer in self-defence.

It seems pretty implausible that Murderer, who would clearly be liable to be killed if Victim did not have a parachute, is not so liable if Victim happens to have a parachute. Murderer is, after all, maliciously trying to kill Victim, chasing him with a gun and shooting at him. If that doesn't render a person liable to be killed, I'm not sure what does. I do not think that if Victim kills Murderer in *Lucky Escape*, he wrongs Murderer. Murderer has no legitimate complaint if Victim decides uses force against him rather than use his parachute. Nor could Murderer permissibly defend himself if Victim decided to use force rather than use his parachute.

Yet killing Murderer is no longer necessary for saving Victim's life. If we think that a person can be liable only to necessary force, Murderer cannot be liable to defensive killing. An upshot of this claim, on both my view and McMahan's, is that Murderer can, therefore, permissibly defend himself against Victim should Victim employ defensive force rather than jump with the parachute.

Of course, McMahan might point out that his account stipulates that defensive harm must be *instrumental* in averting a threat. Killing Murderer still meets this condition, since Victim can save his life either by jumping, or by killing Murderer. Perhaps McMahan's account pronounces Murderer liable to be killed after all. But I would have thought that since Victim can save his life without killing Murderer, McMahan will want to say that Victim ought not to kill him. But if so, McMahan will need to invoke a separate necessity condition that operates independently of Murderer's liability, making it impermissible for Victim to kill Murderer *even though* Murderer is liable to be killed. If he does this, McMahan's view seems to collapse into mine, and the idea that necessity is internal to liability drops out of the picture. There can be cases in which a person's liability to defensive killing persists even though killing them is unnecessary and therefore impermissible. With respect to non-combatants, then, merely pointing to the necessity condition will not show that non-combatants are not liable to defensive harm. It just shows that even though they are liable, killing them can still be impermissible.

Adopting this picture of liability better captures the nature of liability—that it is backwards-looking—and better explains why Victim would suddenly be permitted to kill Murderer if, for example, he discovers that his parachute is not working. It strikes me as odd to think that a person's liability to defensive killing could pop in and out of existence like this as a result of factors entirely beyond their control. Liability is based on facts about what a person has done, and these facts are not changed by variations in the usefulness of killing them. But what *is* plausible is that whilst a person's liability to harm persists, the permissibility of inflicting that harm can vary as a result of factors beyond her control.

10.8 Conclusion

I have argued that many of the arguments commonly assumed to ground the idea of non-combatant immunity fail. They fail because they seek to defend non-combatant immunity by showing that non-combatants cannot be liable to defensive killing even if they contribute to unjust wars. This position is simply implausible. Non-combatants are sometimes liable to defensive killing, because they are sometimes morally responsible for unjust lethal threats. But, as I have argued, liability is distinct from permissibility. There can be other reasons, aside from the absence of liability, that make killing a person impermissible. One such reason is that killing them serves no purpose. It will sometimes be true that killing a non-combatant achieves no military advantage, and is thus impermissible, even though she has, through her actions, rendered herself liable to be killed. But this is, of course, a simply contingent fact. Sometimes, it *will* serve the purposes of the just war to kill a non-combatant. And if she is liable to be killed, killing the non-combatant is not wrong.

References

Alexander, L. (1976) 'Self-Defense and the Killing of Noncombatants: A Reply to Fullinwider', *Philosophy and Public Affairs* 5/4: 408–415.

Fabre, C. (2009) 'Guns, Food and Liability to Attack in War', *Ethics* 120: 36–63.

Frowe, H. (2008) 'Equating Innocent Threats and Bystanders', *Journal of Applied Philosophy* 25/4: 277–290.

—— (2011) 'Self-Defence and the Principle of Non-Combatant Immunity', *Journal of Moral Philosophy* 8/4: 530–546.

—— (forthcoming) *Defensive Killing: An Essay on War and Self-Defence* (Oxford: Oxford University Press).

Fullinwider, R. (1975) 'War and Innocence', *Philosophy and Public Affairs* 5/1: 90–97.

Mavrodes, G. (1975) 'Conventions and the Morality of War', *Philosophy and Public Affairs* 4/2: 117–131.

McMahan, J. (2009) *Killing in War* (Oxford: Oxford University Press).

Rodin, D. (2008) 'The Moral Inequality of Soldiers: Why *jus in bello* Asymmetry is Half Right', in Rodin, D and Shue, H (eds) *Just and Unjust Warriors* (Oxford: Oxford University Press) 44–68.

Rodin, D (2002) *War and Self-Defense* (New York: Oxford University Press).

Ryan, C. (1983) 'Self-Defense, Pacifism, and the Possibility of Killing', *Ethics* 93/3: 508–524.

UK Ministry of Defence (2004) *The Manual of the Law of Armed Conflict* (Oxford: Oxford University Press).

Index

The manufacturer's authorised representative in the EU for product safety is Oxford University Press España S.A. of el Parque Empresarial San Fernando de Henares, Avenida de Castilla, 2 – 28830 Madrid (www.oup.es/en or product.safety@oup.com). OUP España S.A. also acts as importer into Spain of products made by the manufacturer.

www.ingramcontent.com/pod-product-compliance
Lightning Source LLC
LaVergne TN
LVHW011818200926
848484LV00005B/1238
* 9 7 8 0 1 9 9 6 7 3 4 3 8 *